50 of the Best Strolls, Walks,
and Hikes around Reno

50
of the *Best*
Strolls, Walks,
and *Hikes*
around **Reno**

MIKE WHITE

with photographs by M A R K   V O L L M E R

UNIVERSITY OF NEVADA PRESS *Reno & Las Vegas*

University of Nevada Press, Reno, Nevada 89557 USA
www.unpress.nevada.edu
Copyright © 2017 by University of Nevada Press
All rights reserved
Photographs by Mark Vollmer
Images: page 10 © style67; page 9 © ufotopixl10; page 55 © tinica10; page 75 ©
  Salome; page 99 © tinica10; page 167 © mast3r/Adobe Stock

LIBRARY OF CONGRESS CATALOGING-IN-PUBLICATION DATA
Names: White, Michael C., 1952– author. | Vollmer, Mark, illustrator.
Title: 50 of the best strolls, walks, and hikes around Reno / Mike White with
  photographs by Mark Vollmer.
Other titles: Fifty of the best strolls, walks, and hikes around Reno
Description: Reno, Nevada : University of Nevada Press, [2017] | Includes
  bibliographical references and index.
Identifiers: LCCN 2016041695 (print) | LCCN 2016055854 (e-book) |
  ISBN 978-1-943859-30-6 (paperback : alk. paper) |
  ISBN 978-0-87417-471-7 (e-book)
Subjects: LCSH: Walking—Nevada—Reno Region—Guidebooks. | Hiking—Nevada—
  Reno Region—Guidebooks. | Trails—Nevada—Reno Region—Guidebooks. | Reno
  Region (Nev.)—Guidebooks.
Classification: LCC GV199.42.N3 R469 2017 (print) |
  LCC GV199.42.N3 (e-book) | DDC 796.510979355—dc23
LC record available at https://lccn.loc.gov/2016041695

FIRST PRINTING

Manufactured in the United States of America

Contents

Illustrations

Photos

Acknowledgments

Thanks to Robin White for decades of love and encouragement, without whom this book would not have materialized. Joanne O'Hare served as the inspiration for this guide, a project for which she patiently waited many years until it came to fruition after her retirement at the University of Nevada Press. Thanks to Justin Race and his current staff for their usual fine job of creating a real book from my endeavors. I am also very thankful for Mark Vollmer's contribution of his wonderful photos to this guide. Some fellow hikers joined me for many of the hikes, including Dal and Candy Hunter, Keith Catlin, and Bruce Farenkopf.

Introduction

While much of the country regards Reno as the poor man's Las Vegas, those in the know understand the riches of the area's natural wonders at the cross-roads between the high desert of the Great Basin to the east and the lofty mountains of the Sierra Nevada to the west. As a recreational bonanza, the greater Reno-Sparks region offers year-round walking and hiking opportunities, from the floor of the Truckee Meadows to the summits of the Carson Range. While many parts of the country are seeing trails disappearing due to lack of use, or more commonly, underfunded budgets for the managing agencies, the greater Reno area has recently experienced the addition of several trails to its network. Whether you experience the pungent fragrance of damp sagebrush in the foothills after a brief shower, or survey the sweeping views of the lovely Tahoe Basin from the top of a high peak, these paths and trails highlight the area's abundant outdoor resources.

Identifying and describing the best strolling, walking, and hiking routes in and around Reno, this guide provides opportunities for everyone, from wheelchair users to the well-seasoned and well-conditioned hiker. Within these pages are trips spanning the walking spectrum, from short and easy strolls on flat, paved trails to all-out assaults on mountain summits and everything in between. Readers can choose a gentle walk along the Truckee River through downtown Reno, or a rugged trail along one of its tributaries into the heart of a montane forest. Additional highlights include picturesque vistas, areas teeming with wildlife, places of historical interest, and examples of interesting geology. Whether you're a casual walker in search of an easy stroll, a serious hiker looking for a physical challenge, or someone in between, the greater Reno area definitely has you covered.

Note to Parents

In this present age, many people are becoming less and less involved in the outdoor world, especially children. Certainly, the widespread development and increased accessibility of electronics has had an enormous impact on consuming the leisure time of young people. While in previous generations, parents would shoo their children outside to play, nowadays many parents seem content to allow TV, computers, cell phones, and video games to be their children's babysitters. What little time school-age children do spend outside these days is often limited to organized sports rather than free play.

Unfortunately, many physical education (PE) programs have been cut from the curriculum in school systems as well.

The harried nature of family life in the modern era has also wreaked havoc on children's ability to connect to the natural world, especially for families headed by two working parents or a single parent. Suburbia seems filled with time-pressed and frazzled parents, often appearing to be little more than chauffeurs shuttling their kids from one organized activity to another in an attempt to provide them with every opportunity that presents itself. After school, in between soccer practice and music lessons, Mom, Dad, an older sibling, or a sitter, makes a pass through the drive-through of a fast-food restaurant, tossing dinner to the kids in the backseat of an SUV or mini-van. Little wonder the United States is experiencing a child obesity epidemic when poor nutrition is combined with minimal physical activity.

Complicating matters even further is the trend of the population moving away from rural and suburban areas to reside in the inner city, where natural and open space is oftentimes less available. In this environment, parents who want their children to experience the great outdoors face an even bigger challenge than their rural and suburban counterparts.

All is not doom and gloom, however, as parents do have the choice to expose their kids to the wonders of the world that exists outside of our man-made enclosures. Fortunately, those of us who live in the greater Reno-Sparks area don't have to travel very far to experience the outdoors. But the choice has to be made to prioritize encounters with the natural world outside our back door. While the majority of children are more aware of threats to the environment these days than their parents may have been at the same ages, most kids spend less time actually in that environment than previous generations. Heading outside provides many healthy benefits, including but not limited to the following:

VITAMIN D | Healthy children, as well as adults, require a daily dose of this important vitamin, which can be achieved with an exposure of bare skin to sunlight as short as fifteen minutes per day. An adequate amount of vitamin D is essential to help bodies absorb calcium, which results in the production of healthy bones.

IMMUNE SYSTEM | Children who routinely play outside have more active immune systems. While a lot of responsible parents adhere to the belief that it is best to minimize their children's exposure to bacteria to keep them healthy, the opposite is actually true. By exposing children to the outside elements, parents are actually helping to stimulate their immune systems.

EXERCISE | Outside activities such as hiking, running, riding bikes, pick-up games, and playing tag provide a fun way for children to get the necessary exercise they need in order to be healthy. It is recommended that school-age children get an hour of exercise each day. Many children, especially boys, who get labeled as hyperactive just might be seemingly less high-strung if allowed to burn off some of their extra energy by playing outside.

STRESS REDUCTION | Being outdoors can be relaxing and healing to the body, mind, and soul.

HEALTHY AIR | Unless air pollution is a problem, outside air is generally cleaner than the air inside a building, where recycled and stagnant air accumulates dust particles and other contaminants.

HEIGHTENED SENSES | While we use our five senses inside as well as out, being in nature provides a heightened stimulation of our senses.

IMAGINATION/CREATIVITY | Kids who participate in free play in the outdoors are able to stimulate their imaginations in ways that electronic stimuli can't replicate.

PROBLEM-SOLVING SKILLS | Free play in the outdoors also allows children to develop problem-solving skills, as well as improve social skills.

DISCOVERY | The natural world is a laboratory for discovery, which most children will naturally find intriguing. Some kids might need some introductory guidance in this regard, but eventually they'll find the outdoors to be filled with myriad opportunities of unearthing some of life's more fascinating wonders.

PROTECTING THE ENVIRONMENT | While videos and textbooks can teach kids to be environmentally aware, nothing beats having kids want to protect something they find enjoyment in and learn to understand personally.

One of the greatest gifts a parent can give to a child is the freedom to play outside and experience the natural world in a tactile way. Hiking the area's trails is a wonderful way to introduce your kids to the great outdoors. To learn more about this issue, *Last Child in the Woods*, by Richard Louv, is an outstanding resource. The following are some tips for parents when they are hiking with their children:

- Pick an age-appropriate hike that's interesting and fun.
- Remember to focus on the journey, not the destination. Have reasonable expectations about your child's abilities and desires.
- Plan plenty of snack and rest breaks.
- Bring along a playmate for your child.
- Help kids become good observers of the natural world.
- Plan some activities along the way to keep kids engaged.

Note to Dog Owners

Lots of folks love to bring their dogs along on a hike. Trips that allow dogs on the trail have been identified in the introductory section of each trip. Some areas don't allow pets at all, others require that dogs be on a leash, and still others have no restrictions (although all dogs should be well socialized and under voice control). To keep everyone content in areas where dogs are permitted, here is a list of suggestions:

PICK THE RIGHT TRAIL | Not only should you obey the regulations and take your dog just on trails where they are allowed, but select a trail suitable for your pet. Make certain your pet is physically up to the challenge. Select a path where the surface won't damage a dog's paws, or invest in a set of dog booties. Make sure plenty of water is available or pack some along for Fido. Avoid trails congested with mountain bikers and equestrians.

MAINTAIN CONTROL | Your dog should be leashed where required and under voice control when off leash. He or she should be socially well adjusted, as encounters with humans and other dogs are highly likely on most of the trips in this guide. Don't allow your pet to harass wildlife, or disturb equestrians.

POOP SCOOP | Bring a plastic bag and pack out all poops. Don't do what some dog owners are guilty of by leaving the plastic bag alongside of the trail—sanitation workers will not come by to remove your dog's feces.

ID TAGS | Make sure your dog has an identification tag with your current contact information, just in case he or she gets excited and wanders off.

Trail Etiquette and Safety

ETIQUETTE | The primary concern of trail etiquette is twofold: first, to make the hiking experience enjoyable for everyone and second, to protect the environment. These two goals can be accomplished by practicing the following guidelines:

- Leave no trace of your presence.
- In the wilds, dispose of waste properly (human feces should be buried six inches in the ground and at least 200 feet away from water sources. Dog feces should be bagged and removed).
- Stick to the trail—don't cut switchbacks, which causes erosion.
- Refrain from feeding or approaching wildlife.
- Pack out all litter (be a good Samaritan and pick up litter left behind by others).
- Be quiet, inconspicuous, and respectful on the trail to avoid negatively impacting the experience of others.
- Refrain from collecting natural objects—leave them for others to enjoy.
- Yield the right-of-way to uphill hikers.
- Yield the right-of-way to large groups.
- Allow equestrians the right-of-way—step well off the trail on the downhill side.
- Allow mountain bikers the right-of-way, even though signs indicate the opposite. (It's a lot easier for a person on two legs to yield than expecting a rider to get off his or her bike and move off the trail.)

- Report any major problems to land managers (trail washouts, trashed-out hunter's camps, illegal ATV damage, wildlife encounters, etc.).

SAFETY | Staying safe while hiking is of primary importance. Obviously, the requirements for a long hike into the backcountry will be greater than for a stroll through a city park.
- Be prepared.
- Pack plenty of water. When in the backcountry, purify all drinking water obtained from lakes and streams.
- Be cognizant of the weather—avoid exposed ridges and summits during the afternoon when thunderstorms may be a threat.
- Use caution when hiking in areas of unstable footing—loose boulders, small pebbles, icy patches, and so on.
- Dress in layers, stay dry, eat plenty of high-energy snacks, and know the warning signs of hypothermia.
- Use common sense.

In the backcountry, carry the ten essential systems:
1. Navigation (map and compass)
2. Sun protection (sunglasses and sunscreen)
3. Insulation (extra clothing)
4. Illumination (flashlight or headlamp with extra batteries)
5. First-aid kit
6. Fire (waterproof matches, lighter, candle)
7. Repair kit and tools
8. Nutrition (extra food)
9. Hydration (extra water)
10. Emergency shelter

Additional items that may be handy:
1. Insect repellent
2. Toilet paper and hand sanitizer
3. Cell phone
4. Trekking poles
5. Camera
6. Binoculars
7. Trash bag

How to Use This Guide

The trips in this guide have been categorized into five chapters loosely based upon subregions of the greater Reno area. The first region includes trips along or near the Truckee River. The second group is composed of trips on the valley floor of the Truckee Meadows. The third chapter contains routes outside of town in the valleys and hills to the north, in Lemmon, Sun, and Spanish Springs Valleys. Trips in the foothills above the Truckee Meadows make up the fourth chapter. Finally, Chapter 5 includes trips in the higher mountains above the basin in the Carson Range.

After a short introduction, each trip contains pertinent information listed within several important headings.

LEVEL | This entry identifies the type of outing—stroll, walk, or hike—and the one or more levels of skill necessary to safely and enjoyably handle the trip—novice, intermediate, and advanced.

Strolls are classified as essentially flat and short, and demand virtually no navigational skills. The trails are either paved or on very well-graded natural surfaces. These trips require little if any experience and should be able to be enjoyed by just about anyone.

Walks will experience some elevation change and are generally longer than strolls. Some navigation will be required to safely complete the route. Trail surfaces will be natural and typically well graded.

Hikes are longer, steeper, more technically challenging than walks, and require a higher degree of navigation as well. Hiking experience is absolutely essential.

LENGTH | Accurate round-trip distances have been computed for each trip. Out-and-back trips start and end at the same trailhead. Shuttle trips start and end at different trailheads, requiring two vehicles, or being dropped off and picked up at two different locations. Loop trips start and end at the same trailhead but avoid much if any backtracking. Lollipop loops also start and end at the same trailhead, but they have an out-and-back segment necessary to access the loop section.

TIME | The duration of a hike is listed here, based upon the amount of time necessary for the average hiker to complete the trip. People in excellent condition should be able to do these trips in a shorter amount of time, while less physically fit individuals will require more time than what is listed. Longer trips have been categorized into parts of a day rather than hours, which are more general evaluations and may also vary with one's level of physical fitness.

ELEVATION | The amount of elevation gain and loss appears under this heading. The elevation of out-and-back trips is listed as a one-way figure. Shuttle, loop, and lollipop-loop trips are noted as round-trip figures.

DIFFICULTY | Divided into easy, moderate, strenuous, and very strenuous categories, this listing denotes the level of physical effort required to complete a trip. Easy trips should be able to be completed by just about anyone who is ambulatory, while very strenuous trips should be attempted only by people who are extremely physically fit.

USERS | Under this heading are the types of groups allowed to use the trails. These groups include hikers, runners, trail runners, mountain bikers, cyclists, and equestrians. Also noted under this heading is if the trip is particularly kid friendly.

DOGS | Many people wish to include their dogs on trips. In some areas dogs are not allowed, in others they must be on a leash. Where an *OK* appears, dogs are permitted off leash.

SEASON | This heading indicates the time of year when a particular trip is usually free of snow and is suitable for hiking. During winter, some trails listed as open all year may have brief periods when they are snow-covered, depending on current conditions.

BEST TIME | Taking into account such variable factors as weather, water levels, seasonal wildflowers, or autumn color, this entry attempts to identify the time of year when a particular trip might be at its peak of enjoyment.

FACILITIES | Here is where you'll find a listing of any significant facilities near the trailhead.

MAP | Pertinent maps appear here, which may be hard copy maps available from retailers, or maps that can be downloaded onto a computer from land agency or organizational websites.

MANAGEMENT | Government or, on occasion, private entities charged with the oversight of recreational lands appear under this heading, complete with contact information in case there are questions or concerns.

HIGHLIGHTS | Appearing under this heading are short listings of the main attractions for each trip, identifying the reason or reasons why this trip is worth your time and effort.

LOWLIGHTS | In contrast to the previous entry, this heading points out any negative aspects that users should be aware of when contemplating a particular trip.

TIP | Helpful information particular to trips is listed under this category.

KID TIP | For families with children, this entry provides helpful information for enjoying the trip with youngsters, or for determining its suitability.

TRAILHEAD | Following GPS coordinates for the start of the trail, accurate instructions are provided for driving a vehicle to trailheads.

TRAIL | Accurate and detailed trip descriptions are found here.

MILESTONES | This table lists the major and significant points along the route, with numbers corresponding to the accompanying map.

GO GREEN | For those who wish to give back their appreciation of our precious local resources, suggested activities or organizations are featured under this heading with the pertinent contact information.

OPTIONS | The last entry is sort of a catchall of opportunities to add experiences to each trip. Sometimes this includes additional hikes or trail extensions in the immediate area. Other activities might be listed, such as picnic areas. Nearby attractions may also appear here, as well as places close by to grab a bite or a brew.

List of Abbreviations

COS	City of Sparks
HTNF	Humboldt-Toiyabe National Forest
NDOW	Nevada Division of Wildlife
NSP	Nevada State Parks
RPR&CS	City of Reno Parks, Recreation and Community Services
SR	State Route
TPB	Tahoe-Pyramid Bikeway
TRT	Tahoe Rim Trail
TRTA	Tahoe Rim Trail Association
USGS	United States Geological Survey
USFS	United States Forest Service
WCP	Washoe County Regional Parks and Open Space

Legend

— — — — —	Featured Trail	*1140'*	Elevation
— — — —	Secondary Trail	580	Interstate Highway
～～～	Stream	431	State Highway
—·—·—	Intermittent Stream	～～～	200-foot Contour
○	Spring	·········	40-foot Contour
▲	Developed Campground	┝┿┿┿┿┿┥	Railroad
⊤	Trailhead	· · · ·	Powerline
ℙ	Parking*	------------	Boundary
▲	Mountain	⚒	Mine
⌂	Ranger Station	(4)	Trip Number
?	Visitor or Information Center	1	Milestone Number
⊞	Picnic Area	41653A	Forest Service Road
⊞	Restroom	◇	Rock Cairn
■	Point of Interest	●—●	Gate

* Numerous parking lots may be found on the maps. Trailhead directions will take you to the parking lot at the beginning of the trail of interest, indicated by a bold dotted line.

CHAPTER ONE

THE TRUCKEE RIVER CORRIDOR

Clearly the region's most important waterway, the 121-mile-long Truckee River, named for a Paiute chief who guided a party of emigrants, begins as the sole outlet of Lake Tahoe, flows east through Reno-Sparks, and then terminates at Pyramid Lake (a remnant of prehistoric Lake Lahontan). In the more utilitarian era of the nineteenth and twentieth centuries, the river was exploited as a commercial resource. During our more enlightened times, much effort has gone in to reclaiming the river as a natural wonder.

As the Truckee formerly became a major travel corridor for pioneers, the Transcontinental Railroad, and then the nation's highway system, so too the river has become a haven for modern-day recreationists. The area is home to several parks, preserves, and trails dedicated to the enlightenment and enjoyment of the public. Eleven trips are included in this chapter, each one prominently featuring the river or a tributary environment.

Crystal Peak Park Trails

West of Reno in the community of Verdi, Crystal Peak Park occupies the site of a former lumber mill and railroad townsite, providing three short, basically level trails suitable for just about anyone. The 0.6-mile Interpretive Trail follows a loop along a stretch of the Truckee River, providing insights to the human and natural history of the area along the way. The Verdi Mill Pond Trail is an out-and-back path along the old pond, offering spots to sit and watch the wildlife, or drop a line for catch-and-release fishing. The less developed Fisherman's Trail follows along the riverbank through an undeveloped part of the park, which unofficially continues beyond the park boundary farther upstream on an unmaintained path.

1A ▪ Interpretive Trail

LEVEL	Stroll, novice
LENGTH	0.6 mile, loop
TIME	½ hour
ELEVATION	Minimal
DIFFICULTY	Easy
USERS	Hikers; kid friendly
DOGS	No
SEASON	Open all year
BEST TIMES	Spring, fall
FACILITIES	Interpretive signs, picnic tables, restrooms
MAP	Washoe County Parks: *Crystal Peak Park* (web-map at www.washoecounty.us/parks)
MANAGEMENT	Washoe County Regional Parks and Open Space at 775-328-3600, www.washoecounty.us/parks
HIGHLIGHTS	Fishing, history, interpretive signs, river
LOWLIGHTS	Exposed to sun, freeway noise

TIP | The park is open all year during daylight hours.

KID TIP | There is very little shade along the loop, so pack along plenty of sunscreen and water. The Truckee River provides a fascinating environment for

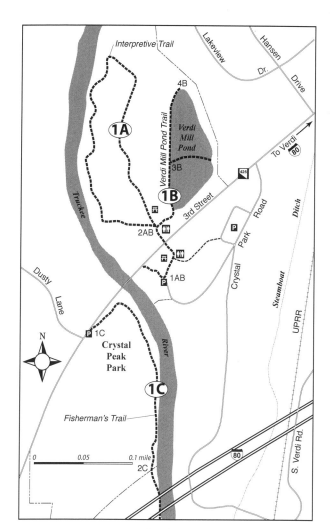

1. Crystal Peak Park Trails

children to experience and explore. However, small children must be closely supervised at all times.

TRAILHEAD | 39°30.773′N, 119°59.851′W From Reno, head westbound on I-80 and take Exit 2 for East Verdi. Follow I-80 Business West to Verdi, where the road becomes Third Street in town. Proceed to Crystal Park Road, 3 miles from the freeway exit, and turn left. After 0.1 mile, turn right at the park entrance and continue on the access road to the parking lot.

TRAIL | Head northeast away from the parking area [**1AB**] and pass through an underpass below Third Street, reaching junction **2AB** with four paths at a circular clearing with a kiosk displaying a map and historical information about the area. The wide, left-hand path travels shortly to the river's edge near the highway bridge. To walk the Interpretive Trail, take the left-hand branch of the middle path for a clockwise circuit around the northwest section of the park, soon approaching the Truckee River. Riparian foliage along the riverbank includes ponderosa pines, black cottonwoods, and willows. Along the way, use trails lead down to the water's edge for exploration of the river, park benches offer scenic spots to sit and enjoy the Truckee rolling by, and periodically placed interpretive signs provide information about the human and natural history of the area. Continuing on the main trail, reach the concrete foundation of the Verdi Glen Resort, where an interpretive sign offers speculation about the building's former use.

Approaching the outlet from the millpond at the north edge of the park, the trail bends away from the river and heads back around toward the south, crossing a large, grassy field. Reach a junction with a side path leading to the last remaining building left from the Verdi Lumber Company, sitting just off the main trail and hidden from view by a cluster of tall shrubs. Traveling a short way down this side path reveals the small concrete and stone structure.

Back on the main trail, you weave across the open field to a picnic area in a small copse of ponderosa pines and cottonwoods at the end of the loop near the kiosk [2AB]. From there, simply retrace your steps through the underpass and continue shortly to the parking area [1AB].

MILESTONES

1AB: Start at parking area; 2AB: Turn left at loop junction;
2AB: Go straight at loop junction; 1AB Return to parking area.

1B ▪ Verdi Mill Pond Trail

LEVEL	Stroll, novice
LENGTH	0.6 mile, out and back
TIME	½ hour
ELEVATION	Minimal
DIFFICULTY	Easy
USERS	Hikers; kid friendly
DOGS	No
SEASON	Open all year
BEST TIMES	Spring, fall
FACILITIES	Interpretive signs, picnic tables, restrooms
MAP	Washoe County Parks: *Crystal Peak Park* (web-map at www.washoecounty.us/parks)
MANAGEMENT	Washoe County Regional Parks and Open Space at 775-328-3600, www.washoecounty.us/parks

HIGHLIGHTS Pond, fishing

LOWLIGHTS Exposed to sun, freeway noise

TIP | The park is open all year during daylight hours.

KID TIP | Small children should be supervised at all times around the mill-pond. The pond is a great spot for introducing young ones to fishing.

TRAILHEAD | 39°30.773′N, 119°59.851′W From Reno, head westbound on I-80 and take Exit 2 for east Verdi. Follow I-80 Business West to Verdi, where the road becomes Third Street. Proceed to Crystal Park Road, 3 miles from the freeway exit, and turn left. After 0.1 mile, turn right at the park entrance and continue on the access road to the parking lot.

TRAIL | Head northeast away from the parking area [**1AB**] and pass through an underpass below Third Street, reaching junction **2AB** with four paths at a circular clearing with a kiosk with a map and historical information about the area. To walk the Mill Pond Trail, veer to the right and follow a wide path past a picnic area on the left and vault toilets on the right. Just past a park bench, the old millpond springs into view and you follow a broad path along the west edge. Pass by some park benches on the way to a junction [**3B**] with a path on the right, where the pond is divided into an upper and lower section. Platforms extending away from this path allow anglers to easily drop a line for catch-and-release fishing.

Continuing ahead from the junction, you follow the broad path to the far end of the millpond [**4B**], passing another fishing platform along the way. From where the path ends near the pond's outtake drain, retrace your steps back to the parking area [**1AB**].

MILESTONES

1AB: Start at parking area; **2AB:** Turn right at junction;
3B: Millpond junction; **4B:** End of trail; **1AB:** Return to parking area.

1C ▪ Fisherman's Trail

LEVEL Stroll, novice (Walk, intermediate beyond park boundary)

LENGTH Up to 2 miles, out and back

TIME 1 hour

ELEVATION Minimal

DIFFICULTY Easy

USERS Hikers; kid friendly

DOGS On leash

SEASON Open all year

BEST TIMES Spring, fall

FACILITIES Picnic tables, restrooms (at main park)

MAP Washoe County Parks: *Crystal Peak Park*
(web-map at www.washoecounty.us/parks)

View across the Verdi Mill Pond

MANAGEMENT Washoe County Regional Parks and Open Space at 775-328-3600, www.washoecounty.us/parks

HIGHLIGHTS Fishing, river

LOWLIGHTS Exposed to sun, freeway noise

TIP | The park is open all year during daylight hours. A path extends beyond the park boundary for a good distance, although travel becomes more difficult where the canyon narrows farther upstream.

KID TIP | There is very little shade along the trail, so pack along plenty of sunscreen and water. This undeveloped stretch of the Truckee provides a fascinating environment for children to experience and explore a river environment. While hiking close to the river, small children must be supervised at all times.

TRAILHEAD | 39°30.767′N, 119°59.859′W From Reno, head westbound on I-80 and take Exit 2 for east Verdi. Follow I-80 Business West to Verdi, where the road becomes Third Street. Proceed past Crystal Park Road on the left, 3 miles from the freeway. Continue another 0.3 mile on Third Street and cross the bridge over the Truckee River. The parking area is on the left-hand shoulder just past the bridge, just across the road from the intersection of Third Street and Dusty Lane.

TRAIL | From a sign near the edge of the road reading "Crystal Peak Park, Fishing Access Trail" **[1C]**, descend a short path down toward the river and the Third Street bridge to a small clearing. On a dirt path, turn upstream and walk through the transition zone between riparian foliage along the riverbank to your left and an open field on the right. Use trails provide access to the river at various locations, as the Fisherman's Trail continues south along the river. At 0.3 mile, you reach the edge of park property [2c], just before the freeway bridge.

A path continues through a gap in a fence and proceeds along the west bank of the river for quite a while until the canyon narrows farther upstream. At whatever point you decide to end the journey, simply retrace your steps back to the trailhead [1c].

TRUCKEE RIVER, TROPHY SECTION The Truckee River upstream of Crystal Peak Park to the California border has been designated as a trophy section, where anglers are allowed only two trout (14 inches minimum) and ten whitefish per day. Only artificial lures with single barbless hooks are permissible.

MILESTONES

1c: Start at trailhead; 2c: Park boundary; 1c: Return to trailhead.

GO GREEN | Washoe County Regional Parks and Open Space has an Adopt-A-Park program, where volunteers can donate their time for working in the parks to keep them clean, attractive, and safe. The program is open to individuals and groups. For more information, visit their website at www .washoecounty.us/parks/volunteer_opportunities.php, or contact the Parks Volunteer Coordinator at 775-785-4512, ext. 107.

OPTIONS | The Sasquatch Tavern and Grill (775 Third St.) in the middle of Verdi is a fine place to stop before or after a visit to Crystal Peak Park for breakfast, lunch, or dinner. When the weather is accommodating, opt for a table outside on the deck. Crystal Peak Park's picnic areas would be fine spots for enjoying a picnic lunch.

TRIP

2 | Verdi Nature Trail

Combined with a visit to the Wildlife Education Center next door, the Verdi Nature Trail near Verdi Elementary School is a fine introduction to the ecology of the transition zone from the eastern Sierra to the Great Basin, especially for children. The loop is easily accomplished by just about anyone and by carrying the downloadable interpretive guide from the Nevada Department of Wildlife keyed to twenty-five stops along the way, you'll have plenty of useful information to share with young and old alike.

LEVEL	Stroll, novice
LENGTH	0.5 mile, loop
TIME	1 hour
ELEVATION	Minimal
DIFFICULTY	Easy
USERS	Hikers; kid friendly
DOGS	On leash
SEASON	Open all year
BEST TIME	Spring
FACILITIES	Verdi Community Library & Wildlife Education Center, restrooms
MAP	Nevada Department of Wildlife: *Verdi Nature Trail* (web-map at www.ndow.org)
MANAGEMENT	Nevada Department of Wildlife at 775-345-8104 (Verdi Community Library), www.ndow.org/Education/Wildlife _Ed/Education_Sites/Verdi_Center
HIGHLIGHTS	Interpretive trail, Verdi Community Library & Wildlife Education Center
LOWLIGHTS	Exposed to sun

TIP | The trail is open all year, from sunrise to sundown. The Wildlife Education Center is open when the public library is open (call for current hours). **KID TIP** | Most kids should find the activities at the Wildlife Education Center to be quite interesting before or after the hike. Although the trail is short, there is very little shade. Be sure to pack along plenty of sunscreen and water.

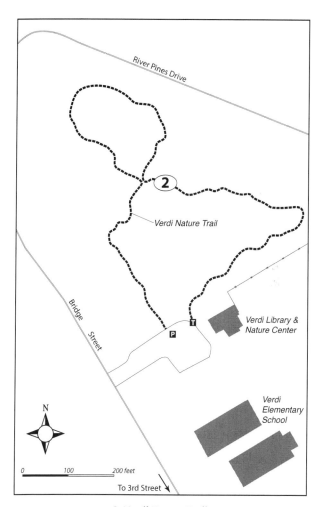

2. Verdi Nature Trail

TRAILHEAD | 39°31.312′N, 119°59.443′W From Reno, head westbound on I-80 and take Exit 2 for east Verdi. Follow I-80 Business West to Verdi, where the road becomes Third Street. Follow Third Street (Business 80) into the center of Verdi and turn northwest onto Bridge Street. Drive past Verdi Elementary School and immediately turn right into the parking area near the Wildlife Education Center.

TRAIL | From the trailhead at the northwest side of the parking lot, head out on the trail as it loops around through pine forest and then more open areas at the far side. Along the way, you pass numbered posts corresponding to the information in the brochure. After a half mile, the trail closes the loop at the trailhead.

A father and son enjoying the Verdi Nature Trail

WESTERN FENCE LIZARD (*Sceloporus occidentalis*) A hike in this area without seeing one of these common reptiles is a rare experience. Dark brown, gray, or black on top, their blue undersides have led to the nickname of blue-belly. The 2½- to 3½-inch-long lizards are most easily seen on rock outcrops, sunning themselves or performing push-ups.

GO GREEN | NDOW has volunteer opportunities for outdoor education instructors and wildlife volunteers. For more information, visit their website and follow the links to "Education" and then "Volunteer."

OPTIONS | The Outlaw Coffee Shop (1155 Third St.) in the middle of Verdi is a good place to grab a cup of coffee or a latte on the way to Crystal Peak Park. They also serve breakfast and lunch on weekdays from 6:30 to 2:30 and Saturdays from 7:30 to 2:30 (closed Sundays).

TRIP 3 | Tom Cooke Trail to Hole in the Wall

Back in the 1980s, public access to the Steamboat Ditch Trail was a hotly contested issue, pitting a few determined homeowners against hikers, runners, dog walkers, equestrians, and bikers. After a lengthy period of acrimony, a settlement was finally reached, which nowadays allows these users to enjoy their pursuits in peace. Reaching the ditch trail after a stiff climb from the Truckee River on the Tom Cooke Trail, the mellow grade is quite enjoyable, following the course of a section of the Steamboat Ditch upstream to Hole in the Wall, a tunnel used to get the ditch water from one side of Ranch Hill to the other.

LEVEL	Hike, moderate
LENGTH	5.6 miles, out and back
TIME	2 to 3 hours
ELEVATION	+450'−150'
DIFFICULTY	Moderate
USERS	Hikers, trail runners, mountain bikers, equestrians
DOGS	On leash
SEASON	All year
BEST TIMES	Spring, fall
FACILITIES	Picnic tables (Mayberry Park)
MAP	United States Geological Survey: *Verdi, Mt. Rose NW*
MANAGEMENT	City of Reno: Parks, Recreation and Community Services at 775-334-2262, www.reno.gov/government/departments /parks-recreation-community-services
HIGHLIGHTS	Irrigation ditch, views
LOWLIGHTS	Exposed to sun

TIP ǀ Summer users should start early in the day to beat the heat.

KID TIP ǀ After the initial, three-quarter-mile-long climb from the river up to the ditch trail, the grade along the ditch is quite gentle (by accessing the ditch trail from Woodchuck Drive, you could avoid the steep climb altogether—see directions to the alternate trailhead below). Adults must constantly supervise young children when water is flowing during irrigation season. Be sure to pack along plenty of sunscreen and water.

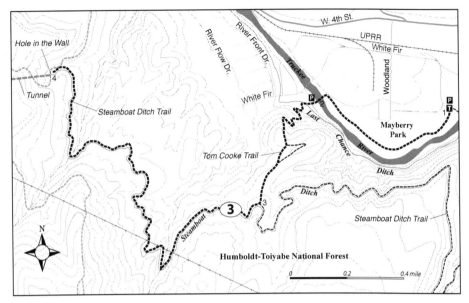

3. Tom Cooke Trail to Hole in the Wall

TRAILHEAD | 39°30.311'N, 119°53.186'W From West McCarran Boulevard, drive west on W. Fourth Street for 1.9 miles and turn left onto Woodland. Take the first left onto White Fir and curve around to the entrance to Mayberry Park and continue to the parking area. Leave your vehicle on the west edge of the parking lot.

ALTERNATE TRAILHEAD | To avoid the steep climb on the Tom Cooke Trail, drive to the Caughlin Parkway/Plumb Lane/McCarran Boulevard intersection in west Reno, head west on Caughlin Parkway for 1.2 miles and then turn left onto Plateau Road. After 0.6 mile, make another left onto Woodchuck and follow this road shortly to where you cross the Steamboat Ditch. Limited parking is nearby on the shoulder. This alternate starting point is about 2.5 miles east of the junction between the ditch trail and the Tom Cooke Trail [**MILESTONE 3**].

TRAIL | From the parking lot in Mayberry Park [1], head west on a paved section of the Tahoe-Pyramid Bikeway for 0.3 mile to a pedestrian bridge [2] spanning the Truckee River. On the far side of the bridge, follow signs up to a short bridge over the Last Chance Ditch and then make a moderate, switchbacking climb up a hillside carpeted with sagebrush scrub. Depending on how much moisture the area has received, springtime visitors may experience dashes of color from seasonal wildflowers, including California poppy, lupine, paintbrush, and phlox. After a while the grade mellows on the way to a saddle, from where you veer southwest to merge briefly with

The Tom Cooke Trail zigzagging up the hillside

an old jeep road. The short stretch of road leads to a junction [3] with the Steamboat Ditch Trail, 1.1 mile from the trailhead.

Turn right and follow the gently ascending grade of the ditch trail as it matches the meandering upstream course of the Steamboat Ditch. Amid fields of high desert flora, the ditch banks are lined with water-loving plants, including willow and wild rose, as well as some invasive species. After 0.4 mile, you bend into the canyon of a lushly lined seasonal stream, where three logs provide a dry crossing when the water is flowing. When the stream is dry, simply dip down into the drainage and climb up the far side. The easy hiking continues away from the canyon for about another mile to a second seasonal stream, where willows line the banks and tall cottonwoods provide some of the only shade along the route. A concrete channel carries the ditch water above the usually dry streambed.

Away from the second drainage, the ditch trail wraps around and comes to what locals refer to as Hole in the Wall [4]. Here Ranch Hill stands in the way of continuing the contour of the ditch, so the builders opted for a quarter-mile-long tunnel (no hiker access). The Steamboat Ditch resumes again on the west side of the hill. While most visitors are content with Hole in the Wall as their turnaround point, ambitious recreationists can climb steeply up the jeep road and over the hill to pick up the resumption of the ditch trail on the far side.

STEAMBOAT DITCH Of all the major irrigation ditches coursing through the Truckee Meadows, the Steamboat Ditch was the last to be completed. Construction of the 31-mile-long ditch began in 1878 and was completed two years later. The ditch flows into Steamboat Creek at the south end of the Truckee Meadows near Steamboat Springs, which then flows northeast to the Truckee River at the east end of the Truckee Meadows, entering the river near a water treatment facility. Beyond Hole in the Wall, the ditch continues another 9 miles to a diversion dam on the Truckee River just inside the California–Nevada state line and just south of Verdi. The Steamboat Ditch Company maintains the ditch.

MILESTONES

1: Start at Mayberry Park trailhead; **2:** Cross pedestrian bridge;
3: Turn right at Steamboat Ditch junction; **4:** Hole in the Wall;
1: Return to trailhead.

GO GREEN ⏐ Washoe County Regional Parks and Open Space has an Adopt-A-Park program, where volunteers can donate their time for working in the parks to keep them clean, attractive, and safe. The program is open to individuals and groups. For more information, visit their website at www .washoecounty.us/parks/volunteer_opportunities.php, or contact the Parks Volunteer Coordinator at 775-785-4512, ext. 107.

OPTIONS ⏐ Old roads and use trails abound in the undeveloped tracts of land bordering the ditch trail, providing countless ways to vary or extend your trip.

Dorostkar Park Nature Trail

Dorostkar Park occupies a slice of riverbank on the south side of the Truckee River in the Mayberry area of west Reno. The short and flat Nature Trail loops through riparian foliage alongside the river and then across sagebrush scrub, followed by a stretch of tall willows near the end. Along the way, interpretive signs provide interesting tidbits about the natural history of the area. Spring and early summer visitors will have the added bonus of flowering shrubs. A short out-and-back extension from the middle of the loop crosses the river on a stout pedestrian bridge and then continues downstream to a turnaround with a lone picnic table.

LEVEL	Stroll, novice
LENGTH	1.4 miles, loop (plus out-and-back extension to picnic table)
TIME	1 hour
ELEVATION	Minimal
DIFFICULTY	Easy
USERS	Hikers, trail runners; kid friendly
DOGS	On leash
SEASON	All year
BEST TIME	Spring
FACILITIES	Picnic tables
MAP	None
MANAGEMENT	Washoe County Regional Parks and Open Space at 775-328-3600, www.washoecounty.us/parks
HIGHLIGHTS	Interpretive signs, river, wildlife
LOWLIGHTS	Close to railroad tracks

TIP | The park is open from sunrise to sunset.

KID TIP | This relatively short and flat trail near the Truckee River is great for kids. However, with easy access to the river, small children must be supervised at all times. Packing along an aquarium net would be a fun tool for helping kids to discover what sort of insects make the river their home.

TRAILHEAD | 39°30.373'N, 119°53.192'W In west Reno, follow I-80 to Exit 10 for McCarran Boulevard West, turn south and travel 0.9 mile to West Fourth

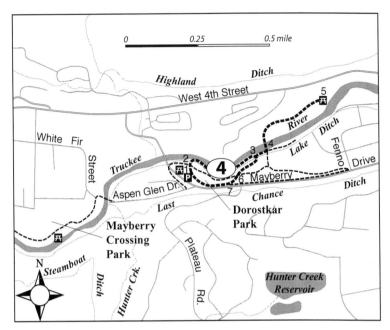

4. Dorostkar Park Nature Trail

Street. Head right (west) on Fourth Street for 1.7 miles and turn left onto Mayberry Drive. The park entrance is 0.3 mile on the left.

TRAIL | From the parking area [1], head toward the Truckee River, crossing a paved section of the Truckee-Pyramid Bikeway and a short bridge over the Lake Ditch. Turn right [2] and follow a thin strip of riparian foliage between the river and the ditch. You will encounter interpretive signs along the way. At one-third mile, you will reach a junction [3] where the Nature Trail crosses a bridge over the ditch and then loops back to the trailhead. (If you're only interested in the short hike on the Nature Trail, follow it west back toward the parking lot.)

To extend the trip beyond the Nature Trail, continue east from the loop on a dirt path to a junction with a paved trail [4]. Turn left and cross a substantial pedestrian bridge across the Truckee River, to admire the upstream and downstream views. On the far bank, the paved path parallels the river on the right and the Southern Pacific Railroad tracks on the left for one-quarter mile to a turnaround with a picnic table in the middle [5]. When the time comes to head back, simply retrace your steps to the Nature Trail junction [3].

From the Nature Trail junction, the route leaves the riparian zone and passes through sagebrush scrub. Additional interpretive signs greet you on the way to a crossing of the paved Tahoe-Pyramid Bikeway [6]. Beyond, the

Dorostkar Park bridge across the Truckee River

path parallels Mayberry Drive and continues a short distance to a three-way junction [7]. Bear right, walk through a stand of tall and dense willows, and then proceed to the end of the loop at the parking area [1].

LAKE DITCH One of several irrigation ditches siphoning water from the Truckee River, the Lake Ditch was built in the 1860s. The 14-mile ditch sends river water to Thomas Creek in south Reno, which then flows east into Alexander Lake north of the present-day Double Diamond subdivision.

MILESTONES
1: Start at Dorostkar Park trailhead; **2:** Cross paved bikeway, first Lake Ditch bridge, turn right; **3:** Cross second Lake Ditch bridge, turn left; **4:** Turn left onto paved trail, cross Truckee River bridge; **5:** Reach turnaround; **4:** Cross Truckee River bridge, turn right; **3:** Go straight at Nature Trail loop; **6:** Cross bikeway; **7:** Turn right at three-way junction; **1:** Return to trailhead.

GO GREEN | Washoe County Regional Parks and Open Space has an Adopt-A-Park program, where volunteers can donate their time for working in the parks to keep them clean, attractive, and safe. The program is open to

individuals and groups. For more information, visit their website at www
.washoecounty.us/parks/volunteer_opportunities.php, or contact the Parks
Volunteer Coordinator at 775-785-4512, ext. 107.

OPTIONS | Alternate routes and short social trails abound in and around the
park, offering opportunities for longer walks. Perhaps the most enticing
alternative is the connection to Mayberry Park: From the parking area at
Dorostkar Park, turn west and follow the paved Tahoe-Pyramid Bikeway a
short distance to an underpass below Mayberry Drive. Loop around east to
Aspen Glen Drive and follow this residential street one-quarter mile past
where Hunter Creek dumps into the river to a pedestrian bridge over the
Truckee. Shortly past the bridge and across from the River School Farm,
a paved bike trail follows above the north bank of the river into Mayberry
Park, passing lawn areas, picnic tables and barbecues grills along the way.
Beyond the park, the paved bike path continues west to the Patagonia prop-
erty, where a pedestrian bridge heads across the river to a connection with
the Tom Cooke Trail (see Trip 3). To leave a second vehicle at Mayberry
Park, head west from the Mayberry Drive/West Fourth Street intersection
for 0.4 mile and turn left onto Woodland Avenue. Take the first left onto
White Fir and curve around to the park entrance.

5 | Oxbow Nature Study Area

As long as a freight train doesn't rumble by during your visit and you can ignore the dwellings on the far side of the river, you'll feel as though you're totally in the wild at the Oxbow Nature Study Area, despite being surrounded by a completely urban setting at the edge of downtown Reno. The area is truly a hidden gem next to the Truckee River, despite the train tracks and nearby residential and industrial development. The riparian environment is captivating, with fine scenery and a diverse assortment of wildlife. Numerous interpretive signs present an abundance of interesting information about the area along the trail and from a couple of overlooks. Oxbow is a wonderful natural escape in the midst of the city.

LEVEL	Stroll, novice
LENGTH	1 mile, out and back
TIME	1 hour
ELEVATION	Minimal
DIFFICULTY	Easy
USERS	Hikers; kid friendly
DOGS	No
SEASON	All year
BEST TIME	Spring
FACILITIES	Interpretive center, picnic tables, park benches, restrooms
MAP	Nevada Department of Wildlife brochure (web-map at www.ndow.org)
MANAGEMENT	Nevada Department of Wildlife at 775-334-3808, www.ndow.org/Education/Wildlife_Ed/Education_Sites /Oxbow_Nature_Study_Area
HIGHLIGHTS	Interpretive signs, river, wildlife
LOWLIGHTS	Close to railroad tracks, interpretive signs in disrepair

TIP | The park is open from sunrise to sunset; in the winter the entrance gate closes at 4:00 PM. The trail can be muddy in spots following storms.

KID TIP | The Oxbow Nature Study Area is a great place for kids to learn about riparian ecology in a fun setting along the banks of the Truckee River. However, with the river so close by, small children should be under constant supervision. NDOW offers education programs for groups.

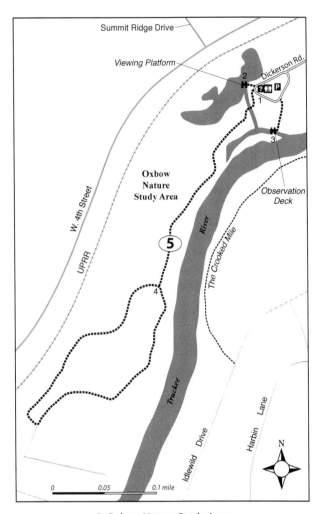

5. Oxbow Nature Study Area

TRAILHEAD | 39°31.117′, 119°50.774′ Follow Interstate 80 west from downtown Reno to the Keystone Exit and head south 0.4 mile to West Second Street. Turn right and proceed west for a half mile, where Second Street becomes Dickerson Road. Continue on Dickerson another 0.6 mile to the end of the road and the entrance to Oxbow Nature Study Area. Park in the gravel parking lot as space allows.

TRAIL | The well-signed trail begins on the northwest side of the parking area [1]. Before heading out on the trail, though, a couple of diversions are worth a little time. First, walk over to the observation deck [3] perched above the north bank of the Truckee River for an up-close look at the only watercourse exiting Lake Tahoe. In 1997 a major flood swept through this area, causing massive destruction of the park and leaving behind tons of debris—destructive evidence hard to imagine after almost two decades of recovery. Watch for mallards and Canada geese along the river's edge. On hot summer days, you may see rafters drifting along in the current. Second, an elevated viewing platform [2] on the opposite side of the park provides a good look at a fair-size pond bordered by willows and cattails.

Heading out on the trail, you soon come to a bridge over one of the park's namesake oxbows, which presently connects the pond on the right to the river on the left. Continue a short distance through dense foliage to where the path breaks out into more open habitat. Here you'll notice the residual effects from a 1999 windstorm and a 2008 fire, which flattened or charred some of the park's mature cottonwoods. The wire placed around the base of some of the still-living trees is there to deter destruction by beavers. Continuing west, a bevy of informative signs offers plenty of information about the natural history of the area. Periodically placed park benches encourage you to linger and enjoy the surroundings. Near the west end of the park, a short loop [4] pushes on to the boundary and then arcs back around to the main trail again. From there, retrace your steps to the parking lot [1].

COTTONWOODS Members of the willow family, Fremont cottonwoods (*Populus fremontii*) are found along the Truckee River intermixing with black cottonwoods (*Populus trichocarpa*). Fremont cottonwoods have light green, triangular-shaped leaves with teeth along the margins, while the leaves of black cottonwoods are heart-shaped, shiny on top and with smoother margins. The leaves of both of these cottonwoods provide vibrant color in autumn. While on the trail, you may notice chicken wire wrapped around the trunks of these trees to prevent beavers from toppling them.

GO GREEN ǀ Volunteer opportunities do exist through the NDOW. Contact them at 775-334-3808, or send an e-mail to rkeller@ndow.org for more information.

OPTIONS ǀ Through a car windshield headed for Oxbow Park, the Dickerson Road area first appears like a dingy mix of hodgepodge industrial properties peppered with some out-of-place apartment buildings. However, upon closer inspection, a burgeoning arts community is taking shape here, accompanied by an unexpected enterprise—the Oxbow Café and Bistro. Open for breakfast, lunch, and dinner every day except Monday, this relatively inexpensive little gem would be a fine spot for a meal before or after a visit to the park. Check out their website at www.oxbowcafebistro.com.

Alum Creek– Caughlin Ranch Trail

The Caughlin property was once a large ranch in West Reno extending from the Truckee River up into the foothills of the Carson Range. Nowadays, much of the land has been used for one of Reno's more upscale housing developments. However, unlike many higher-end neighborhoods in town, Caughlin Ranch is not a gated community, which allows residents and non-residents alike to walk the network of paved trails winding through the property. This trip begins in Chrissie Caughlin Park and follows a greenbelt along Alum Creek from the river to Betsy Caughlin Park and then upstream through a more picturesque greenbelt across the heart of the housing development to undeveloped Forest Service lands beyond.

LEVEL	Walk, novice
LENGTH	3 miles, shuttle; 6 miles, out and back
TIME	1 to 2 hours
ELEVATION	+500'–0'
DIFFICULTY	Easy (lower section), moderate (upper section)
USERS	Hikers
DOGS	On leash
SEASON	All year
BEST TIMES	Spring, fall
FACILITIES	Interpretive signs, picnic tables, restroom (Chrissie Caughlin Park)
MAP	Caughlin Ranch HOA: *Caughlin Ranch Trail Map* (www.caughlinhoa.com/pdf/trailmap.pdf)
MANAGEMENT	City of Reno: Parks, Recreation and Community Services at 775-334-2262, www.reno.gov/government/departments/parks-recreation-community-services; Caughlin Ranch HOA
HIGHLIGHTS	Greenbelt, stream
LOWLIGHTS	Traffic noise

TIP | As this route mostly passes over private and not public land, visitors should be courteous and respectful at all times.

KID TIP | Children should be well behaved and polite while walking by the private homes of the Caughlin Ranch neighborhood.

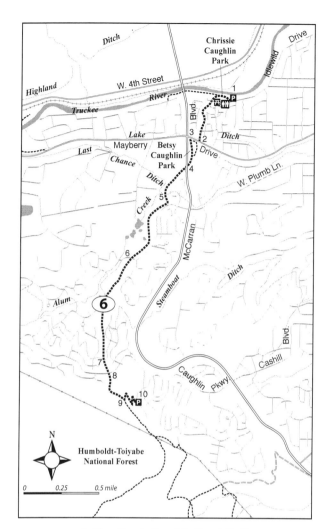

6. Alum Creek–Caughlin Ranch Trail

TRAILHEAD | 39°30.636′N, 119°51.186′W From Mayberry Drive, 0.2 mile east of the West McCarran Boulevard intersection, turn north onto River Run Parkway. Take the first right onto Riverberry Drive and follow it around to Idlewild Drive. Turn left and drive a short distance to the parking lot for Crissie Caughlin Park on the right.

For the shuttle, head south on McCarran Boulevard to the upper intersection with Caughlin Parkway and turn right. After 0.8 mile, turn left onto Turning Leaf Way and continue 0.1 mile to the vicinity of the walking path (39°30.636′N, 119°51.186′W). Park your vehicle on the side of the road as space allows.

Along the Caughlin Ranch Trail

TRAIL | From the parking lot [1], follow the paved path that weaves west through Crissie Caughlin Park, with the Truckee River flowing to your right. Immediately after crossing a pedestrian bridge over Alum Creek, turn left (south) onto a section of dirt trail shortly followed by a paved path heading upstream through a greenbelt bordering the creek between housing units on either side. Pass through an underpass below River Bend Drive and continue to a short bridge over the Lake Ditch to the sidewalk on the north side of Mayberry Drive [2]. Turn right (west) to follow the sidewalk to the West McCarran intersection, use the crosswalk to reach the southeast corner of the intersection, and then proceed through the entrance into Betsy Caughlin Park [3].

Shortly reach the paved loop circling through the park near an interpretive sign about the history of the ranch. You can go either direction here, but heading in a clockwise direction will lead past more interpretive signs. The eventual goal is to reach the underpass [4] beneath McCarran Boulevard toward the southwest corner of the park.

Beyond the underpass on the far side of McCarran, the paved path continues upstream along Alum Creek through a thin strip of greenbelt bordered by a split-rail fence. Here, the natural vegetation along the narrow creek is bordered by the landscaping of the Caughlin Ranch development, a scene that will continue all the way through the neighborhood. At 0.9 mile, you cross a bridge over the Last Chance Ditch [5], beyond which the greenbelt widens to include some scenic ponds. On the way through Caughlin Ranch, a number of intersecting side paths will come and go, but your route continuously follows Alum Creek upstream through the greenbelt. Periodically placed picnic tables offer tempting spots for breaks and snacks. The steadily rising path eventually leads across the boundary between City of Reno and Washoe County, where the Juniper Trails section of the development begins. The path crosses Caughlin Parkway [6] at 1.5 miles from Crissie Caughlin Park.

Continue up the greenbelt alongside Alum Creek, passing the tennis courts and swimming pool of Caughlin Club on the right. As you proceed upstream, the paved path repeatedly crosses the stream, which courses through culverts below the pathway. Near the 2-mile mark is a copse of native Jeffrey pines, where a picnic table and a memorial park bench offer a fine location for a rest stop. The greenbelt narrows and, at 2.4 miles, crosses the Steamboat Ditch [7] and the associated trail. A short way past the crossing, you walk through an underpass below Caughlin Parkway [8].

Although not quite as dramatic as when Dorothy opens the farmhouse door and gazes upon the colorful land of Oz in the beloved classic movie, the transformation of the landscape on the far side of the underpass is marked. The more natural vegetation of sagebrush scrub on the hillsides and Jeffrey pines lining Alum Creek replaces the manicured grounds of upscale Caughlin Ranch. After passing by the last two homes of the subdivision, the transformation is even more pronounced, as the paved path curves to the southeast to match the course of the creek. Reach a junction [9] at 2.9 miles, where the paved path turns left and a dirt path continues up the creek.

To reach the upper trailhead, turn left, cross a short bridge over Alum Creek, and then head up the asphalt path on a steep, switchbacking climb out of the canyon. At the canyon rim, follow the path between two houses to the edge of Turning Leaf Way [10].

HUMBOLDT-TOIYABE NATIONAL FOREST The trail beyond the junction to Turning Leaf Way enters national forest land, a small portion of the nearly 6.3 million acres of the Humboldt-Toiyabe National Forest that encompasses ten noncontiguous ranger districts across Nevada and a slice of eastern California. The Carson Ranger District administers the land upstream along Alum Creek.

1: Start at Crissie Caughlin Park trailhead; **2:** Turn right at Mayberry Drive; **3:** Cross Mayberry Drive and enter Betsy Caughlin Park; **4:** Pass through McCarran Boulevard underpass; **5:** Cross Last Chance Ditch; **6:** Cross Caughlin Parkway; **7:** Cross Steamboat Ditch; **8:** Pass through Caughlin Parkway underpass; **9:** Turn left at junction; **10:** End at Turning Leaf Way.

GO GREEN | The Truckee River Fund is a tax-exempt, nonprofit organization established by the Truckee Meadows Water Authority to support works that protect the Truckee River watershed. A tributary of the Truckee River, Alum Creek was so named by early residents of Reno for the presence of alum (a chemical compound) in solution in the water. Alum may not be the only thing in the water, as recent efforts sponsored by the Truckee River Fund have focused on reducing pollutants entering the stream and eventually the river. Sampling and testing have identified specific pollutants, which may lead to remediation efforts to reduce their presence and increase water quality. Caughlin Ranch has voluntarily switched to an organic fertilizer to assist these efforts. Learn more about the mission at www.truckeeriverfund.org.

OPTIONS | Anyone interested in turning this walk into a longer hike can easily do so by continuing up Alum Creek beyond the junction [9] with the paved path to Turning Leaf Way (see Trip 25).

TRIP 7
Tahoe-Pyramid Bikeway: Wingfield Park to Rock Park

Somewhat neglected and abused for decades, the Truckee River through downtown Reno is finally receiving its due as a wonderful community resource. The implementation of a variety of improvements has created a pleasant environment for tourists and residents alike. This stretch of the Tahoe-Pyramid Bikeway connects a string of city parks, interspersed with residential, commercial, and industrial lands. This section of concrete and asphalt path begins in the heart of downtown's Riverwalk District and then heads east along the river to a terminus at Rock Park in Sparks. On a normal day a wide variety of people use this popular trail, including joggers, cyclists, dog walkers, rollerbladers, wheelchair users, and families with strollers.

LEVEL	Stroll, novice
LENGTH	3.4 miles, shuttle
TIME	1½ to 2 hours
ELEVATION	Minimal
DIFFICULTY	Easy
USERS	Hikers, runners, bikers; ADA accessible
DOGS	On leash
SEASON	All year
BEST TIMES	Spring, fall
FACILITIES	Amphitheater, basketball and tennis courts, picnic tables, restrooms; whitewater park (Wingfield Park); picnic tables (Fisherman's Park); port-a-potties, picnic area, playground, whitewater park (Rock Park)
MAP	Tahoe-Pyramid Bikeway: *Verdi to Sparks: Section 3* (web-map at www.tpbikeway.org)
MANAGEMENT	City of Reno: Parks, Recreation and Community Services at 775-334-2262, www.reno.gov/government/departments /parks-recreation-community-services; City of Sparks: Parks and Facilities at 775-691-9130, www.cityofsparks.us
HIGHLIGHTS	Fishing, river
LOWLIGHTS	Homeless camps, litter, traffic noise

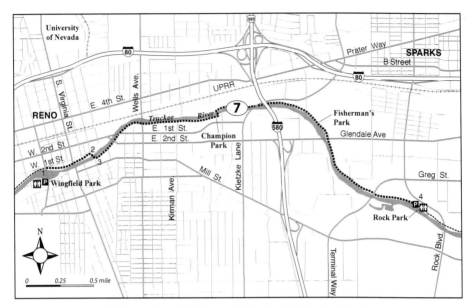

7. Tahoe-Pyramid Bikeway: Wingfield Park to Rock Park

TIP | At certain times of the year, you may see homeless camps spread across the far bank of the river outside of the downtown core, despite a posted camping ban. During the height of the tourist season, the camps are routinely cleared out.

KID TIP | Depending on individual sensibilities, parents may want to keep a close eye on youngsters on this section of the bike trail.

TRAILHEAD

START | 39°31.487′N, 119°48.996′W Wingfield Park is in the heart of Reno's Riverwalk District, bisected by South Arlington Avenue between West First Street and Island Avenue. Parking close to the park can be difficult at times, particularly in the warmer months of the year. Limited parking may be available inside the park along Island Avenue to the west of Arlington.

END | 39°31.253′N, 119°45.943′W Rock Park is located on the north bank of the Truckee River off of Rock Boulevard, between Greg Street and Mill Street.

TRAIL | From wherever you found a parking spot [1], head to the start of the Riverwalk, a concrete sidewalk on the southeast corner of the North Arlington Avenue and West First Street intersection. Follow the sidewalk along the north bank of the Truckee River through downtown Reno, following crosswalks at N. Sierra Street, N. Virginia Street, and N. Center Street. At Lake Street [2], turn right, walk over the bridge to the far side, and then cross the street near the old Reno Arch [3] to the start of an asphalt path on the north side of the National Automobile Museum.

Night view of downtown Reno from the Tahoe-Pyramid Bikeway

Follow the asphalt path along the river, passing beneath bridges at E. Second Street and Kuenzli Street. Beyond the second bridge, you pass an access path from Kuenzli and proceed into William A. Broadhead Memorial Park, named in honor of a former Reno Assistant Police Chief. Pass another access path from S. Park Street near the east end of the park, walk below the Wells Avenue overpass, and then stroll by apartment buildings on the way to an underpass below the Sutro Street bridge. After the bridge, you encounter the Reno Gazette Journal property, an industrial building, and then an undeveloped parcel before arriving at the small site of John Champion Memorial Park, named for a local businessman and a staunch advocate of the Truckee River. At the east end of the park, walk across a pedestrian bridge over the river to the north bank.

Continue the downstream journey along an asphalt path by industrial properties and beneath a tangle of highway bridges at N. Kietzke Lane and Interstate 580. Soon you enter the thin strip of greenbelt at Fisherman's Park and follow alongside Galletti Way to where the path curves and dips below Glendale Avenue. From there, stroll past a water treatment facility and continue toward an underpass below the bridge at Greg Street. On the far side of the bridge is a small patch of lawn at Gateway Park with an access point at Greg Street. Proceed past an RV park to the north edge of Rock Park and the end of this segment of the Tahoe-Pyramid Bikeway [4].

BLACK-BILLED MAGPIE (*Pica hudsonia*) Members of the crow family, black-billed magpies are common residents of the Truckee Meadows and are frequently seen in the Truckee River corridor. Easily identified by an abnormally long tail, black head, and white belly, they also sport iridescent green, blue, and violet colors on wings and tail. Typically living up to six years, magpies generally mate for life.

MILESTONES

1: Start at N. Arlington Avenue/W. First Street intersection;   **2:** Turn right at Lake Street;   **3:** Turn left at old Reno Arch;   **4:** End at Rock Park trailhead.

GO GREEN | The Tahoe-Pyramid Bikeway organization is dedicated to facilitating the completion of the 116-mile bike and foot trail from Lake Tahoe to Pyramid Lake along the Truckee River. Only three sections remain unfinished, a stretch of the Truckee River canyon in California, a section between east Sparks and Mustang, and from USA Parkway to Wadsworth. The public can donate to the nonprofit organization and volunteer for projects. For more information, visit their website at www.tpbikeway.org.

OPTIONS | You could easily extend your journey by 1.2 miles with a start at Idlewild Park, where finding a parking spot might be easier than at Wingfield Park. Simply walk west through the park, cross the Booth Street bridge, continue west along Riverside Drive, and then follow the bikeway through Bicentennial Park and along W. First Street to N. Arlington Avenue. If you want to shorten the walk, access points along the way as noted in the description make this an easy task.

Tahoe-Pyramid Bikeway: Rock Park to East Sparks

This segment of the Tahoe-Pyramid Bikeway follows a paved path along the Truckee River through the industrial zone of south Sparks, starting at Rock Park, passing through Cottonwood Park, and ending near the mouth of the lower Truckee River canyon. Much of the route follows a flood control dike along the north side of the river. Undeveloped lands on the second half of the trip offer more peace and quiet than the section of the bikeway through downtown Reno as described in Trip 7.

LEVEL	Stroll, novice
LENGTH	4.7 miles, shuttle
TIME	2 hours
ELEVATION	Minimal
DIFFICULTY	Easy
USERS	Hikers, runners, bikers; ADA accessible
DOGS	On leash
SEASON	All year
BEST TIMES	Spring, fall
FACILITIES	Port-a-potties, picnic area, playground, whitewater park (Rock Park); picnic area, restrooms (Glendale Park); fitness station, picnic tables, restrooms (Cottonwood Park)
MAP	Tahoe-Pyramid Bikeway: *Verdi to Sparks: Section 3* (web-map at www.tpbikeway.org)
MANAGEMENT	City of Sparks: Parks and Facilities at 775-691-9130, www.cityofsparks.us
HIGHLIGHTS	Fishing, river
LOWLIGHTS	Homeless camps, litter, traffic noise, slight odors from wastewater treatment plant near the end

TIP | Although typically less numerous than on the section through Reno, you may see homeless camps spread along the banks of the river, despite a posted camping ban. During the height of the tourist season, the camps are routinely cleared out.

KID TIP | Depending on individual sensibilities, parents may want to keep a close eye on youngsters on this section of the bike trail.

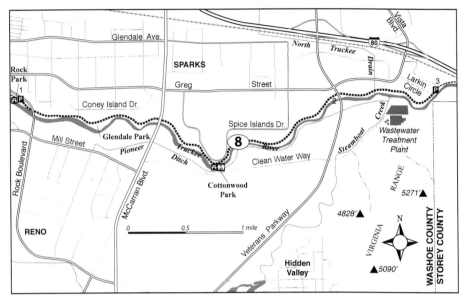

8. Tahoe-Pyramid Bikeway: Rock Park to East Sparks

TRAILHEAD START | 39°31.253′N, 119°45.943′W Follow Interstate 80 to Exit 17 for Rock Boulevard and head southbound for 1 mile to Rock Park, located on the north bank of the Truckee River between Greg Street and Mill Street.

END | 39°31.288′N, 119°41.764E Follow Interstate 80 to Exit 21 for Greg St./ Vista Blvd. and head south on Greg Street for 0.2 mile and turn left onto Larkin Circle. Proceed another 0.3 mile to where the road curves and park on the left shoulder near the asphalt bikeway as space allows.

TRAIL | Follow a sidewalk southeast through the manicured grounds of Rock Park [1] to where the surface changes to asphalt and pass underneath the Rock Boulevard bridge and then below a set of power lines on the far side. Continue eastbound with industrial properties on the left and the cottonwood-lined river to the right. At 0.6 mile is an access point at Marietta Way and a short way farther is Glendale Park with access from Coney Island Drive. Beyond Glendale Park, the path follows the winding river to an underpass below McCarran Boulevard, 1.5 miles from Rock Park.

As you continue beyond McCarran, the land on the far side of the river transitions from industrial use to agricultural at University Farms. However, the north side of the river is still covered with industrial buildings, as you curve around to come alongside Spice Islands Drive and reach Cottonwood Park.

The trees diminish beyond the park, creating a more open environment with views of the surrounding hills. Farther on, the trail passes through

The Truckee River in east Sparks

parcels of undeveloped land and reaches a junction [2] with a paved path on the left, just prior to where the bikeway passes below the new Veterans Parkway bridge. Beyond the bridge, the ambiance is a little wilder, at least on the south side of the river, where a natural landscape sweeps along the base of the Virginia Range foothills and up Steamboat Creek. Cross a bridge over the North Truckee Drain, 4.1 miles from Rock Park, and continue east across from where Steamboat Creek pours into the river. Another half mile along the asphalt leads underneath a set of power lines and a tramway before curving around toward Larkin Circle, where a short path dips down on the left to the edge of the road [3]. The asphalt path ahead continues another quarter mile to the end near the railroad tracks.

BRAZILIAN FREE-TAILED BATS (*Tadarida brasiliensis*) From June to September, you can catch an evening show for free by heading west from Rock Park on the Tahoe-Pyramid Bikeway one-quarter mile to the McCarran Boulevard bridge. Each summer evening near dusk, a colony of around 40,000 Brazilian free-tailed bats descend out of the cracks of the bridge and fly through the air at speeds up to 47 miles per hour to consume between 200 and 600 insects per evening before returning to the bridge. The bats aren't the only winged animals in the show, as hawks and owls may grab a bat or two for their evening meal.

MILESTONES

1: Start at Rock Park; **2:** Go straight at junction; **3:** End at Larkin Circle.

GO GREEN | The Tahoe-Pyramid Bikeway organization is dedicated to facilitating the completion of the 116-mile bike and foot trail from Lake Tahoe to Pyramid Lake along the Truckee River. Only three sections remain unfinished, a stretch of the Truckee River canyon in California, a section between east Sparks and Mustang, and from USA Parkway to Wadsworth. The public can donate to the nonprofit organization and volunteer for projects. For more information, visit their website at www.tpbikeway.org.

OPTIONS | Until the bikeway is extended, there are no options for extending this trip farther east. Cyclists can make a connection to north-south routes along Veterans Parkway and Sparks Boulevard.

Tahoe-Pyramid Bikeway: Mustang to Patrick

This segment of the Tahoe-Pyramid Bikeway leads into the Nature Conservancy's McCarran Ranch Preserve, where an extensive restoration program is underway along the Truckee River. So far, the multimillion-dollar project has been a great success, restoring the river to a more natural course after decades of man-made "improvements" that channelized the river and led to habitat and species loss. Considered its flagship project for river restoration, the Nature Conservancy has recently opened these lands to the public, creating a fine spot to enjoy the riparian environment and appreciate the recuperative powers of nature.

LEVEL	Walk, intermediate
LENGTH	5.2 miles, shuttle
TIME	2 to 3 hours
ELEVATION	Minimal
DIFFICULTY	Easy
USERS	Hikers, trail runners, mountain bikers
DOGS	On leash
SEASON	All year
BEST TIMES	Spring, fall
FACILITIES	None
MAP	Tahoe-Pyramid Bikeway: *Mustang to USA Parkway* (web-map at www.tpbikeway.org)
MANAGEMENT	The Nature Conservancy at 775-322-4990, www.nature.org
HIGHLIGHTS	Fishing, river, wildlife
LOWLIGHTS	Close to railroad tracks and freeway

TIP | Wildlife viewing will probably be most productive just after sunrise and before sunset. You may be surprised by the presence of horse dung along the way, as the trail is not open to equestrians. However, herds of wild horses are often present in this area.

KID TIP | Children usually find flowing water to be a quite captivating environment and this section of the Truckee will be no exception. The opportunity to see various species of wildlife should be fascinating as well. A fun activity

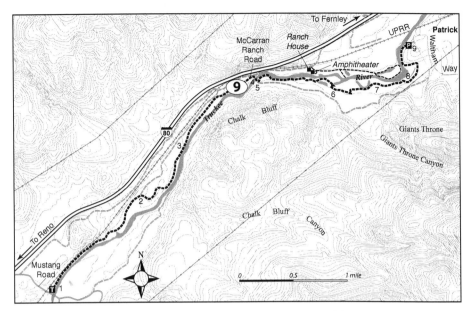

9. Tahoe-Pyramid Bikeway: Mustang to Patrick

would be to get a book from the library or an online source that helps children identify the animal tracks they may see on the way. The river, while beautiful, can be dangerous when flows are high and fast, requiring parents to keep a close eye on their progeny.

TRAILHEAD START | 39°31.170′N, 119°37.133′W From Reno, follow Interstate 80 east to Exit 23 for Mustang. At the stop sign, turn left and go 0.3 mile and take the first left. Pass under the freeway, take the next left and continue ahead on the frontage road for 0.3 mile and then follow Mustang Road as it bends toward the river for another 0.4 mile. Just after passing below a railroad trestle, watch for the graveled Tahoe-Pyramid Bikeway parking area on the left.

END | 39°33.062′N, 119°33.452′W Follow Interstate 80 east from Reno-Sparks to Exit 28 for Patrick. Turn right and head southeast on Waltham Way, cross a bridge over the Truckee, and come to a four-way intersection just beyond the bridge. Turn right to remain on Waltham, pass through a railroad crossing, and immediately turn right onto Wild Horse Canyon Drive, 0.2 mile from the intersection. Continue another 0.1 mile and look for a paved road on the right, just south of a building. Turn down this road, which soon turns to dirt, and proceed to the parking area at the end.

TRAIL | Leaving the gravel parking area [1], you pass through a gap in a fence and follow the compacted dirt path of a road on the north side of the Truckee River, with the railroad tracks a short way up the hill to the left.

The Truckee River as seen from the Tahoe-Pyramid Bikeway

The scenery is quite pleasant, with the Truckee River winding and drifting through the canyon and the Clark Hills rising above to the east. At least on the initial segment, the road noise from the freeway is muted by a row of hills between the river and the interstate. At a pair of signs you enter the Nature Conservancy's McCarran Ranch Preserve at 0.6 mile.

About 0.2 mile from the preserve's boundary is an area where restoration work was ongoing in 2015. Farther on, around the 1.25-mile mark, the road bends toward the river and ascends a low rise. The road comes alongside and follows a diversion ditch for a while before veering away to the left. After passing through a gap in a barbed wire fence, 2.5 miles from the trailhead, you reach a three-way junction [2] and turn right toward the river, crossing over the ditch on the way.

The steady drone of traffic becomes more noticeable where the river bends closer to the freeway, and passing trains rumble along occasionally on the even-closer railroad tracks. Proceed ahead at a junction [3] with a road down to the riverbank and continue to a junction [4] with the McCarran Ranch Road.

Turn right onto the well-graded gravel road and walk across a bridge over the river to the far side and then turn left at a junction [5] with the continuation of the bikeway.

Follow the dirt road closer to the river and around a short "S" bend. After a while, you pass beneath a set of power lines and continue to a junction [6], where a single-track path veers away from the road and follows a backwater finger of the river. A set of interpretive signs nearby offers information about the plants and animals in this riparian environment. Eventually the path merges again with the Tahoe-Pyramid Bikeway [7] across open sagebrush scrub with good views of the surrounding terrain, including Giants Throne.

At a junction [8], 4 miles from the trailhead, leave the road and follow a single-track trail again, reaching another set of signs after 0.3 mile. Beyond the signs, you pass to the left of a motocross park and to the right of an overflow pond. At the north end of the pond, the trail bends sharply west, passes through a gap in a fence, and then curves north along the main channel of the river. Eventually, the trail bends away from the river on a short climb up to the ending trailhead [9].

> **BALD EAGLE** (*Haliaeetus leucocephalus*) Although far from a common sight in the skies of western Nevada, bald eagles are occasionally seen in the Truckee River canyon, usually during the winter months. With recent improvements to the river's health, primarily under the guidance of the Nature Conservancy, the hope is that our national bird will become a more frequent visitor. The characteristic white, or "bald," head does not appear until the birds are about five years old. Despite a wingspan of 6 to 7 feet that makes them appear to be quite large for birds, bald eagles only weigh between 10 and 14 pounds. When not nesting, they tend to be communal, with large groups roosting in tall trees.

MILESTONES

1: Start at Mustang trailhead; **2:** Turn right at three-way junction; **3:** Go straight at junction; **4:** Turn right at McCarran Ranch Road (bridge); **5:** Turn left at junction; **6:** Turn left at junction; **7:** Merge with bikeway; **8:** Turn left at junction; **9:** End at Patrick trailhead.

GO GREEN | The Nature Conservancy has done an excellent job restoring portions of the lower Truckee River to a more natural course with projects at the McCarran Ranch, 102 Ranch, Lockwood, and Tracy Ranch. To learn more about their work, volunteer for projects, or make a donation, check out their website at www.nature.org and follow the "Our Work" and "Where We Work" link to Nevada.

OPTIONS | Extending the hike along the next section of the bikeway to the USA Parkway trailhead is possible, although walking or biking sections of road on Wild Horse Canyon Drive and Waltham Way between the west and east Tracy trailheads will be necessary.

10 Lockwood Trails

Near the mouth of the Truckee River canyon east of Sparks, this trip combining the Interpretive and Lockwood Loops provides a short and easy jaunt along the banks of the river.

LEVEL	Stroll, novice
LENGTH	1.5 miles, loop
TIME	1 hour
ELEVATION	Minimal
DIFFICULTY	Easy
USERS	Hikers, runners; ADA accessible
DOGS	On leash
SEASON	All year
BEST TIMES	Spring, fall
FACILITIES	Interpretive signs, picnic area, restroom
MAP	Washoe County Parks: *Lockwood Trailhead Park* (web-map at www.washoecounty.us/parks)
MANAGEMENT	Washoe County Regional Parks and Open Space at 775-328-3600, www.washoecounty.us/parks
HIGHLIGHTS	Interpretive signs, river, wildlife
LOWLIGHTS	Close to railroad tracks and freeway

TIP | Lockwood Park is open from sunrise to sunset. Although there is some shade along the circuit next to the Truckee River, the vast majority of the route is exposed to the sun. Walk here in the morning or evening if you plan to hike this trail during the summer months.

KID TIP | This short and easy trail can be a great spot to bring the kids for exploring the riparian zone along the Truckee, but the close proximity to the river means adults will need to continuously supervise small children. As the chances of seeing waterfowl, especially ducks, on this trip are high, this might be a great place for children to start compiling a bird life list. Numerous online resources can help you get started. The signs along the Interpretive Trail provide opportunities to inform children about the river's environment.

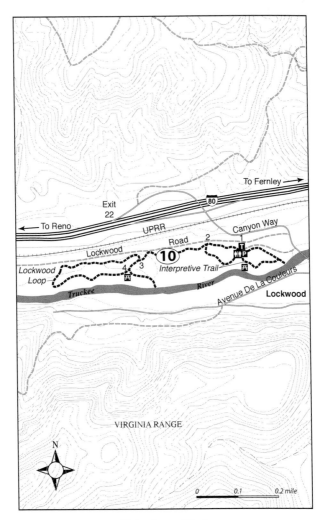

10. Lockwood Trails

TRAILHEAD ❘ 39°30.594′N, 119°39.107′W From Reno, head eastbound on I-80 to Exit 22, 7.5 miles from the Interstate 580 interchange. Turn right onto Canyon Way and drive 0.2 mile past Lockwood Road to the entrance road on the right just before the bridge over the river, marked by a small Washoe County Regional Parks sign. Follow the road a short way to the parking lot.

TRAIL ❘ From the vicinity of the restroom [1], follow the wide, level track of the trail west to start a counterclockwise loop. You will soon encounter a junction [2], where the Interpretive Trail veers to the left and the Lockwood Loop Trail goes straight ahead. Continue ahead past a picnic table near an

View from the Lockwood Loop

old cottonwood tree to a signed junction [3] with the loop portion, 0.25 mile from the trailhead.

From the junction, follow the right-hand path through open areas of sagebrush scrub, and attempt to ignore the constant hum of traffic speeding by on the interstate. Nearing the west edge of the property, the trail bends south toward the river and reaches a wide spot, where a conveniently placed park bench offers the opportunity to sit and enjoy watching the current of the Truckee River glide by you. Amid scattered cottonwoods, with their trunks wrapped with chicken wire as protection against the beavers, you head east above the riverbank. You will reach a junction [4] with the River Access Trail at 0.75 mile, where another picnic table is nearby. The extremely short path leads right to the very edge of the river at River Vista for a fine view. When you've seen enough, simply retrace your steps shortly back to the junction [4].

From the junction, follow the left-hand trail west through a copse of scattered, young cottonwoods and then sagebrush scrub. A narrow use trail on the right leads along the finger of a slough and then follows the main river channel back to the parking area. Remaining on the main trail, you soon close the loop section at the junction [3] and retrace your steps east for a short distance to the junction [2] with the Interpretive Trail. If you're pressed for time, simply head back toward the parking area.

For the full trip, turn right at the junction [2] and follow the Interpretive Trail toward the north bank of the river. As you follow the river's edge, keen eyes may spot a variety of waterfowl. Pass another well-placed picnic table with a nice view of the river and an interpretive sign nearby about the Truckee River Basin. From there, the trail bends slightly away from the river and comes to a crossing of the park access road, which heads to the boat launch on the right. After crossing the road, head south above the river to a junction, where a short path leads over to the river's edge and a view of some rapids. Back on the main trail, walk past more picnic areas and interpretive signs as you loop around, cross the access road, and proceed to the end [1] near the restroom building.

> **MALLARDS** (*Anas platyrhynchos*) Along with Canada geese, mallards are the most common waterfowl in the waterways of the Reno-Sparks area. Males are easily identified by their iridescent-green heads, bright yellow bills, gray bodies, and black tails. The less colorful females have mostly brown bodies. These ubiquitous birds are found throughout North America. Although a common practice, humans should avoid feeding bread to wild ducks, as doing so could inadvertently lead to malnutrition, overcrowding, pollution, loss of natural behavior, and susceptibility to diseases.

MILESTONES

1: Start at trailhead; 2: Go straight at Interpretive Trail junction; 3: Turn right at loop junction; 4: Turn right at River Access Trail junction; 3: Go straight at loop junction; 2: Turn right at Interpretive Trail junction; 1: End at trailhead.

GO GREEN | The Nature Conservancy has done an excellent job restoring portions of the lower Truckee River to a more natural course with projects at the McCarran Ranch, 102 Ranch, Lockwood, and Tracy Ranch. To learn more about their work, volunteer for projects, or make a donation, check out their website at www.nature.org and follow the "Our Work" and "Where We Work" link to Nevada.

OPTIONS | Plenty of picnic tables around the loop offer fine places to watch the river while you enjoy lunch or a snack. Otherwise, there's little in the way of amenities in this section of the Truckee River canyon, but nearby sections of the Tahoe-Pyramid Bikeway are good options for additional hikes.

11 | McCarran Ranch Preserve

Over the years, the presence of modern man has not been kind to the Truckee River. Among other detrimental effects, channelization of the river east of Sparks resulted in loss of vegetation, introduction of nonnative species, habitat loss, and loss of animal species. Thanks to the Nature Conservancy and its partners, restoration efforts have made a huge impact in reversing these effects. Due to the willingness of the Conservancy to open the property to the public, visitors can learn about these efforts firsthand while enjoying a stretch of the river on the site of the old McCarran Ranch. Utilizing a combination of new trails, old roads, and a new bridge across the Truckee, hikers can follow the river upstream along the south bank and then downstream along the north bank to the old ranch house. Additional trails on the property provide the opportunity for further wanderings from there.

LEVEL	Walk, intermediate
LENGTH	5.5 miles, out and back
TIME	2 to 3 hours
ELEVATION	Minimal
DIFFICULTY	Easy to moderate
USERS	Hikers, trail runners, mountain bikers
DOGS	On leash
SEASON	All year
BEST TIMES	Spring, fall
FACILITIES	Amphitheater, port-a-potty, picnic table (at ranch)
MAP	The Nature Conservancy: *McCarran Ranch Preserve* (web-map at www.nature.org)
MANAGEMENT	The Nature Conservancy at 775-322-4990, www.nature.org
HIGHLIGHTS	Fishing, interpretive signs, history, river, wildlife
LOWLIGHTS	Freeway and railroad noise

TIP | Wildlife viewing will probably be most productive just after sunrise and before sunset. You may be surprised by the presence of horse dung along the way, as the trail is not open to equestrians. However, herds of wild horses

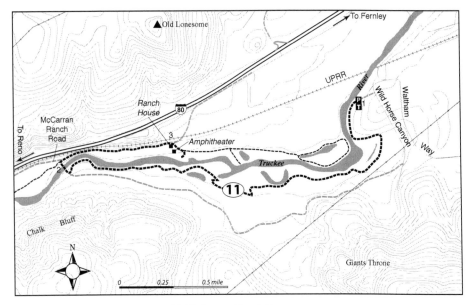

11. McCarran Ranch Preserve

are often present in this area. If you're fortunate enough to see mustangs on your trip, keep your distance, speak in a low voice, and don't even contemplate the idea of feeding them. Packing along a pair of binoculars or a spotting scope might be a good idea.

KID TIP | This gently graded trail can be a great spot to bring the kids for exploring the riparian zone along the Truckee, but the close proximity to the river means adults will need to continuously supervise small children. The river, while beautiful, can be dangerous when flows are high and fast. Since 2008 the Nature Conservancy has been very proactive in providing opportunities to educate students about conservation. To participate in their program, or for more information, contact nevada@tnc.org. Identifying Giants Throne and guessing how this feature got its name might stimulate younger kids.

TRAILHEAD | 39°33.062′N, 119°33.452′W Follow Interstate 80 east from Reno-Sparks to Exit 28 for Patrick. Turn right and head southeast on Waltham Way, cross a bridge over the Truckee, and come to a four-way intersection just beyond the bridge. Turn right to remain on Waltham, pass through a railroad crossing, and immediately turn right onto Wild Horse Canyon Drive, 0.2 mile from the intersection. Continue another 0.1 mile and look for a paved road on the right, just south of a newer building. Turn down this road, which soon turns to dirt, and follow it to the parking area at the end.

TRAIL | Next to a trio of signs providing information about the Truckee River and the Nature Conservancy's restoration projects, you drop away from the parking area [1] and follow the riverbank on an upstream course. Soon, the trail bends away from the river, passes through an opening in a fence and by another sign with a timeline for the McCarran Ranch, and then curves back to the west. Walk to the right of a motocross park and draw closer to the river again near a stand of mature cottonwoods. Just to the right of the trail, at 0.9 mile from the trailhead, are more signs about the restoration project and the river's ecology. Farther on, the trail bends around and merges with the Tahoe-Pyramid Bikeway at 1.2 miles. Follow the wide track of the bike route across open topography, which allows views of the surrounding hills, including Giants Throne to the southeast. Soon, your route veers off the roadbed and back onto a narrower trail that curves down alongside a backwater finger of the river. Another set of signs nearby provides information about some of the flora and fauna. Beyond the area of the signs, the trail comes alongside the main river channel and proceeds upstream. After passing beneath a set of power lines, the river and trail move closer to the freeway and the railroad tracks, with a corresponding increase in noise levels. After a short "S" curve, you merge with a well-graded gravel road and cross the river on a modern bridge [2], 2.3 miles from the trailhead.

Now on the north bank of the river, merge with the course of the old McCarran Ranch Road and head eastward below the railroad tracks and the freeway above. After about a half mile, the road brings you to the old ranch house [3], a small, white building now used as a field office by the Nature Conservancy. A lone picnic table is near the house and a port-a-potty is

---

TRUCKEE RIVER Along with Pyramid Lake, the Truckee helped sustain the native Paiutes for generations, especially two species of fish, the cui-ui and Lahontan cutthroat trout. In the mid-1800s, the craze of the Comstock Lode soiled the river and its tributaries with sawdust and logging debris. During the same period, much of the water in the river was diverted for irrigation purposes, with eight major ditches supplying ranches in the Truckee Meadows. In the early 1900s, additional water was diverted at Derby Dam east of Mustang, transported via the Truckee Canal, and then delivered to farms and ranches around Fallon. These improvements were done as part of the Bureau of Reclamation's maiden endeavor, the Newlands Project. Later, in the mid-1900s, the Army Corps of Engineers embarked on plans to channelize portions of the Truckee River for flood protection. The work of the Nature Conservancy and its partners has mitigated some of these more misguided "improvements."

usually just across the way. Toward the river is an amphitheater with three rows of natural stone benches. From the south side of the amphitheater, a path heads upstream along the river for a bit to the vicinity of a pond. When your visit is over, retrace your steps back to the trailhead [1].

MILESTONES

1: Start at trailhead; **2:** Bridge over Truckee River; **3:** McCarran Ranch house; **1:** Return to trailhead.

GO GREEN | The Nature Conservancy has done an excellent job restoring portions of the lower Truckee River to a more natural course with projects at the McCarran Ranch, 102 Ranch, Lockwood, and Tracy Ranch. To learn more about their work, volunteer for projects, or make a donation, check out their website at www.nature.org and follow the "Our Work" and "Where We Work" link to Nevada.

OPTIONS | An old road heads downstream from the ranch house to a side road to an overflow pond and then continues east to a short loop around another pond at the far end of the property.

CHAPTER TWO

THE TRUCKEE MEADOWS

Although formerly referring to the series of meadows bisected by the Truckee River and some of its tributaries, in modern times the term *Truckee Meadows* has become interchangeable with the principal valley of the Reno-Sparks community. Situated within an approximately 100-square-mile basin between the Carson and Virginia ranges, much of the area has been developed over the last 150 years. Except for the north part of Rancho San Rafael Regional Park, the rest of the trails described in this chapter pass through developed parks or urban settings.

12 Rancho San Rafael Regional Park

Potentially slated to become another cookie-cutter neighborhood of sub-division homes, Rancho San Rafael Regional Park was saved from such ignominy in the late 1970s. Since then, additional properties have been added or transferred to create this nearly 600-acre gem of a park in north-west Reno. A number of trails and old roads form a modest network of routes for walkers, hikers, and bikers throughout the park, from concrete sidewalks across manicured lawns to single-track dirt trails along wetlands and across sagebrush scrub. A walk through the Wilbur D. May Arboretum and Botanical Garden can be a serene journey through gardens filled with native and introduced species of plants able to thrive in the challenging cli-mate of the high desert. Combining the Evans Creek Trail and Nature Trail takes you away from the developed part of the park into a unique wetlands environment along an intermittent creek, which is home to a variety of wild-life. The Pasture Loop encircles a large pastureland containing an expansive dog park, with fine views across the open field of the surrounding moun-tains. Along with the trail system, the park offers much more to see and do.

12A ▪ Arboretum Loop

LEVEL	Stroll, novice
LENGTH	Varies, up to 1.5 miles loop
TIME	1 to 2 hours
ELEVATION	+75′–75′
DIFFICULTY	Easy
USERS	Hikers; ADA accessible (parts)
DOGS	No
SEASON	All year
BEST TIMES	Spring through early summer, fall
FACILITIES	Dog park, museum, picnic areas, playground, restrooms
MAP	Washoe County Parks: *Wilbur D. May Arboretum and Botanical Garden Trail Map* (available near trailhead)
MANAGEMENT	Washoe County Regional Parks and Open Space at 775-328-3600, www.washoecounty.us/parks

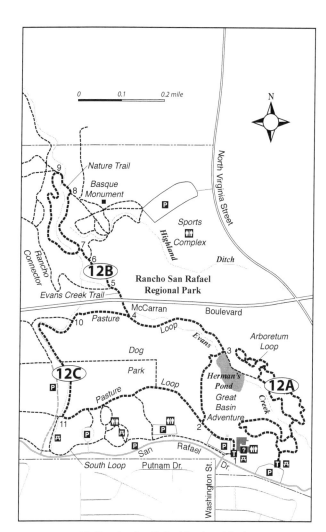

12. Rancho San Rafael Regional Park

HIGHLIGHTS Flora, interpretive signs, views

LOWLIGHTS Traffic noise

TIP ⏐ As park hours vary, changing as often as every two weeks in the spring, check the park's voicemail message for updates at 775-785-4512.

KID TIP ⏐ As stated on a sign near the entry, the arboretum is intended to be a quiet place. Therefore, if you plan to take small children, make sure they can be kept under control.

TRAILHEAD ⏐ 39°32.788′N, 119°49.537′W Take Exit 13 from Interstate 80, signed for Downtown Reno/S. Virginia Street. Proceed ahead on Eighth

Street to Sierra Street and turn right. Head north on Sierra for 0.7 mile to a left-hand turn onto Putnam Drive and continue a short distance to the east entrance into the park on your right. Follow the park access road to the second parking lot on the right and park your vehicle as space allows.

TRAIL | The well-marked entry to the Arboretum Loop is near the northwest corner of the structure housing the May Museum. Following a network of concrete, asphalt, and natural paths, the trail wanders through a variety of differently themed gardens, allowing you to see as much or as little of the botanical areas as you choose. Shortly beyond the entry, a kiosk has maps available to help guide you through the labyrinth of gardens within the 13-acre living museum. Park benches, water fountains, shade structures, water features, and a gazebo enhance the journey, while interpretive signs aid in understanding the human and natural history of the area and botanical signs help identify the plants. The arboretum is definitely a place not to be in a hurry, so take your time and enjoy the botanical diversity. The south and north sides of the arboretum are separated by Evans Creek flowing east out of Herman's Pond, where a wooden bridge is the only way across the creek between the two sections. The trail system on the north side ascends a hillside to an overlook above Herman's Pond, where a set of interpretive signs identifies the surrounding mountains in view.

12B ▪ Evans Creek Trail and Nature Trail

LEVEL	Walk, intermediate
LENGTH	2 miles, lollipop loop
TIME	1 hour
ELEVATION	+125'−125'
DIFFICULTY	Easy
USERS	Hikers, trail runners
DOGS	On leash
SEASON	All year
BEST TIME	Spring to early summer
FACILITIES	Dog park, museum, picnic areas, playground, restrooms
MAP	Washoe County Parks: *Rancho San Rafael Park* (web-map at www.washoecounty.us/parks)
MANAGEMENT	Washoe County Regional Parks and Open Space at 775-328-3600, www.washoecounty.us/parks
HIGHLIGHTS	Interpretive signs, stream, wetlands, wildlife
LOWLIGHTS	Traffic noise

TIP | As park hours vary, changing as often as every two weeks in the spring, check the park's voicemail message for updates at 775-785-4512.

KID TIP | This should be a fun hike for kids. The interpretive signs along the Nature Trail provide an opportunity to expose them to the wonders of the natural world.

TRAILHEAD | 39°32.785′N, 119°49.592′W Take Exit 13 from Interstate 80, signed for Downtown Reno/S. Virginia Street. Proceed ahead on Eighth Street to Sierra Street and turn right. Head up Sierra for 0.7 mile to a left-hand turn onto Putnam Drive and continue a short distance to the east entrance into the park on the right. Follow the park access road to the second parking lot on the right and park your vehicle as space allows.

TRAIL | The trail begins at the northwest corner of the parking lot [1] and follows the wide track of a compacted gravel road and soon comes to a junction [2] with a narrower road on the right. Turn right and follow a gently graded path along a white fence bordering the large pasture on the left, and the site of the closed Great Basin Adventure beyond the trees to your right. Where the road bends to the right, you pass a park bench and an interpretive sign near the shore of Herman's Pond. You will cross a bridge over Evans Creek and immediately reach a junction [3]. Here, the right-hand path travels around the pond and connects with the Arboretum Trail.

Turn left and follow the nearly level trail that crosses another bridge and eventually arcs west below the embankment of McCarran Boulevard. At 0.5 mile, reach a T-junction [4] between the continuation of the Pasture Loop ahead and the Evans Creek Trail turning right.

Turn right (north) and walk through the underpass below McCarran Blvd. to the far side, where the path bends around and reaches a junction [5] with the Rancho Connector. Proceed on the right-hand trail from the junction, passing to the right of a broad area of wetlands filled with cattails and dotted with cottonwoods. Come to the next junction [6] with the lower segment of the Nature Trail on the right coming from the parking area near the park's sports complex. Veer left and walk a short distance on a narrower dirt path to the loop junction [7].

Proceed ahead at the junction and head upstream along the course of Evans Creek beneath the shade of a stand of cottonwoods and past the first interpretive signs describing the natural and human history of the area. At 1 mile you reach a junction with the upper segment of the trail from the sports complex and very shortly a second, signed junction [8], where the Evans Creek Trail continues ahead and the Nature Trail turns sharply left.

Remaining on the Nature Trail, you head left and then turn downstream. Cross over a concrete swale at the site of the former Highland Ditch flume and continue down the canyon past more interpretive signs, eventually winding around to a wood-railed bridge over a tributary. Proceed to a signed junction [9], where the right-hand trail provides a short link to the Rancho Connector.

Dog walkers in Rancho San Rafael Regional Park

Turn sharply left at the junction and soon come to a wood-plank bridge. On the far side is the close of the loop [7]. From there, simply retrace your steps back to the trailhead.

> **GREAT HORNED OWL** (*Bubo virginianus*) Common across North America and much of South America, this aggressive, powerful, and usually nocturnal hunter also goes by the name of "tiger owl." Rabbits, snakes, lizards, and smaller birds appear to be their most common prey in our area, but they have been known to go after larger mammals, such as skunks, as well. Characteristic ear tufts, glowing yellow or orange eyes, and haunting hoots easily identify this raptor.

MILESTONES

1: Start at trailhead; **2:** Turn right at Pasture Loop junction; **3:** Turn left at junction near Herman's Pond; **4:** Turn right at underpass junction; **5:** Turn right at Rancho Connector junction; **6:** Turn left at lower Nature Trail junction; **7:** Go straight at loop junction; **8:** Turn left at Evans Creek Trail junction; **9:** Turn left at junction; **7:** Turn right at loop junction; **1:** Return to trailhead.

12C ▪ Pasture Loop

LEVEL	Stroll, novice
LENGTH	1.4 miles, loop
TIME	1 hour
ELEVATION	+100'–100'
DIFFICULTY	Easy
USERS	Hikers, runners, bikers
DOGS	On leash
SEASON	All year
BEST TIMES	Spring to early summer
FACILITIES	Dog park, museum, picnic areas, playground, restrooms
MAP	Washoe County Parks: *Rancho San Rafael Park* (web-map at www.washoecounty.us/parks)
MANAGEMENT	Washoe County Regional Parks and Open Space at 775-328-3600, www.washoecounty.us/parks
HIGHLIGHTS	Pasture, views
LOWLIGHTS	Traffic noise

TIP ı As park hours vary, changing as often as every two weeks in the spring, check the park's voicemail message for updates at 775-785-4512.

KID TIP ı Kids who like dogs should be well entertained on this loop while watching them cavort around the popular dog park.

TRAILHEAD ı 39°32.785′N, 119°49.592′W Take Exit 13 from Interstate 80, signed for Downtown Reno/S. Virginia Street. Proceed ahead on Eighth Street to Sierra Street and turn right. Head up Sierra for 0.7 mile to a left-hand turn onto Putnam Drive and continue a short distance to the east entrance into the park on the right. Follow the park access road to the second parking lot on the right and park your vehicle as space allows.

TRAIL ı The trail begins at the northwest corner of the parking lot **[1]**. It follows the wide track of a compacted gravel road and soon comes to a junction **[2]** with a narrower road on the right. Turn right and follow a gently graded path along a white fence bordering the large pasture on the left, and the site of the closed Great Basin Adventure beyond the trees to your right. Where the road bends to the right, you pass a park bench and an interpretive sign near the shore of Herman's Pond. You will cross a bridge over Evans Creek and immediately reach a junction **[3]**. Here, the right-hand path travels around the pond and connects with the Arboretum Trail.

Turn left and follow the nearly level trail that crosses another bridge and eventually arcs west below the embankment of McCarran Boulevard. At 0.5 mile, reach a T-junction [4] between the continuation of the Pasture Loop ahead and the Evans Creek Trail turning right.

Beyond the junction, the Pasture Loop embarks on the only significant climb on the entire circuit, ascending to a high point near the edge of McCarran Boulevard, where a memorial bench tempts passersby to sit and enjoy the view of the surrounding mountains. The trail drops away from the high point and curves around to meet a section of the Highland Ditch. A short way farther, a bridge across the ditch leads to a path [10] that continues up to the edge of McCarran Boulevard. The Pasture Loop continues to follow the curve of the ditch around the west side of the fenced dog park. Reach a junction [11] where a second bridge spans the ditch on the right and turn left onto a concrete sidewalk.

With the pasture/dog park to your left, you walk on the sidewalk across manicured lawns on the right, past picnic tables, a playground, and a pond, to meet the compacted gravel surface of the old road once again. Follow the road along the white fence as it curves back to the junction [2], and then retrace your steps the short distance back to the parking lot [1].

MILESTONES

1: Start at trailhead; **2:** Turn right at Pasture Loop junction. **3:** Turn left at junction near Herman's Pond; **4:** Go straight at underpass junction; **10:** Turn left at junction; **11:** Turn left at Pasture Loop junction; **1:** Return to trailhead.

GO GREEN | Washoe County Regional Parks and Open Space has an Adopt-A-Park program, where volunteers can donate their time for working in the parks to keep them clean, attractive, and safe. The program is open to individuals and groups. For more information, visit their website at www .washoecounty.us/parks/volunteer_opportunities.php, or contact the Parks Volunteer Coordinator at 775-785-4512, ext. 107.

OPTIONS | Extensions are possible for both the Evans Creek Trail and Nature Trail trip and the Pasture Loop trip. You could continue up Evans Canyon from the upper junction of the Nature Trail as described in Trip 21. The South Park Loop could easily be added to the Pasture Loop.

Adding a picnic to the agenda could be an enjoyable way to spend a day in the park. Those who prefer a meal at a restaurant have plenty of options nearby. Archie's is a 24/7 diner serving breakfast all day and specializing in their "world famous" giant hamburgers. Located across from the University of Nevada, Reno, at 2195 S. Virginia Street, the establishment is a favorite hangout of college students.

Bartley Ranch Loop and Anderson Trail

There's plenty to do at Bartley Ranch Regional Park, including walking on some of the park's trails. The premier route is the Bartley Ranch Loop, a 1.5-mile circuit leading to grand views and interesting glimpses into the history of Reno's ranching days. Park activities during the summer include free concerts at the Robert Z. Hawkins Amphitheater during Reno's Artown festival. Combining your walk with exploration of the historic buildings, a visit to the interpretive center, and a picnic lunch would be a fine way to spend a day.

Anderson Park preserves 70 acres of ranchland in the shadow of Windy Hill, where old roads have been converted into recreational trails for a variety of users. The essentially flat property makes for easy walking and the open fields allow for fine views of the mountains bordering the Truckee Meadows. Land acquisitions finalized in the early 2000s created a straight-forward connection to Bartley Ranch Regional Park (see Trip 13A).

13A ▪ Bartley Ranch Loop

LEVEL	Walk, intermediate
LENGTH	1.5 miles, loop
TIME	1 hour
ELEVATION	+175′–175′
DIFFICULTY	Easy
USERS	Hikers, runners, mountain bikers, equestrians; kid friendly
DOGS	On leash
SEASON	All year
BEST TIMES	Spring, fall
FACILITIES	Amphitheater, equestrian facilities, historical buildings, interpretive center, picnic area, restrooms
MAP	Washoe County Parks: *Bartley Ranch Regional Park and Anderson Park* (web-map at washoecounty.us/parks)
MANAGEMENT	Washoe County Regional Parks and Open Space at 775-328-3600, www.washoecounty.us/parks
HIGHLIGHTS	History, views
LOWLIGHTS	Traffic noise

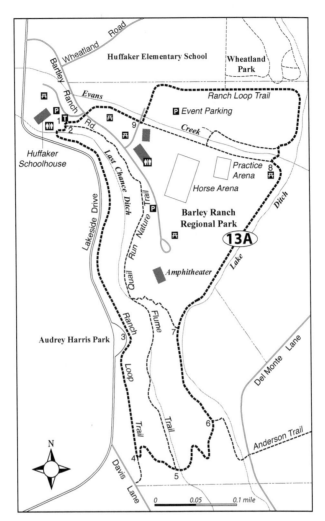

13A. Bartley Ranch Loop

TIP | The park is open from dawn to dusk.

KID TIP | Bartley Ranch Regional Park has plenty of interesting diversions for kids of all ages.

TRAILHEAD | 39°28.121′N, 119°48.417′W From S. McCarran Boulevard, turn south onto Lakeside Drive and proceed for 0.4 mile to Bartley Ranch Road on the left. After crossing through the covered bridge just beyond the park entrance, turn right into the parking lot near the old Huffaker Schoolhouse.

TRAIL | The well-signed trail begins on the south side of the parking area [1] and immediately comes to a junction [2] with the Quail Run Nature Trail on the left. Go straight at the junction and head uphill on the Ranch Loop Trail, soon crossing the Last Chance Ditch on a wood-railed bridge. Immediately past the bridge, the trail bends to the left and slices across an open hillside below curving Lakeside Drive. Make a steadily rising ascent while enjoying the surrounding scenery. The structure just below the ditch is the Robert Z. Hawkins Amphitheater, site of many noteworthy performances, especially during Artown's July run. The climb reaches its apex at Audrey Harris Park [3], a tiny park with an enormous view. Here the whole park spreads out below you, as well as most of the Truckee Meadows, against a backdrop in the east of the tan hills of the Virginia Range. A section of the flume on the Last Chance Ditch below is also visible. Back in the day, this little aerie on Windy Hill was the premier nighttime make-out location for amorous Reno residents.

The trail drops away from Audrey Harris Park and continues a southbound course. Eventually, you reach a three-way junction [4], where the path ahead shortly reaches the shoulder of Davis Lane.

Angle back sharply to the left at the junction and make a slightly winding descent to the south junction [5] with the Flume Trail immediately prior to a bridged crossing of the Last Chance Ditch. Proceed ahead across the ditch and follow a switchbacking descent across the open hillside to the junction [6] with the trail from Anderson Park (see Trip 13B).

Turn left and head northwest to remain on the Bartley Ranch Loop. Soon the trail draws nearer to the Lake Ditch and follows it to a Y-junction [7] near a white fence and a fenced display of an old wagon. The left-hand trail heads toward the amphitheater.

Veer right at the junction and follow the Bartley Ranch Loop around a fenced field. Along the way are several pieces of old ranch equipment with interpretive signs identifying their names and uses. Follow the old road to the end of the fence, where another road splits off to the left to head toward the equestrian area. Near this junction are numerous pieces of old, unidentified ranch equipment. Proceed ahead, soon following the road around a bend to the next significant junction near a picnic table [8].

A sign at the junction directs walkers to leave the road, turn right, and take a narrow path down to and across the usually dry channel of Evans Creek. On the far side, you intersect another old roadbed. Turn to the right and curve around the northeast boundary of the park, encountering more fenced exhibits of ranch equipment on the way. Follow the park boundary to the south of the more manicured grounds of Wheatland Park, where two sidewalks provide access points. Beyond the park, pass the grounds of Huffaker Elementary School on the right and a large parking area on the left. The trail ends near the far (west) edge of the parking lot, where you should head south-southwest across the parking area and a road bridge across the creek bed to an intersection [9] with a road on the right.

Turn right and walk through a parking lot for a picnic area to a closed steel gate. Continue past the gate and follow a gravel path to a crosswalk over the main park access road. A short section of trail on the far side leads back to the Huffaker Schoolhouse parking lot and the close of the loop [1].

MILESTONES
1: Start at Huffaker Schoolhouse trailhead; 2: Go straight at Quail Run Nature Trail junction; 3: Audrey Harris Park; 4: Turn left at junction; 5: Go straight at Flume Trail junction; 6: Turn left at Anderson Park Trail junction; 7: Turn right at junction; 8: Turn right at junction; 9: Turn right at intersection; 1: Return to trailhead.

> **GRANVILLE W. HUFFAKER** (1831–1892) Mr. Granville, originally from Kentucky, drove five hundred head of cattle from Salt Lake City to the Truckee Meadows in the late 1850s. He sold beef during the early days of the Comstock Lode from his ranch in south Reno, which became a stop on the V&T Railroad, which was also the terminus of a flume bringing lumber from the mountains around Lake Tahoe. The Huffaker Schoolhouse was built in 1868 on land he donated and was later transported to the park in 1992.

13B ▪ Anderson Trail

LEVEL	Stroll, novice
LENGTH	1.8 miles, lollipop loop
TIME	1 hour
ELEVATION	Minimal
DIFFICULTY	Easy
USERS	Hikers, runners, mountain bikers, equestrians; ADA accessible, kid friendly
DOGS	On leash
SEASON	All year
BEST TIMES	Spring, fall
FACILITIES	Picnic area, port-a-potty
MAP	Washoe County Parks: *Bartley Ranch Regional Park and Anderson Park* (web-map at www.washoecounty.us/parks)
MANAGEMENT	Washoe County Regional Parks and Open Space at 775-328-3600, www.washoecounty.us/parks
HIGHLIGHTS	Pastureland, views
LOWLIGHTS	Near commercial and residential properties

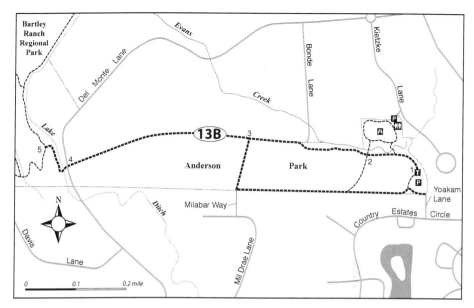

13B. Anderson Trail

TIP | The gate at the park entrance is open from dawn to dusk.

KID TIP | The flat topography should make an easy hike, but the pastures are fenced and unavailable for exploration by inquisitive children. Spring and early summer may be the most interesting times for kids when the streams and ditches are flowing.

TRAILHEAD | 39°27.755′N, 119°47.349′W Follow S. Virginia Street to the Huffaker Lane/Longley Lane intersection. Turn west and follow Huffaker Lane for 0.2 mile to Country Estates Circle on the right, just past the I-580 underpass. Proceed on Country Estates Circle for 0.6 mile and then turn right onto Yoakam Lane and continue to the parking lot.

TRAIL | Take the trail from the north end of the parking area [1] and follow the wide path as it bends around, passing between a row of commercial buildings on the right and a fenced pasture to the left. Where the trail turns west, you reach a path on the left that crosses a seasonal stream on a wooden bridge and then shortly enters the manicured lawn of Anderson Park's picnic area. Continue ahead along the drainage to a four-way junction [2], where another path heads right across a bridge and into the picnic area and the path to the left arcs across the pasture to connect with the trail on the far side (taking this route would create a short, half-mile loop back to the parking lot).

Remaining on the main trail, you proceed ahead from the junction, continuing to follow the streambed, which is lined with cottonwoods and

Along the Anderson Trail

willows. The open pastureland allows fine views of Mount Rose and Slide Mountain to the southwest. Where the trail makes a slight bend, a narrow road on the right heads shortly to access Bonde Lane, as the stream channel makes a sharp bend to the north. Now dividing two sections of pasture, you head west on the wide track of a gravel road between two barbwire fences. The top of Peavine Peak comes into view on the way to the next junction [3] at 0.4 mile, where a trail on the left heads across the pasture.

Go straight at the junction and continue across the pasturelands, approaching some private homes on the right as you near the west edge of the park and a road. Pass around a closed steel gate and follow the crosswalk across Del Monte Lane [4] to the resumption of trail on the far side. A very brief climb leads to the crossing of the Lake Ditch on a wood-railed bridge. The trail follows above the ditch for a short distance and then bends up to a three-way junction with the Bartley Ranch Loop [5], 0.9 mile from the trailhead.

Extending your hike by following the 1.5-mile Bartley Ranch Loop is straightforward (see 13a). Otherwise, retrace your steps to the junction [3].

To vary your return slightly, turn right at the junction and follow a narrower path across the pasture to the south side of Anderson Park. At the far side, bend sharply east and follow the trail along the park boundary. Continue ahead at a junction with a path crossing the pasture and proceed back to the parking lot [1].

LAST CHANCE DITCH Built in the mid-1870s, this 17-mile-long irrigation ditch transferred water from the Truckee River near Mogul to Whites Creek in south Reno. Farmers George Andrews, Enoch Morrill, and Winslow Nay created the ditch as the "last chance" to secure water from the river to irrigate their farms. Over the years, many legal battles over water rights were waged until the settlement of the Orr Ditch Decree in 1944.

MILESTONES

1: Start at Anderson Park trailhead; **2:** Go straight at four-way junction; **3:** Go straight at junction; **4:** Go straight across Del Monte Lane; **5:** Bartley Ranch Loop junction; **3:** Go right at junction; **1:** Return to trailhead.

GO GREEN | Washoe County Regional Parks and Open Space has an Adopt-A-Park program, where volunteers can donate their time for working in the parks to keep them clean, attractive, and safe. The program is open to individuals and groups. For more information, visit their website at www .washoecounty.us/parks/volunteer_opportunities.php, or contact the Parks Volunteer Coordinator at 775-785-4512, ext. 107.

OPTIONS | The 0.2-mile Park Loop circles around the grass picnic area of Anderson Park. Sheltered picnic tables offer fine locations for a picnic lunch. Connecting to the Ranch Loop Trail in Bartley Ranch (see 13a) allows you to extend the journey by up to 1.5 miles, slightly shorter if you incorporate the Flume Trail and Quail Run Nature Trail instead.

Huffaker Park Lookout Trail

The Huffaker Park Lookout Trail circles around a pair of hills topped with rock outcrops in southeast Reno. Short side paths to the top of both outcrops offer fine vistas of the Truckee Meadows, the Carson Range to the west, and the Virginia Range to the east. The wide, well-graded, ADA-accessible loop is a favorite path with dog walkers, joggers, families, and workers from the neighboring businesses on their lunch break. Interpretive signs, picnic tables, and a gazebo offer some diversions along the way.

LEVEL	Walk, novice
LENGTH	2 miles, loop
TIME	1 hour
ELEVATION	+250′–250′
DIFFICULTY	Easy
USERS	Hikers, runners; ADA accessible, kid friendly
DOGS	On leash
SEASON	All year
BEST TIMES	Spring, fall
FACILITIES	Interpretive signs, picnic area, recreational facilities, restrooms
MAP	None
MANAGEMENT	City of Reno: Parks, Recreation and Community Services at 775-334-2262, www.reno.gov/government/departments /parks-recreation-community-services
HIGHLIGHTS	Interpretive signs, views
LOWLIGHTS	Lack of shade

TIP | The park is open from sunrise to sunset. Summer users should go early or late in the day to beat the heat.

KID TIP | Pack plenty of water and sunscreen for your children. As the Huffaker Hills region of south Reno is an interesting geologic area, you may want to explore the Nevada Bureau of Mines website (www.nbmg.unr.edu) and follow links to Science Education and K-12 Earth Science Educational Resources for help in finding stimulating ways to engage kids with earth science.

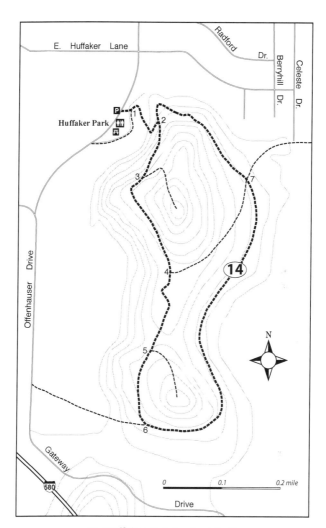

14. Huffaker Park Lookout Trail

TRAILHEAD | 39°27.352′N, 119°46.070′W From I-580, take the S. Virginia Street Exit and head north on S. Virginia Street to E. Patriot Boulevard. Turn right onto E. Patriot Boulevard and then take the first right-hand turn onto Bluestone Drive. Continue ahead onto Portman Avenue, where Bluestone bends left, and proceed to the intersection with Offenhauser Drive. Turn left and follow Offenhauser Dr. to Huffaker Park on the right. Park your vehicle on the shoulder as space allows.

TRAIL | Find the start of the trail [1] on the east side of the park to the north of the group picnic area. After walking across a short bridge spanning a ditch, you climb stiffly up the hillside and switchback up to a junction [2] with the loop trail. Turn right at the junction to begin a counterclockwise loop across sagebrush scrub–covered slopes, with good views of the surrounding landscape. Soon reach a gazebo on a low ridge offering a fine vista of the Carson Range. Immediately past the gazebo is a junction [3] on the left, where a short, dirt path winds up to the crest of the rock outcrop on the north hill, with an even better view. Continue south on the main trail to a junction [4] near a group picnic area. Anyone interested in a shorter trip could turn left here to intersect the far side of the loop and then return to the trailhead.

For the full trip, continue southbound on the main trail. Around a half mile from the start, you reach a junction [5] with a dirt path on the left winding up to the top of the south hill, where a picnic table and a fine vista offer the opportunity to sit and enjoy the scenery. Back on the main trail, head south for a short distance to the next major junction [6], with a wide path coming in from the right providing an alternate access point from Offenhauser Drive below.

Veer east from the junction and circle around the south hill through more open sagebrush scrub. Soon the trail winds around to the north, passing above the buildings of an industrial park on the way to a four-way junction [7], with the shortcut trail on the left and a side path on the right to access points at Celeste Court and Double R Boulevard.

Remaining on the main trail, proceed ahead and bend around the north hill to the close of the loop [2]. From there, retrace your steps back to the start of the trail [1].

> **HUFFAKER HILLS** Nestled into the southeast region of the Truckee Meadows is a series of mounded hills known as the Huffaker Hills. Unlike the Virginia Range to the east, which are uplifted fault-block mountains, the Huffaker Hills are volcanic in origin. Through faults in the earth, highly viscous rhyolitic lava erupted and piled up over time to form these low peaks.

MILESTONES

1: Start at trailhead; 2: Turn right at loop junction; 3: North hill junction; 4: Go straight at shortcut junction; 5: South hill junction; 6: Turn left at junction to Offenhauser Drive; 7: Go straight at four-way junction; 2: Turn right at loop junction; 1: End at trailhead.

GO GREEN | Plenty of volunteer opportunities are available to assist the City of Reno parks department. Access information on their website.

OPTIONS | With a near cult-like following, In-N-Out Burger has been serving their simple menu of burgers, fries, and shakes since 1948, but not until 2004 in Reno. Prior to 2004, hearing about Renoites on pilgrimages to the closest In-N-Out in Auburn, California, was not uncommon. Located on the southwest corner of S. Virginia Street and Patriot Boulevard, the Reno In-N-Out is just minutes from Huffaker Park.

Additional Trips

TEGLIA'S PARADISE PARK LOOP | 39°32.591'N, 119°46.599'W Surrounding a series of ponds in an urban setting in east Reno, Teglia's Paradise Park is a favorite haunt of locals. The 1-mile circuit around the ponds offers a straightforward walk suitable for just about anyone.

SPARKS MARINA LOOP | 39°32.088'N, 119°43.892'W Previously, a giant hole known as the Helms Pit occupied this part of east Sparks. The gravel pit was forced to pump out seeping groundwater in order to continue operations. Eventually the plant closed, the City of Sparks took over the property, and a beautiful park with a lake (Helms Lake) in the middle was created. Nowadays, residents and visitors flock to the area during pleasant weather to boat, fish, swim, picnic, and play. The nearly 2-mile paved path around the shore is a favorite of walkers and joggers.

VIRGINIA LAKE PARK LOOP | 39°30.205'N, 119°48.402'W The urban trail around Virginia Lake is one of the most popular walking paths in the Truckee Meadows thanks to a level grade, relatively short length, and location in the midst of one of Reno's original neighborhoods. Not far from the hubbub of traffic and commercial properties along the S. Virginia corridor, the park is an oasis for city dwellers of all stripes.

MIRA LOMA PARK URBAN TRAIL | 39°29.300'N, 119°44.859'W This paved, ADA-accessible walkway is suitable for just about anyone, young and old alike. Looping around the perimeter of Mira Loma Park, the urban trail is not without some natural landscape, as it follows a stretch of Boynton Slough on the north and east sides and provides the option of a 0.7-mile extension along the slough to the east of the park. With plenty of additional diversions, remaining in the park would be a splendid way for families to spend part of a day.

SOUTH MEADOWS URBAN TRAILS

LAKE LOOP | 39°26.620'N, 119°45.617'W The short Lake Loop provides a mile-long route around a good-size lake in a manicured, park-like setting, with moments of fine scenery and good views.

SOUTH MEADOWS LOOP | A quarter of a century ago, South Meadows was sprawling ranchland. Nowadays, subdivisions and commercial and industrial properties have supplanted the bucolic scene of cattle grazing on verdant, green pasturelands. Modern-day residents can still find traces of the natural environment along two strips of wetlands slicing through the subdivisions by walking the 4-mile South Meadows Loop. However, walking along the sidewalks of some major arterials for short distances will be necessary to complete the whole circuit.

CHAPTER THREE

THE NORTHERN VALLEYS

A series of valleys lie to the north of the Reno-Sparks metropolitan area, bordered by intervening ridges and ranges, where small pockets of land have been set aside for the public. The undeveloped land around the valleys, most of which is under the purview of the Bureau of Land Management (BLM), offers very little to the hiker searching for maintained trails, with much of the land open to off-highway vehicles (OHVs). Within this chapter is a trip halfway around Swan Lake in a nature study area, a pair of nature trails in regional parks, and a couple of climbs to beautiful vista points.

Swan Lake Nature Study Area

The Swan Lake area was destined to become a subdivision before a broad coalition of the BLM, City of Reno, Lahontan Audubon Society, Nevada Army National Guard, Nevada Department of Wildlife, Nevada Land Conservancy, Washoe County Regional Parks and Open Space, and Washoe County School District came together to save the area from development. Using reclaimed wastewater from the nearby Reno-Stead Sewage Treatment Plant to pair with natural runoff, the marshland has been sustained as an important stop for over a hundred different bird species traveling the Pacific Flyway. Partially dependent on how much moisture falls out of the sky each year, the lake level varies from season to season, from a high-water line extending across nearly the entire basin to a much smaller surface area during periods of drought. No matter the water level, Swan Lake is a unique and special place in the middle of an urban setting.

The Swan Lake Nature Study Area boasts a pair of options for bipeds. From the south parking area, a short gravel path leads north to a fenced, ADA-accessible boardwalk made from recycled materials that spans across the marshland and surface of Swan Lake, complete with interpretive signs to explain the area's ecology. Eventually, the Master Plan calls for a loop trail around the entire lake but, for the time being, a 2-mile trail arcs around the west part of the lake, offering beautiful vistas and plenty of wildlife-viewing opportunities.

LEVEL Stroll, intermediate
LENGTH 2.2 miles, shuttle; 4.0 miles, out and back
TIME 1 hour (shuttle); 2 hours (out and back)
ELEVATION Minimal
DIFFICULTY Easy
USERS Hikers, trail runners; ADA accessible (boardwalk), kid friendly
DOGS No
SEASON All year
BEST TIME Spring
FACILITIES Boardwalk, interpretive signs, picnic area, port-a-potty

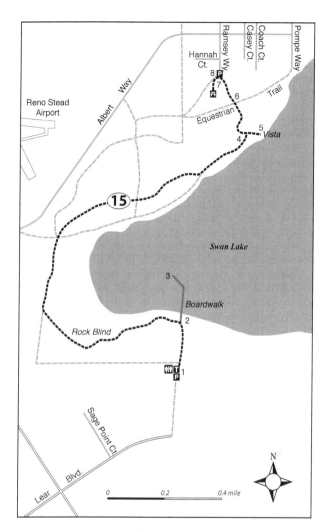

15. Swan Lake Nature Study Area

MAP United States Geological Survey: *Reno NE*

MANAGEMENT Washoe County Regional Parks and Open Space at
775-328-3600, www.washoecounty.us/parks

HIGHLIGHTS Lake, views, wildlife

LOWLIGHTS Initial sections of trail may be muddy.

TIP | The park is open from dawn to dusk.

KID TIP | The boardwalk is an excellent place to bring small children, who
should receive plenty of entertainment from the abundant bird life. The
Lahontan Audubon Society based in Reno offers field trips and classroom

visits to help educate students about birds and conservation. Their website (www.nevadaaudubon.org) is a good place for information about birds in our area.

TRAILHEAD | 39°39.027′N, 119°51.390′W Head north from Reno on US 395 to Exit 74 for Lemmon Drive, about 6 miles from Interstate 80. Follow Lemmon Drive north for three-quarter mile and turn left onto Military Road. After 1.6 mile, turn right at Lear Boulevard and proceed 0.4 mile to the end of the pavement and make a left-hand turn onto a gravel road, marked by a small sign for Swan Lake Nature Study Area. Proceed one-quarter mile to the parking area.

For the shuttle option, continue on Military Road another 0.8 mile past Lear Boulevard and turn right at Echo Avenue. Take the next left at Mount Limbo Street, turn right at Bravo Avenue, and proceed a mile to where it becomes Albert Way. Drive to a stop sign at Ramsey Way, turn right, and continue to the end of the pavement (39°39.876′N, 119°51.249′).

TRAIL | From the parking area [1], head north on a closed section of gravel road alongside a ditch for 0.2 mile to a junction [2] at the South Side Interpretive Area, where you'll find a kiosk, park benches, and trashcans. Ahead is a path leading to a fenced boardwalk that jogs above a marsh filled with cattails. Interpretive signs along the way provide information about the area's ecology. Depending on the amount of rainfall and snowmelt from the previous winter season, you will reach the edge of Swan Lake sooner or later. A section of boardwalk at the end [3] provides plenty of viewing opportunities to observe the waterfowl. When your observations are complete, retrace your steps back to the junction at the South Side Interpretive Area [2].

To hike the trail around the lake, head west on compacted gravel alternating with sections of dirt path past additional interpretive signs to a rock blind, where birdwatchers can remain hidden while peering at the usually plentiful wildlife through slits in the wall. Beyond the blind, as the trail bends more to the north, you move out of the wetlands environment and climb briefly into typical sagebrush scrub vegetation. The slightly elevated vantage allows for grand views across Swan Lake to the brown hills on the east side of Lemmon Valley. Moving away from the large industrial building on the southeast corner, the hills above the Swan Lake basin hide much of the surrounding development, creating a wilder ambiance to the area. However, you may notice that birds aren't the only things flying across the sky, as small planes make their approach for landings at the Reno-Stead Airport, located on the bench just west of the lake. About a half mile from the junction, the trail merges with a road coming in from the south, the first of many unmarked junctions with old jeep roads that crisscross the area. Always follow the gravel sections of road and trail and you won't get off track. About 0.2 mile farther is one such example, where you reach a junction with

On the boardwalk at Swan Lake Nature Study Area

a half-dozen dirt roads heading off in a variety of directions, one of which heads west to Bravo Avenue. Remain on the gravel road, which bends around to the east. Reach an opening in a fence at 1.3 miles and proceed another 0.2 mile to a signed junction [4].

Turn right and follow the short side path to the edge of a low rise and the designated observation point [5]. Along with the good view of Swan Lake, Peavine Peak to the west, and Mount Rose in the distance, you'll find an interpretive sign, bench, and a short pole with a perch at this site. Springtime and early-season visitors should be able to observe a large number of birds from this vantage. If you're doing the out-and-back trip, simply retrace your steps 1.8 miles back to the trailhead [1].

For the shuttle option, return shortly to the junction [4] and turn right, following signed directions toward Ramsey Way and Pompe Way. Proceed straight ahead at the junction [6] with the equestrian trail (a right turn here would lead shortly to Pompe Way). Soon reach another junction [7] near an interpretive sign, where the path ahead curves around to a lone, metal picnic table. The right-hand path goes shortly to a steel gate at the edge of Ramsey Way [8].

TUNDRA SWAN (*Cygnus columbianus*) Smallest members of the swan family, tundra swans migrate thousands of miles from the Arctic to our area each winter and then back again for the summer. With white bodies and black feet and bills, they congregate in flocks during the winter months but breed as solitary pairs in the tundra. They can live up to twenty years.

MILESTONES (SHUTTLE):

1: Start at south trailhead; 2: Turn right at South Side Interpretive Area junction; 3: End of boardwalk; 4: Turn right at junction; 5: Observation point; 4: Turn right at junction; 6: Go straight at equestrian junction; 7: Turn right at junction; 8: Reach Ramsey Way trailhead.

MILESTONES (OUT AND BACK):

1: Start at south trailhead; 2: Turn right at South Side Interpretive Area junction; 3: End of boardwalk; 4: Turn right at junction; 5: Observation point; 4: Turn left at junction; 2: Turn right at junction; 1: Return to trailhead.

GO GREEN | The success of the Swan Lake Nature Study Area was due to the collaboration of many conservation and governmental agencies. The Nevada Land Trust was one such agency, with a mission to preserve and protect open space within the state. The mission at Swan Lake continues with annual cleanups, usually in the fall. Many other volunteer opportunities are available. Check out their website at www.nevadalandtrust.org for more information.

OPTIONS | The Swan Lake Master Plan calls for additional trails and alternate parking areas creating a network of paths that will one day almost form a complete loop around Swan Lake.

TRIP
16 | Sun Valley Regional Park

Nestled into the hills above Sun Valley, this 343-acre regional park provides a gateway to the undeveloped BLM lands blanketing the mountains between Sun and Golden Valleys. Beautiful vistas abound and picturesque rock outcrops add visual interest to a land carpeted with sagebrush scrub and dotted with Utah junipers. Casual hikers and families will find plenty of enjoyment along the Sun Rock Trail, a 0.6-mile loop with interpretive signs about the flora, fauna, and geology of the area. More adventurous hikers have a plethora of possible routes to explore, as myriad roads crisscross the park and lead west and north onto BLM land. Among the many potential hikes in the area is the climb to Peak 5356 described below.

16A ▪ Sun Rock Trail

LEVEL	Stroll, intermediate
LENGTH	0.6 mile, loop
TIME	½ hour
ELEVATION	+50′–50′
DIFFICULTY	Moderate
USERS	Hikers
DOGS	On leash
SEASON	All year
BEST TIMES	Spring, fall
FACILITIES	Disc golf course, equestrian parking, picnic area, vault toilets
MAP	United States Geological Survey: *Reno*
MANAGEMENT	Washoe County Regional Parks and Open Space at 775-328-3600, www.washoecounty.us/parks
HIGHLIGHTS	Interpretive signs, views
LOWLIGHTS	Exposed to sun

TIP ǀ Although not a problem on the Sun Rock Trail, motorized vehicles seem to use the old roads within the park with some regularity, despite a posted ban. Obviously, violators are accessing the park from neighboring BLM lands. Report any sightings to park officials.

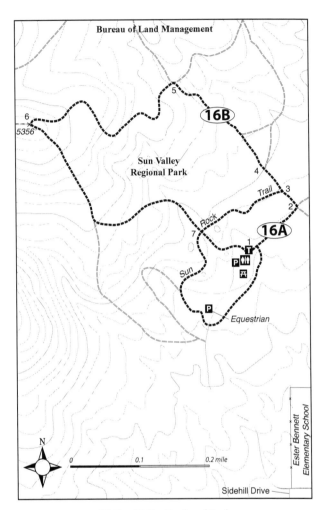

16. Sun Valley Regional Park

KID TIP | The short and relatively easy Sun Rock Trail is well signed and should provide groups with small children a good option for a family hike. However, with roads heading off in virtually every direction, some supervision will be required to keep children from wandering off on the wrong path.

Although the chances are quite slim of seeing one, mountain lions thrive in undeveloped areas across Nevada. For more information go to the "Living With Mountain Lions" page on the Nevada Department of Wildlife's website (www.ndow.org/uploadedFiles/ndoworg/Content/public_documents/Wild life_Education/Publications/mountain_lion.pdf).

TRAILHEAD | 39°36.723′N, 119°47.194′W Heading north from Interstate 80 on US 395, take Exit 69 signed for Sun Valley/Clear Acre Lane. Continue north on Clear Acre, which becomes Sun Valley Drive and proceed about 3.5 miles to a left-hand turn onto Quartz Lane, just past a City of Reno fire station. Proceed for 0.2 mile and turn right at Sidehill Drive. Find the park entrance road on the left, opposite the access into Esther Bennett Elementary School. Follow the park road for 0.75 mile to the parking area.

TRAIL | Find the start of the trail near a kiosk by the vault toilets at the northeast edge of the parking lot [1] and follow signed directions onto the wide path of an old road that climbs up a hillside covered with sagebrush scrub and dotted with widely scattered Utah junipers. Turn left at a four-way signed junction [2] and climb a short distance to a signed T-junction [3], where the Sun Rock Trail turns left onto a single-track path.

Gently graded trail soon leads to the first interpretive sign about some of the plants in the area. A park bench is just beyond the sign. Follow a slightly winding course through interesting rock formations to the next interpretive sign about wildlife, where a park bench nearby offers an inviting spot to sit and enjoy the view. Continue the pleasant stroll past yet another park bench to the third interpretive sign, this one with information about the area's geology. Beyond the interpretive sign, the trail crosses a couple of dirt roads [7], where trail signs help to keep you on track. From there, the Sun Rock Trail descends generally southeast toward the park access road, crosses it, and then heads northeast back to the developed part of the park [1].

MILESTONES

1: Start at trailhead; 2: Turn left at four-way junction; 3: Turn left at T-junction; 1: Return to trailhead.

16B ▪ Peak 5356

LEVEL	Hike, advanced
LENGTH	1.2 miles, lollipop loop
TIME	1 hour
ELEVATION	+300′–300′
DIFFICULTY	Moderately strenuous
USERS	Hikers
DOGS	On leash
SEASON	All year
BEST TIMES	Spring, fall
FACILITIES	Disc golf course, equestrian parking, picnic area, vault toilets
MAP	United States Geological Survey: *Reno*
MANAGEMENT	Washoe County Regional Parks and Open Space at 775-328-3600, www.washoecounty.us/parks
HIGHLIGHTS	Peak, views
LOWLIGHTS	Exposed to sun

Rock formation in Sun Valley Regional Park

TIP | Motorized vehicles seem to use the old roads within the park with some regularity, despite a posted ban. Obviously, violators are accessing the park from neighboring BLM lands. Report any sightings to park officials.

KID TIP | The longer and steeper routes through the park and BLM land beyond are ill suited for young children, but older kids in good shape should be able to handle the hike to Peak 5356. Although getting off track is quite possible with so many old roads crisscrossing the area, becoming totally lost would be hard to do in the open terrain. Bring plenty of water and sunscreen.

TRAILHEAD | 39°36.723′N, 119°47.194′W Heading north from Interstate 80 on US 395, take Exit 69 signed for Sun Valley/Clear Acre Lane. Continue north on Clear Acre, which becomes Sun Valley Drive and proceed about 3.5 miles to a left-hand turn onto Quartz Lane, just past a City of Reno fire station. Proceed for 0.2 mile and turn right at Sidehill Drive. Find the park entrance road on the left, opposite the access into Esther Bennett Elementary School. Follow the park road for 0.75 mile to the parking area.

TRAIL | Find the start of the trail near a kiosk by the vault toilets at the northeast edge of the parking lot [1] and follow signed directions onto the wide path of an old road that climbs up a hillside covered with sagebrush scrub and dotted with widely scattered Utah junipers. Turn left at a four-way signed junction [2] and climb a short distance to a signed T-junction [3], with the Sun Rock Trail.

Proceed ahead from the junction and climb stiffly northwest up the hillside to a Y-junction [4]. Take the left-hand road and continue the ascent to a four-way junction [5], about 0.2 mile from the junction with the Sun Rock Trail.

Now heading generally west, you follow a road on a winding uphill climb to a low rock outcrop on the top of Peak 5356 [6]. Here a marvelous view unfolds south down Sun Valley to the Truckee Meadows, east across Spanish Springs to the Pah Rah Range, west to Peavine Peak, and southwest to the crest of the Carson Range.

When the time comes to leave this wonderful vista, head southeast on a steep descent, veer left about midway downslope, and then arc around to the southeast again on the way toward the developed part of the park. Just before you get there, cross the Sun Rock Trail [7] and continue straight down the hillside to the cut slope above the parking area, veer to the left and wrap around toward the kiosk [1].

UTAH JUNIPER (*Juniperus osteosperma*) The Utah juniper is the most widely distributed conifer within Nevada. As in the park, this tree is often found on the low hills above the desert, able to survive in dry conditions where other conifers cannot. With red-brown bark that peels off its trunk in leathery strips and ragged foliage, the tree looks like it belongs in these harsh environs.

MILESTONES

1: Start at trailhead; 2: Turn left at four-way junction; 3: Turn left at T-junction; 4: Turn left at Y-junction; 5: Turn left at four-way junction; 6: Peak 5356; 7: Go straight at Sun Rock Trail; 1: Return to trailhead.

GO GREEN | Washoe County Regional Parks and Open Space has an Adopt-A-Park program, where volunteers can donate their time for working in the parks to keep them clean, attractive, and safe. The program is open to individuals and groups. For more information, visit their website at www .washoecounty.us/parks/volunteer_opportunities.php, or contact the Parks Volunteer Coordinator at 775-785-4512, ext. 107.

OPTIONS | The alternate routes through the park and across the BLM land beyond are too numerous to mention, limited only by one's imagination and endurance. The longer hike to the top of the highest peak northwest of the trailhead would be a fairly challenging affair.

17 | Pah Rah Interpretive Trail

This short and easy stroll on paved trail provides an interesting contrast from the developed lands of Golden Eagle Park and the undeveloped natural lands beyond. Interpretive signs offer interesting tidbits about the region's ecology along the way.

LEVEL	Stroll, novice
LENGTH	0.6 mile, loop
TIME	½ hour
ELEVATION	Minimal
DIFFICULTY	Easy
USERS	Hikers, bikers; ADA accessible
DOGS	On leash
SEASON	All year
BEST TIMES	Spring, fall
FACILITIES	Picnic area, vault toilets (at trailhead); athletic fields, concessions, picnic areas, playground, pro shop, restrooms (at sports field complex)
MAP	None
MANAGEMENT	City of Sparks: Parks and Facilities at 775-691-9130, www.cityofsparks.us
HIGHLIGHTS	Interpretive signs, views
LOWLIGHTS	None

TIP I The park is open from 8:00 AM to sunset.

KID TIP I This easy trip should be short enough to keep the attention of young children.

TRAILHEAD I From Exit 21 on Interstate 80 for Vista Boulevard/Greg Street, drive north on Vista Boulevard for 8 miles to a right-hand turn onto Home Run Drive, signed for Golden Eagle Regional Park. After 0.6 mile, turn right and follow Hans Berry Road for another 0.6 mile to the entrance into the Pah Rah Interpretive Trail parking lot on the right.

TRAIL I The trail begins on the far side of the covered picnic area near a three-sided kiosk [1]. Follow the asphalt path in a counterclockwise direction on

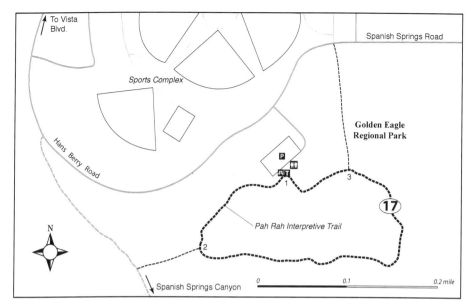

17. Pah Rah Interpretive Trail

a loop across a rising slope filled with sagebrush. You will soon reach a signed junction [2], where a dirt path on the right marked "Trail Access" leads shortly to a dirt road heading into Spanish Springs Canyon (see Trip 18). Shortly past the junction, you reach the first of three interpretive signs spread around the loop and a park bench nearby. Continue east for a while, enjoying the sweeping view up the canyon and then follow the asphalt path as it bends back around toward the trailhead. Along the way is a T-junction [3] with an asphalt path to the sports fields to the north shortly before you reach the close of the loop at the kiosk [1].

> **BLACK-TAILED JACKRABBIT** (*Lepus californicus*) Not in the rabbit but the hare family, these mammals are found in the desert and foothill environments of western Nevada. With their characteristic long ears, which can grow up to 8 inches, and long hind legs with large feet, they are easily distinguished from the smaller cottontail rabbits common to the area. Jackrabbits are most likely to be seen by hikers around dusk, as they emerge from their hollows to forage under low-light conditions.

MILESTONES

1: Start at kiosk; **2:** Go straight at junction; **3:** Go straight at junction; **1:** Return to kiosk.

GO GREEN | The City of Sparks: Parks and Recreation Department has an Adopt-A-Park program, where groups or individuals can donate their time to help support the parks. For more information, visit the City of Sparks website and follow the link for the Adopt-A-Park program, or contact the Parks Volunteer Coordinator at 775-353-2376.

OPTIONS | More ambitious hikers can follow the path over to the road up the canyon to a junction with a single-track trail created by mountain bikers that climbs into the hills (see Trip 18). Although an encounter is unlikely if you remain on the single-track, the area is open to OHV vehicles. Discharging firearms is also allowed.

18 | Zipper Trail

A trail has been created in the hills above Spanish Springs Canyon by some dedicated mountain bikers that will hopefully be given official recognition by the BLM in the very near future. Undoubtedly named for the way the trail zigzags up the west wall of the canyon via tight switchbacks, the Zipper heads away from the Pah Rah Interpretive Loop for a couple of miles to the start of a loop that runs along the top of Canoe Hill and dips down the west side before regaining the ridge and closing the loop. Along the way, you have some fantastic views of the surrounding hills and valleys along the ridge, as well as some interesting scenery closer at hand.

LEVEL	Hike, advanced
LENGTH	8.8 miles, lollipop loop
TIME	Half day
ELEVATION	+1,425′–1,425′
DIFFICULTY	Moderate to strenuous
USERS	Hikers, trail runners, mountain bikers
DOGS	On leash (first quarter mile)
SEASON	March through November
BEST TIMES	Spring, fall
FACILITIES	Picnic area, vault toilets (at trailhead); athletic fields, concessions, picnic areas, playground, pro shop, restrooms (at sports field complex)
MAP	Great Basin Bicycles Trail Maps: *Pah Rah Mountain Range* (web-map at www.greatbasinbicycles.com/trailmaps)
MANAGEMENT	City of Sparks: Parks and Facilities at 775-691-9130, www.cityofsparks.us; Bureau of Land Management at 775-861-6400, www.blm.gov/nv/st/en/fo/carson_city_field .html
HIGHLIGHTS	Views
LOWLIGHTS	Target shooting, trails not marked, trash

TIP ǀ You might be able to avoid some of the noise from OHVs and target shooting by getting an early start and hiking on weekdays.

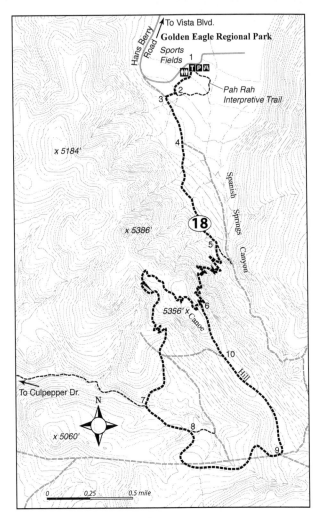

18. Zipper Trail

KID TIP | Combined with target shooting and OHV use, the long and some-times steep trail makes this trip ill suited for small children. Families with older kids might enjoy the initial stretch of trail up to the first viewpoint at the loop junction.

TRAILHEAD | 39°35.730′N, 119°40.098′W From Exit 21 on Interstate 80 for Vista Boulevard/Greg Street, drive north on Vista Boulevard for 8 miles to a right-hand turn onto Home Run Drive, signed for Golden Eagle Regional Park. After 0.6 mile, turn right and follow Hans Berry Road for another 0.6 mile to the entrance into the Pah Rah Interpretive Trail parking lot on the right.

TRAIL | The trail begins on the far side of the covered picnic area near a three-sided kiosk [1]. Follow the asphalt path in a counterclockwise direction on the Pah Rah Loop across a rising slope filled with sagebrush. You will soon reach a signed junction [2], where you turn right onto a dirt path at a sign marked "Trail Access." This path leads shortly to a dirt road [3] heading into Spanish Springs Canyon, where you turn left. Keeping an eye out for vehicles, cross a cattle guard (a structure typically built over a ditch using parallel bars to prevent cattle from crossing) and head down the dirt road past two side roads heading right to where an unmarked single-track trail [4] heads south away from the road to the right, 0.5 mile from the trailhead.

You follow a single-track path on a moderate, rolling ascent across the right-hand side of Spanish Springs Canyon, steadily climbing above the dirt road through Spanish Springs Canyon below. Pass through typical sagebrush scrub on the way to a small rock outcrop and a junction with a faint path just beyond [5], 1.3 miles from the trailhead.

Rather than continue ahead up the canyon, turn right and begin a tightly switchbacking, steeper climb toward the top of Canoe Hill. After a few switchbacks, reach a Y-junction, where a less steep path switchbacks across the slope on the left and a steeper path heads directly up to the right. While the paths shortly converge again higher upslope, the left-hand one is the designated route. Continue the zigzagging climb to the top of a knoll, where a metal stake marks the loop junction [6] at 2.3 miles. A good view of the canyon and the surrounding ridges unfolds here, which makes a fine turnaround point for a shorter out-and-back trip for those not wishing to complete the full loop trip.

Veer to the right at the junction and continue the climb, soon reaching the crest of Canoe Hill, where an even more magnificent view opens up to the south of the Truckee Meadows, bordered by the mountains of the Carson Range. Heading northwest, wind around along the long ridge crest for a while, crossing a jeep road at 2.75 miles. At a junction with a shortcut trail on the left, proceed ahead and follow a serpentine path around a rocky promontory, a technically challenging stretch of trail for mountain bikers. Beyond the promontory, cross back over the jeep road crossed previously, this time farther down the hillside, and then continue on a winding descent to an intersection with a jeep road near the 4-mile mark. Cross over the road and continue down a usually dry wash, reaching a junction [7] marked by a small cairn, where the trail on the right heads west down the canyon for about a mile to an alternate access point at Culpepper Drive.

Turn left and climb up the south side of the canyon. After a while, you dip into and climb more steeply out of a side gully and then proceed to a Y-junction, 0.4 mile from the previous junction [8].

Wintertime view of Mount Rose from the Zipper Trail

Bend right at the junction to veer away from the canyon and ascend open slopes for one-quarter mile, as the trail arcs around to the south on the way to the crossing of a well-traveled dirt road. Cross the road and head east up an old jeep track that roughly parallels this dirt road. Initially, the track follows a gently rising grade up the hillside until encountering steeper terrain on the way toward the crest of the ridge, where the route angles across the dirt road, switchbacks, and then meets the road again. You climb steeply up the main road to the top of the ridge and a four-way intersection [9], 5.3 miles from the trailhead.

At the intersection, turn left onto the least traveled road and follow the rising crest to the top of a low rise, where a fine view unfolds of the northwest section of the Truckee Meadows, Peavine Peak, and a stretch of the Carson Range running south to Mount Rose. Dip down away from the rise and follow a single-track path along the slightly rolling ridge, as the views expand to include Slide Mountain to the southwest and the north part of Spanish Springs Valley. Merge with the track of an old jeep road for a while and proceed to a junction [10] marked by a small cairn, where a single-track trail veers away from the road to the right and climbs stiffly uphill toward the high point of Canoe Hill. Before reaching the high point, the trail slices across the east side of the hill and then descends back to the top of the knoll at the close of the loop junction, 6.5 miles from the trailhead [6].

From the loop junction, retrace your steps 2.3 miles to the trailhead [1].

GOLDEN EAGLE (*Aquila chrysaetos*) The largest and most impressive raptor you might see in the western Nevada skies is the golden eagle, with a wingspan of up to nearly 8 feet. Their range can extend up to 75 square miles, preferring open, undeveloped habitats. Opportunistic hunters, the chief prey of golden eagles are rabbits and other rodents. A smaller percentage of their diet comes from other birds, and they will consume snakes and lizards when available.

MILESTONES

1: Start at Pah Rah trailhead; **2:** Turn right at junction; **3:** Turn left at junction with Spanish Springs Canyon Road; **4:** Turn right at junction with single-track trail; **5:** Turn right at junction; **6:** Turn right at loop junction; **7:** Turn left at junction with trail to Culpepper Drive; **8:** Turn right at Y-junction; **9:** Turn left at four-way intersection; **10:** Turn right at single-track junction; **6:** Loop junction; **1:** Return to trailhead.

GO GREEN | The City of Sparks: Parks and Recreation Department has an Adopt-A-Park program, where groups or individuals can donate their time to help support the parks. For more information, visit the City of Sparks website and follow the link for the Adopt-A-Park program, or contact the Parks Volunteer Coordinator at 775-353-2376.

While the chances of actually seeing one are slim, rattlesnakes thrive in undeveloped areas across Nevada. If you encounter one, allow the snake plenty of room for escape. Keep dogs (especially small breeds) on a leash, or at least under close observation in rattlesnake country. Although poisonous, these snakes are a vital part of the ecosystem and should not be exterminated in the wild. For more information go to the "Venomous Reptiles of Nevada" page on the Nevada Department of Wildlife's website (www.ndow .org/uploadedFiles/ndoworg/Content/Nevada_Wildlife/Animals/Concerns /NV_Ven_rept.pdf).

OPTIONS | You can create a shorter, 6-mile trip by starting at the Culpepper Drive trailhead and accessing the loop portion after 0.9 mile.

The BLM was considering formally adopting the Zipper as an official trail and adding another 11 miles to the network. If this comes to pass, expect some signage and trail improvements in the future. Hopefully, some of the trash will get picked up as well.

TRIP

19 | Sugarloaf Peak

A few decades ago, Spanish Springs Valley was relatively undeveloped, without industrial plants and with only scattered ranchettes peppering the valley floor. Nowadays, all of that has changed, as subdivisions, commercial properties, and industrial complexes have left only a fraction of the former open space. Plopped down toward the north end of Spanish Springs is Sugarloaf Peak—a lump of granite with a basalt summit that affords a sweeping 360-degree view of the valley and the surrounding hills and mountains. The first half of the 2.8-mile route is fairly flat and easy, but the second half is a steep climb on a sometimes-rocky path. However, the 500-foot climb is well worth the effort for those up to the task, as the view is exceptional, even with all of the recent development.

LEVEL Hike, advanced

LENGTH 5.6 miles, out and back

TIME 2 to 3½ hours

ELEVATION +750′–50′

DIFFICULTY Moderately strenuous

USERS Hikers

DOGS OK

SEASON All year

BEST TIMES Spring, fall

FACILITIES None

MAP United States Geological Survey: *Vista*

MANAGEMENT Washoe County Regional Parks and Open Space at 775-328-3600, www.washoecounty.us/parks

HIGHLIGHTS Peak, views

LOWLIGHTS Operational gravel pit nearby, exposed to sun, rough sections of trail

TIP | Plan on a very early start if you come during the summer to beat the heat. The gravel pit is always an eyesore on the second half of the trip, but you may be able to avoid the accompanying noise from the operating equipment by hiking the trail on weekends.

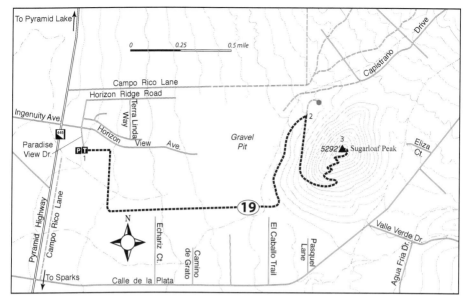

19. Sugarloaf Peak

KID TIP | You'll likely hear few complaints from the young ones on the first half of the trail, as the grade is easy. The steep and rocky second half of the climb is a different story altogether. One way to add some variety to the experience would be to ride bikes to the red gate and then go on foot to the top. Pack plenty of water and sunscreen.

TRAILHEAD | 39°40.521′N, 119°41.906′W Follow Pyramid Highway (SR 445) north from Interstate 80 for 10.5 miles and turn right onto Horizon View Avenue. After 0.1 mile turn right again onto Paradise View Drive and drive the short distance to the end of the cul-de-sac and park as space allows.

TRAIL | A county parks sign marks the beginning of the trail [1], which follows the nearly flat grade of a dirt road east through sagebrush scrub for a short while before curving south and then east again near the half-mile mark. The grade increases slightly on the way to a fence corner at 0.8 mile from the trailhead. Just inside the fence, a dirt berm conceals from view a part of the large gravel pit to the west of Sugarloaf Peak. Continue the pleasant walk another half mile along the fence line to a red steel gate and pass through the opening to the right of the locked gate, where only foot traffic is allowed farther up the road. Continue east toward the southwest base of Sugarloaf Peak.

The road turns north and makes a short climb, where, thanks to the gain in elevation, the massive scar of the gravel pit pops into view on the left. You give up most of the hard-won elevation on a short descent before

Sugarloaf Peak

the road resumes a less steep ascent on the way to a signed junction [2], where a narrower segment of trail angles uphill to the right, 1.8 miles from the trailhead.

Turn right and follow the single-track trail on a steeply rising traverse across the west flank of Sugarloaf Peak. After a quarter mile, the trail curves up the southwest slope and follows a series of switchbacks toward the top. Improving views of Spanish Springs Valley and the surrounding mountains propel you onward toward the summit. Following the last switchback, a spiraling segment of trail delivers you to the top of Sugarloaf Peak [3], where previous visitors have built a rock pile and some low rock walls. As billed, the 360-degree vista encompassing Spanish Springs Valley is quite impressive, with Spanish Springs Peak and the Pah Rah Range to the east, the Junction House Range to the west, and the massive hulk of Peavine Peak to the southwest.

At the conclusion of your stay, retrace your steps 2.8 miles back to the trailhead.

PAH RAH RANGE The mountains to the east of Sugarloaf Peak are part of the Pah Rah Range, so named after a Shoshone word for river. The wishbone-shaped range extends from the Truckee River in the south to Mullen Pass in the north. While the prominent peak to the south-southeast is 7,401-foot Spanish Springs Peak, the highest peak in the range, 8,367-foot Virginia Peak, is farther north. The Pah Rahs are primarily volcanic in origin.

MILESTONES

1: Start at trailhead; **2:** Turn right at junction; **3:** Top of Sugarloaf Peak.

GO GREEN | Washoe County Regional Parks and Open Space has an Adopt-A-Park program, where volunteers can donate their time for working in the parks to keep them clean, attractive, and safe. The program is open to individuals and groups. For more information, visit their website at www.washoecounty.us/parks/volunteer_opportunities.php, or contact the Parks Volunteer Coordinator at 775-785-4512, ext. 107.

OPTIONS | There are very few distractions in the immediate vicinity, but you can power up for the climb to the top of Sugarloaf Peak with a signature omelet at the Sparks Squeeze In (4670 Sparks Boulevard) on the way to the trailhead. The summit is a fine lunch spot, if you don't mind parking your behind on one of the boulders.

CHAPTER FOUR

THE FOOTHILLS

Where the valley of the Truckee Meadows reaches the base of the Carson Range to the west, the Virginia Range to the east, the Steamboat Hills to the south, and the unnamed hills to the north, the foothills begin. A transition zone between the sagebrush scrub typical of the flatlands and the forests of the upper mountains, the foothills hold a diverse mixture of flora. A transition of human habitation is also prevalent, as the high-density communities of the Truckee Meadows give way to the less densely populated hillsides above. Trips in this chapter range from paved urban paths through a housing development to rugged dirt trails into the lonely hills.

TRIP

20 | Halo Trail

Under the supervision of the Forest Service, volunteers have devoted a lot of hours to the construction of miles and miles of well-marked, single-track trail on the south slope of Peavine Peak. Primarily used by mountain bikers, the Halo Trail has become the premier piece of single-track trail on the mountain. While plans call for a complete circumnavigation of Peavine via the Halo Trail eventually, hikers and riders nowadays have shorter options, including the nearly 9-mile lower loop described here and an upper loop of almost 13 miles in length, plus many other variations. The open terrain offers plenty of gorgeous views of the Truckee Meadows and the surrounding mountains along the way. In years of abundant moisture, wildflower displays can be stunning in late spring and early summer.

LEVEL	Hike, advanced
LENGTH	8.7 miles, loop
TIME	Half day
ELEVATION	+1,200'−1,200'
DIFFICULTY	Moderate
USERS	Hikers, trail runners, mountain bikers
DOGS	On leash
SEASON	March to December
BEST TIMES	April to May, October
FACILITIES	None
MAP	Poedunks: *Peavine Trails* (web-map at www.poedunk.org /poeville-89503/peavine-trail-maps)
MANAGEMENT	USFS Humboldt-Toiyabe Forest, Carson Ranger District at 775-882-2766, www.fs.usda.gov/htnf
HIGHLIGHTS	Views, seasonal wildflowers
LOWLIGHTS	Short road walk, exposed to sun

TIP ǀ Hiking on weekdays may find the trail less crowded with mountain bikers. The south facing side of Peavine can be incredibly hot in summer, so start early in the day to beat the heat when high temperatures are forecasted.

KID TIP ǀ The nearly 9-mile loop will be too much for small children. For older kids, pack plenty of water and sunscreen. Since the Halo Trail is a

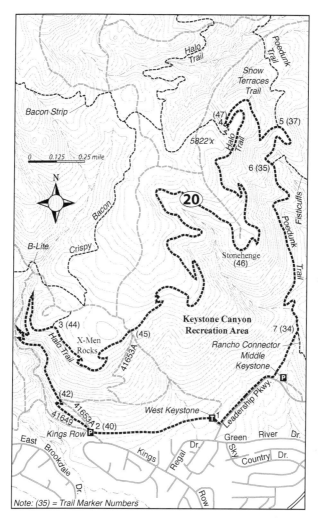

Note: (35) = Trail Marker Numbers

20. Halo Trail

very popular mountain bike route, kids should be well coached for possible encounters. Also, instruct them to avoid any of the old mine areas that may be passed along the way.

TRAILHEAD I 39°32.970′N, 119°51.594′W Follow Interstate 80 west from Reno to Exit 10 for McCarran Boulevard West and go north on McCarran for 2.1 miles to a left turn onto Victory Lane. Follow Victory for 0.1 mile to a T-intersection with Leadership Parkway and turn left. Continue another 0.7 mile to a roundabout and veer right onto a gravel road. Immediately turn right again and drive a short distance to the West Keystone trailhead parking area.

TRAIL | From the West Keystone trailhead [1], traverse west on the Kings Row Trail, which follows the course of an old road for a half mile to a closed steel gate and a junction [2] just beyond at Trail Marker 40. The gravel road on the left goes a short distance to an access point from Kings Row, while Forest Service (FS) Road 41649 heads west, and FS Road 41653A heads north.

Turn northwest at the junction and follow the single-track path of the Halo Trail on a moderate, slightly winding climb up the slope, merging with an old road at Trail Marker 42. Continue climbing above Bud Canyon to the left, as the trail snakes up into the hills. Farther on, switchbacks wind up the slope, beyond which the trail veers east away from the canyon, merges with a stretch of road, and then proceeds across the hillside to a junction [3] with the Crispy Bacon Trail at Trail Marker 44, 1.9 miles from the trailhead.

Veer right, remaining on the Halo Trail, and continue winding up across open, sagebrush-covered slopes. Views improve with the gain in elevation, which now include a view of the summit of Peavine Peak. Follow the switchbacking trail around X-men Rocks and proceed northeast to the crossing of twin-tracked FS Road 41653A at Trail Marker 45, 2.6 miles from the trailhead.

Remaining on the Halo Trail, you continue northeast for a short while, climb up the slope via a set of short-legged switchbacks, and then wind around above the canyon of a seasonal drainage. Climb up the west lip, wrap around a side canyon, and continue the ascent to the head of the main canyon. Here the trail bends southeast and descends down the far side of the canyon, passing the site of an old mine shaft along the way to Trail Marker 46 near the Stonehenge viewpoint. Just above the trail here is a turnaround for a jeep road at the boundary of the nonmotorized zone of the Keystone Canyon Recreation Area. A switchbacking, three-quarter-mile climb leads to the trip's high point, just south of Peak 5822. From there, the trail descends roughly northward, with views of the radio towers and the Hoge Road area. After a switchback, you reach the next junction [4], 6.2 miles from the trailhead, at Trail Marker 47.

Leaving the Halo Trail, you veer to the right onto the Snow Terraces Trail and proceed 0.2 mile to the crossing of an old jeep road. Continue the descent to the next junction at Trail Marker 37 [5], 6.75 miles from the trailhead.

Turn right onto the Poedunk Trail and proceed downhill, curving into a side canyon of Keystone Canyon. After one-quarter mile, you reach a junction at Trail Marker 35 [6], where the Fisticuffs Trail veers off to the left. Continue ahead on the Poedunk Trail, crossing a couple of side drainages on the way to the crossing of an unmarked trail. A short distance farther downhill, at 8 miles, you reach a junction [7] with the Rancho Connector at Trail Marker 34.

Wildflowers along the Halo Trail on Peavine Peak

Veer left at the junction, immediately crossing the drainage, and then following a rocky road down toward Leadership Parkway. Upon reaching the asphalt, head southwest along the road a short distance back to the West Keystone trailhead and the close of the loop [1].

CARSON RANGE The Halo Trail provides a grand opportunity to witness the geology of the Carson Range and the Truckee Meadows. The mountains to the southwest are part of a subrange of the Sierra with similar rocks of similar ages. The range begins at Carson Pass (CA 88) and continues north to the Truckee River. As seen from the trail, the Sierra Frontal Fault lies between the base of the range and the west edge of the valley. Simply put, the Carson Range, made up primarily of granodiorite, continues to rise while the valley continues to drop.

MILESTONES

1: Start at West Keystone trailhead; **1:** Return to trailhead.

GO GREEN ǀ The Poedunks are an International Mountain Bike Association–affiliated club with a focus on building, maintaining, and riding sustainable single-track trail on Peavine Peak. Working in cooperation with the USFS, Washoe County, and the City of Reno, they have built, improved, and maintained many of the area's trails, including the Halo Trail. When fully complete, the Halo Trail will encircle Peavine on a 36-mile circuit. For more information, check out their website at www.poedunk.org.

OPTIONS ǀ Connecting to additional trails in the area provides an almost unlimited number of options for trip variations and extensions.

Evans Canyon and Miners Trail Loop

As part of the nonmotorized zone on Peavine Peak, combining the Evans Canyon and Miners Trail creates a loop offering a sense of remoteness that belies its close proximity to civilization. Away from the occasional hubbub around Rancho San Rafael Regional Park's sports complex, the route enters the steep canyon of seasonal Evans Creek and proceeds upstream with a feeling of seclusion. This illusion eventually disappears when signs of civilization return in the form of an apartment complex in the upper canyon. Here the trail makes a U-turn and heads down the opposite side of the canyon and eventually back to the trailhead. Springtime visitors are most likely to see water in the creek and wildflowers along the banks.

LEVEL Hike, intermediate

LENGTH 3.5 miles, loop

TIME 1½ to 2 hours

ELEVATION +325′−325′

DIFFICULTY Moderate

USERS Hikers, trail runners, mountain bikers

DOGS On leash

SEASON March to December

BEST TIMES Spring, fall

FACILITIES Athletic fields, disc golf course, port-a-potty (restrooms at athletic fields)

MAP Washoe County Parks: *Rancho San Rafael Park* (web-map at www.washoecounty.us/parks)

MANAGEMENT Washoe County Regional Parks and Open Space at 775-328-3600, www.washoecounty.us/parks; Humboldt-Toiyabe National Forest, Carson Ranger District at 775-882-2766, www.fs.usda.gov/htnf

HIGHLIGHTS Canyon, seasonal stream, views

LOWLIGHTS Exposed to sun

TIP ⏐ This is a popular trip with mountain bikers and trail runners, so solitude is at a premium. Summer visitors should get an early start, as the route is exposed to the sun all the way.

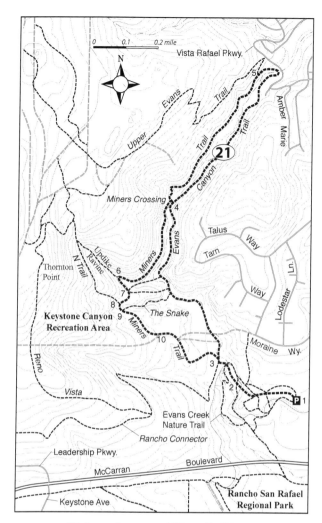

21. Evans Canyon and Miners Trail Loop

KID TIP | Older kids should be OK with the climb up the canyon, but the shorter and better-maintained Evans Creek Nature Trail nearby is perhaps a better option for smaller children.

TRAILHEAD | 39°33.224′N, 119°49.769′W From Exit 13 off I-80 in downtown Reno, head north on N. Virginia Street to the McCarran Boulevard intersection. Continue northbound on N. Virginia another 0.3 mile and turn left into the parking lot for Rancho San Rafael Regional Park sports complex. The trailhead begins at the northwest corner of the parking lot.

TRAIL | Take the middle of a trio of routes leaving the northwest corner of the parking lot [1] and head west on a dirt path to the junction of the wide gravel path at the entrance to the National Monument to the Basque Sheepherder. Continue west to a junction [2] with the Nature Trail and then head northwest toward Evans Creek. Ignore an unmarked path heading north to Moraine Way and immediately cross a bridge over the Highland Ditch just beyond. Upon reaching the canyon bottom, you enter a remarkably lush environment, where a variety of plants and trees line the banks of seasonal Evans Creek. Stroll through this greenbelt for a bit, cross the creek on a wooden bridge, and pass through a junction with the Nature Trail. Away from the creek, you encounter an open area, where paths seem to head in virtually every direction. Walk a short distance northwest to a trail sign and map at 0.4 mile from the parking area. Nearby is the junction between the Evans Canyon Trail heading north and the Miners Trail heading west [3].

Veer to the right (north) and follow the Evans Canyon Trail through a fence and beneath a set of power lines, ignoring a lesser path on the left heading west along the power lines. Soon the main trail narrows to single-track width and weaves up the canyon on a mild to moderate grade. Ignore another old road on the left and continue to a junction with The Snake route on the left, 0.8 mile from the parking lot. Remaining on the Evans Canyon Trail, continue ahead and follow the intermittent creek through a deep gorge. After a while, you cross to the east bank and proceed up the canyon, ignoring a couple of lesser paths branching to the left along the way. Reach a signed junction [4] known as Miners Crossing, 1.0 mile from the trailhead, with a very short connector to the Miners Trail on the opposite side of the creek (turning left here and heading downstream on the Miners Trail offers a shortcut back to the trailhead).

For the next half mile, you follow the trail through the winding canyon. Signs of civilization appear on the approach to Vista Rafael Parkway, where townhomes line the east canyon wall and the trail comes alongside a paved walkway. At the base of the road's fill slope, the trail arcs around to the west side of the canyon beneath a rock wall and across culverts before turning downstream. Walk across a pile of yellow tailings leftover from the old mining days and reach a pair of 4 × 4 posts. At the second post, 1.6 miles from the trailhead, is a junction [5] with the Miners Trail ahead and the route to Keystone Canyon (Upper Evans Trail) on the right (see Trip 22).

Continue ahead on the Miners Trail down the west side of the canyon across typical sagebrush scrub vegetation, which contrasts sharply with the riparian vegetation along seasonal Evans Creek. Midway down the canyon, you pass below a set of power lines, the first hint of civilization since the apartments at the head of the canyon. You reach an unsigned junction with a path climbing west out of the canyon and continue downstream, soon drawing near to the creek and reaching a junction with a very short piece of trail heading across the creek at Miners Crossing [4].

Continue ahead along the west side of the creek for a while before the trail moves a bit farther up the hillside. After passing below another set of power lines, the trail bends into a side canyon known as Updike Ravine, crosses its seasonal drainage near a path [6] on the right continuing up the ravine, and then heads down to a four-way junction [7].

Turn right at the junction and soon come to another junction [8] with the Thornton Point "N" Trail on the right, just below the site of the old Updike Mine.

Veer to the left, cross a shallow ravine and drop down to a junction [9] with The Snake on the left, a challenging mountain bike trail heading northeast toward the Evans Canyon Trail. Remaining on the Miners Trail, continue downslope to merge with an old road, which you follow briefly to another junction [10] near a power line. Proceed ahead (southeast) from this area and then bend more to the east on the way down to the close of the loop section [3] at the open area with trails heading in virtually every direction.

From there, retrace your steps across the creek, along the Nature Trail to the junction [2], and then past the Basque Monument on the way back to the trailhead [1].

BIG SAGEBRUSH (*Artemisia tridentata*) No other plant is more associated with the Great Basin than the big sagebrush, which carpets the foothills of the vast number of mountain ranges within the state. This gray-green shrub produces small yellow flowers (Nevada's state flower) that appear in late summer or early fall. Average height is 2 to 4 feet. Perhaps the most notable aspect of this plant is the pungent fragrance it emits, especially after a rain shower.

MILESTONES

1: Start at sports complex trailhead; **2:** Turn right at Nature Trail junction; **3:** Turn right at Evans Canyon Trail junction; **4:** Go straight at Miners Crossing; **5:** Go straight at Keystone Canyon (Upper Evans Trail) junction; **4:** Go straight at Miners Crossing; **6:** Go straight at Updike Ravine junction; **7:** Turn right at four-way junction; **8:** Veer left at Thornton Point "N" Trail junction; **9:** Turn right at Snake junction; **10:** Turn right at power line junction; **3:** Go straight at Nature Trail junction; **2:** Turn left at junction near Basque Monument; **1:** Return to trailhead.

GO GREEN | Washoe County Parks and Open Space has an Adopt-A-Park program, where volunteers can donate their time for working in the parks to keep them clean, attractive, and safe. The program is open to individuals and groups. For more information, visit their website at www.washoecounty.us /parks/volunteer_opportunities.php, or contact the Parks Volunteer Coordinator at 775-785-4512, ext. 107.

OPTIONS | A shorter loop is easily accomplished by crossing Evans Creek at Miners Crossing and then heading down the Miners Trail back to the lower junction with the Nature Trail.

TRIP 22

Evans Canyon and Keystone Canyon Loop

The Evans Canyon and Keystone Canyon Loop provides a physical challenge for a wide range of recreationists. A while back the Forest Service closed this section of Peavine Peak to motorized travel and, with the help of volunteers like the Poedunks, improved the trail system within this nonmotorized zone. In spring, water runs through upper Evans Canyon, which helps produce a nice variety of wildflowers. Views of Peavine Peak, the Truckee Meadows, and the Carson Range are always in season.

LEVEL	Hike, advanced
LENGTH	6.8 miles, loop
TIME	Half day
ELEVATION	+700'–700'
DIFFICULTY	Moderately strenuous
USERS	Hikers, trail runners, mountain bikers
DOGS	On leash
SEASON	Late March to December
BEST TIMES	Spring, fall
FACILITIES	Athletic fields, disc golf course, port-a-potty (restrooms at fields)
MAP	Poedunks: *Peavine Trails* (web-map at www.poedunk.org /poeville-89503/peavine-trail-maps)
MANAGEMENT	Washoe County Regional Parks and Open Space at 775-328-3600, www.washoecounty.us/parks; Humboldt-Toiyabe National Forest, Carson Ranger District at 775-882-2766, www.fs.usda.gov/htnf
HIGHLIGHTS	Canyon, stream, views
LOWLIGHTS	Rough trail sections, trails and roads crisscrossing route, exposed to sun

TIP | This is a popular trip with mountain bikers and trail runners, so solitude is at a premium. Summer visitors should get an early start, as the route is exposed to the sun all the way.

KID TIP | Older kids should be OK with the rough sections of trail, but the shorter and better-maintained Evans Creek Nature Trail nearby is perhaps a better option for smaller children. Many slightly older kids seem to be

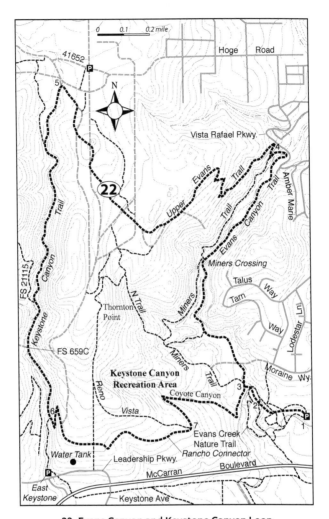

22. Evans Canyon and Keystone Canyon Loop

natural climbers and, as you'll pass by several rock formations on this loop, perhaps a visit to Rocksport's indoor climbing gym (1901 Silverada Boulevard #10) to practice their skills prior to your hike might be in order.

TRAILHEAD | 39°33.224′N, 119°49.769′W From Exit 13 off I-80 in downtown Reno, head north on N. Virginia Street to the McCarran Boulevard intersection. Continue northbound on N. Virginia another 0.3 mile and turn left into the parking lot for Rancho San Rafael Regional Park sports complex. The trailhead begins at the northwest corner of the parking lot.

TRAIL | Take the middle of a trio of routes leaving the northwest corner of the parking lot [1] and head west on a dirt path to the junction of the wide gravel path at the entrance to the National Monument to the Basque Sheepherder. Continue west to a junction [2] with the Nature Trail and then head northwest toward Evans Creek. Ignore an unmarked path heading north to Moraine Way and immediately cross a bridge over the Highland Ditch just beyond. Upon reaching the canyon bottom, you enter a remarkably lush environment, where a variety of plants and trees line the banks of Evans Creek. Stroll through this greenbelt for a bit, cross the creek on a wooden bridge, and pass through a junction with the Nature Trail. Away from the creek, you encounter an open area, where paths seem to head in virtually every direction. Walk a short distance northwest to a trail sign and map at 0.4 mile from the parking area. Nearby is the junction between the Evans Canyon Trail heading north and the Miners Trail heading west [3].

Veer to the right (north) and follow the Evans Canyon Trail through a fence and beneath a set of power lines, ignoring a lesser path on the left heading west along the power lines. Soon the main trail narrows to single-track width and weaves up the canyon on a mild to moderate grade. Ignore another old road on the left and continue to a junction with The Snake route on the left, 0.8 mile from the parking lot. Remaining on the Evans Canyon Trail, continue ahead and follow the intermittent creek through a deep gorge. After a while, you cross to the east bank and proceed up the canyon, ignoring a couple of lesser paths branching to the left along the way. Reach a signed junction known as Miners Crossing, 1.0 mile from the trailhead, with a very short connector to the Miners Trail on the opposite side of the creek.

For the next half mile, you follow the trail through the winding canyon. Signs of civilization appear on the approach to Vista Rafael Parkway, where townhomes line the east canyon wall and the trail comes alongside a paved walkway. At the base of the road's fill slope, the trail arcs around to the west side of the canyon beneath a rock wall and across culverts before heading downstream. Walk across a pile of yellow tailings leftover from the old mining days and reach a pair of 4 × 4 posts. At the second post, 1.6 miles from the trailhead, is a junction [4] with the Miners Trail ahead and the route to Keystone Canyon (Upper Evans Trail) on the right.

Turn right and climb moderately up the slope toward Vista Rafael Parkway. Immediately before reaching the road, the trail switchbacks away and then makes a 0.3-mile upward traverse across the west wall of Evans Canyon amid widely scattered Jeffrey pines. Beyond the traverse, you follow short-legged switchbacks up the slope past some low rock outcroppings. Continue climbing, enjoying improving views of the city and the mountains along the way. The climb abates for a while near the lip of Evans Canyon, until the trail merges with an old jeep road for a short stretch and then veers away toward a set of power poles. Cross the power line road and follow a single-track trail on a moderate climb across open slopes of sagebrush scrub toward a rock

Flowers enhance the view of Reno on the Evans Canyon
and Keystone Canyon Loop.

outcropping (shown as point 5350 on the USGS *Reno* map). Before reaching
the outcropping the trail merges with a well-used road running along a fence
and power line for a few steps and then follows a single-track path past the
outcropping, the high point of your journey.

Head across the road and through a gap in the fence and follow the trail
on a winding descent in the general direction of the radio towers at the head
of Keystone Canyon. Cross a well-traveled dirt road and then wind around
to intersect a less used road for a while. Where the road curves north, you
follow single-track on an arcing route bending south to eventually merge
with the old Keystone Canyon Road [5], 3.4 miles from the trailhead.

Keystone Canyon starts out low and broad but soon narrows and
deepens as you descend, which forces the route across the streambed several times on the way down the canyon. At 3.6 miles is a junction on the right
with a single-track trail (FS 21115) angling in from the north. Continue
down the canyon on a meandering route, eventually passing FS Road 659C
on the right, and then passing below a set of power lines. Shortly beyond,
you leave Forest Service land and enter Washoe County land. Reach a signed
junction with the Rancho Connector [6], 4.7 miles from the trailhead.

Unless you've made shuttle arrangements for pickup at the Keystone
East trailhead, turn left and climb moderately away from Keystone Canyon
via a couple of switchbacks. Cross an old jeep road on the way to the lip of
the canyon, soon enjoying views of the city and the Virginia Range beyond.
Beyond the stiff but short climb, the grade eases as the trail crosses another
old jeep road, passes above a water tank, heads through an opening in a
fence, and reaches a park bench near a rock outcropping. Beginning the final
descent back toward Evans Canyon, you continue eastward until the Rancho

Connector curves northwest near the junction [7] with the Thornton Point "N" Loop at 5.7 miles.

Continue on the Rancho Connector as it drops into a side canyon, switchbacks, and then descends the drainage east toward the bottom of Evans Canyon. Nearing Evans Creek, you reach a junction and bear left (the right-hand trail leads to the main part of Rancho San Rafael Park south of McCarran Boulevard). Soon reach the close of the loop at the open area where trails go seemingly every which way [3]. From there, bear right and retrace your steps over Evans Creek and follow the Nature Trail back to the junction with the trail leading past the Basque Monument and across to the parking lot [1].

CALIFORNIA QUAIL (*Callipepla californica*) These plump, highly sociable birds are most easily identified by their top-knot, a teardrop-shaped head plume, which is black on the males and brown on females. Ground dwellers, these birds prefer to run rather than fly and when they do take to the air, they don't seem to go very far. In the winter, quail tend to band together in groups called coveys. During mating season they pair up and remain monogamous until the following year, when new mates are found. After the chicks are able to fly, in about two weeks, California quail tend to form large family groups again.

MILESTONES

1: Start at sports complex trailhead; 2: Turn right at Nature Trail junction; 3: Turn right at Miners Trail/Evans Canyon junction; 4: Turn right at Miners Trail junction; 5: Turn left at Keystone Canyon Road; 6: Turn left at Rancho Connector junction; 7: Veer right at Thornton Point junction; 8: Turn left at Nature Trail junction; 3: Turn right at Miners Trail and Evans Canyon junction; 1: End at sports complex trailhead.

GO GREEN I Washoe County Parks and Open Space has an Adopt-A-Park program, where volunteers can donate their time for working in the parks to keep them clean, attractive, and safe. The program is open to individuals and groups. For more information, visit their website at www.washoecounty.us /parks/volunteer_opportunities.php, or contact the Parks Volunteer Coordinator at 775-785-4512, ext. 107.

OPTIONS I Numerous jeep roads and trails crisscross the slopes of Peavine, making extending your trip quite easy. However, make sure you have an adequate map and good navigational skills.

If you're famished for a burger following your trip, Archie's (2195 N. Virginia Street) across from the University of Nevada, Reno, offers "world famous" burgers seven days a week.

23 | Thornton Point "N" Loop

A short but sometimes steep trail, the Thornton Point "N" Loop offers an alternative to the popular Evans Canyon and Keystone Canyon trails, with fine views of the Truckee Meadows and the Carson Range along the way.

LEVEL	Hike, intermediate
LENGTH	3.2 miles, loop
TIME	1 to 2 hours
ELEVATION	+600'–600'
DIFFICULTY	Moderately strenuous
USERS	Hikers, trail runners, mountain bikers
DOGS	On leash
SEASON	Late March to December
BEST TIMES	Spring, fall
FACILITIES	Athletic fields, disc golf course, port-a-potty (restrooms at fields)
MAP	Washoe County Parks: *Rancho San Rafael Park* (web-map at www.washoecounty.us/parks)
MANAGEMENT	Washoe County Regional Parks and Open Space at 775-328-3600, www.washoecounty.us/parks
HIGHLIGHTS	Canyon, views
LOWLIGHTS	Steep sections of trail, exposed to sun

TIP | Summer visitors should get an early start, as the route is exposed to the sun all the way.

KID TIP | Older kids should be OK with the rough sections of trail, but the shorter and better-maintained Evans Creek Nature Trail nearby is perhaps a better option for smaller children.

A fun activity for the trail may be a scavenger hunt. Before the hike, create a list of things you might see on the trail and then see how many the kids in your group can identify.

TRAILHEAD | 39°33.224'N, 119°49.769'W From Exit 13 off I-80 in downtown Reno, head north on N. Virginia Street to the McCarran Boulevard intersection. Continue northbound on N. Virginia another 0.3 mile and turn left

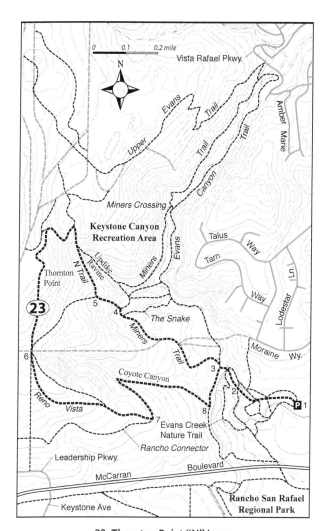

23. Thornton Point "N" Loop

into the parking lot for Rancho San Rafael Regional Park sports complex. The trailhead begins at the northwest corner of the parking lot.

TRAIL | Take the middle of a trio of routes leaving the northwest corner of the parking lot [1] and head west on a dirt path to the junction of the wide gravel path at the entrance to the National Monument to the Basque Sheepherder. Continue west to a junction [2] with the Nature Trail and then head northwest toward Evans Creek. Ignore an unmarked path heading north to Moraine Way and immediately cross a bridge over the Highland Ditch just beyond. Upon reaching the canyon bottom, you enter a remarkably lush environment, where a variety of plants and trees line the banks of Evans Creek. Stroll through this greenbelt for a bit, cross the creek on a wooden bridge, and pass through a junction with the Nature Trail. Away from the creek, you encounter an open area, where paths seem to head in virtually every direction. Walk a short distance northwest to a trail sign and map at 0.4 mile from the parking area. Nearby is the junction between the Evans Canyon Trail heading north and the Miners Trail heading west [3].

Continue ahead on the Miners Trail climbing moderately up the open hillside. Soon your route merges with the wide track of an old road on the left coming in from the southeast. The trail curves northwest and climbs at a gentler grade for a while, coming alongside a line of power poles. As you ascend, the white "N" higher on the slope comes into view, as well as a few tailing piles left over from the mining period. Watchful eyes will see quite a bit of evidence of the Updike Mine scattered across this part of the landscape—the trail is very well named. Proceed ahead on the main trail at junctions with lesser-used trails on the right and left. At about 0.7 mile from the trailhead, you reach a junction with The Snake on the right, a challenging mountain bike route that weaves steeply down a ravine back to a union with the Evans Canyon Trail. Once again, the Miners Trail continues ahead toward a horseshoe bend across a side canyon. Right where the trail starts to bend to the north before crossing this ravine, you come to an unmarked junction [4] with a broad path climbing up the hillside to the northeast past the site of an old mine.

Leave the Miners Trail and ascend the broad path past the old mine and proceed toward the "N" above. Soon you reach another junction [5] with a single-track trail on the right heading steeply uphill to the north. (If you're not feeling up to the full loop, you can continue ahead toward the base of the "N" and then loop back around to the Miners Trail below).

To do the full loop, turn right (north) and climb stiffly up the hillside. Soon the trail bends northwest and climbs above a ravine on the right, where another tailings pile comes into view below. Keep climbing past some low rock outcrops to the right and then follow the trail as it curves around to the southwest toward a rock knob. The trail passes just below the top of the knob, requiring a short jaunt to reach the splendid view of the Truckee Meadows, Carson Range, and Virginia Range from Thornton Point.

With the major climb behind, you snake down the slope past more evidence of old mining activity on the way to a jeep road. Proceed shortly to a fence corner [6] near where a utility line makes a 90-degree bend and you're faced with a trio of possible routes. Take the middle path, a twin-tracked old jeep road that initially heads south and then bends east to reach a junction [7] with the Rancho Connector after 0.5 mile.

Turn left at the junction and drop into a usually dry ravine known as Coyote Canyon. Upon reaching the bottom, the trail turns east and follows the canyon downslope. Just before the Highland Ditch [8], the Rancho Connector turns south and heads toward Rancho San Rafael Park. However, your route back to the sports complex trailhead turns north and continues to the junction [3] between the Miners Trail and Evans Canyon Trail. Once there, retrace your steps 0.4 mile to the parking lot [1].

BASQUE SHEPHERDERS Many Basque sheepherders found their way to Northern Nevada in the last quarter of the 1800s. Most came here by way of South America, sailing north for the California gold rush. As the majority were unsuccessful in the pursuit of gold, they dispersed to areas around the West where the traditional sheepherding practices could be employed, including the greater Reno area. While herding sheep eventually became less lucrative by the mid-twentieth century, many Basque descendants have attempted to keep their cultural traditions intact in modern times, including celebrating the sheepherding heritage.

MILESTONES

1: Start at sports complex trailhead; **2:** Turn right at Nature Trail junction; **3:** Go straight at Miners Trail and Evans Canyon junction; **4:** Turn left at junction near old mine; **5:** Turn right at junction with trail to "N"; **6:** Go straight at fence corner junction; **7:** Turn left at Rancho Connector junction; **8:** Junction to Rancho San Rafael Regional Park; **3:** Turn right at Miners Trail and Evans Canyon junction; **1:** End at sports complex trailhead.

GO GREEN | Washoe County Parks and Open Space has an Adopt-A-Park program, where volunteers can donate their time for working in the parks to keep them clean, attractive, and safe. The program is open to individuals and groups. For more information, visit their website at www.washoecounty.us /parks/volunteer_opportunities.php, or contact the Parks Volunteer Coordinator at 775-785-4512, ext. 107.

OPTIONS | Two downtown Reno establishments have kept Basque cuisine alive in the Reno area. Traditional family-style meals are served for both lunch and dinner at the Santa Fe (235 Lake Street) and Louie's Basque Corner (301 E. Fourth Street), where lamb is the cultural favorite. Adults can enjoy a Picon Punch, the time-honored Basque cocktail, either at the bar or with their meal.

Wedekind Regional Park

Tucked into a hilly parcel of land between the north edge of old Sparks and the south end of Spanish Springs Valley, and bordered by Pyramid Highway on the west and the Orr Ditch to the east, this chunk of undeveloped land within Wedekind Regional Park is a hidden gem in the midst of suburbia. Not that this area hasn't seen its share of human activity, as old mining sites are scattered about, transmission lines run across the property, and numerous old roads and trails crisscross the landscape. The City of Sparks has done an adequate job of delineating some official trails in an attempt to concentrate recreational use, but more work needs to be done.

The prime attractions, other than the close proximity for Sparks residents, are the fine views of the Truckee Meadows, Virginia Range, and Carson Range from various high points scattered about the park. Among the many possible routes, two of the more significant trails are described below. The first trip loops through the southern part of the park with an optional steep ascent to the park's highpoint for an excellent vista. The second is a short but sometimes steep climb from the north trailhead to the top of an unnamed peak with a 360-degree view.

24A ▪ South Park Loop

LEVEL	Hike, intermediate
LENGTH	2.8 miles, lollipop loop with out-and-back climb to Peak 4784
TIME	2 hours
ELEVATION	+425'–425'
DIFFICULTY	Moderately strenuous (moderate without climb to Peak 4784)
USERS	Hikers, trail runners, mountain bikers
DOGS	OK
SEASON	All year
BEST TIMES	April to mid-May
FACILITIES	Outdoor classroom, picnic area, port-a-potties
MAP	United States Geological Survey: *Vista*

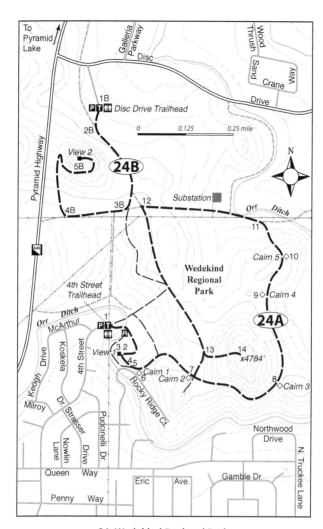

24. Wedekind Regional Park

MANAGEMENT   City of Sparks: Parks and Facilities at 775-691-9130,
www.cityofsparks.us

HIGHLIGHTS   Views

LOWLIGHTS   Exposed to sun

TIP | Pack water, as none is available at the park. Curiously, the photo-map at the trailhead is oriented with north heading down.

KID TIP | Small children may not enjoy the nearly 3-mile trip, but older kids should do fine. Pack along plenty of water and sunscreen, though.

TRAILHEAD | 39°34.003′N, 119°44.565′W From Interstate 80, take Exit 18, head north on Pyramid Highway (SR 445) for 1.8 miles to a right turn at McCarran Boulevard. Follow McCarran for 0.2 mile and then turn left at Fourth Street. Proceed for 0.8 mile to the end of the road and the parking lot for the Fourth Street trailhead for Wedekind Regional Park.

TRAIL | Immediately cross over the Orr Ditch [1] on a stout bridge and come to a modestly developed area of the park with a picnic area, horseshoe pits, and an outdoor classroom. Myriad routes fan out from this end of the park and when combined with a dearth of signs creates some confusion among first-time visitors as to which way to proceed. The loop as described here begins on a distinct path headed generally south up a hillside. Other than a faint section of single-track, your trail is the wide, right-hand path. Heading toward the left side of the shade structure on the knoll southeast of the trailhead, merge with an old road and follow an arcing course shortly to a junction [2], where a short side path on the right climbs west to the top of the hill and View 1 [3]. Beneath a metal shade structure, a placard with a picture identifying some of the key features seen from the viewpoint is at the top. From this slightly elevated perch, you have a good view looking south over the Truckee Meadows. After fully admiring the view, retrace your steps back to the road [2].

Turn right, follow the road briefly to a junction [4] with a fairly well-defined trail on the left and continue another 5 yards to a second junction [5]. Veer to the left here and head toward a very large rock pile (Cairn 1) [6]. As you proceed, you can see some tailings on the hillside above from the by-gone mining days. Soon the trail angles back a bit and comes to yet another junction, where your trail reunites with the trail from junction 4. Traverse around the hillside and pass by more trails on a climb toward another large rock pile (Cairn 2) [7] near a saddle directly southwest of Peak 4784, the park's high point, where a number of trails head off in a variety of directions.

Proceed ahead on the most well-used trail, as views of Reno-Sparks and the Carson and Virginia ranges open up on the way across the saddle. Pass below some interesting-looking low rock formations and above an old mining pit on the way toward the next rock pile (Cairn 3) [8] in a saddle sandwiched between Peak 4784 to the northwest and a low knoll to the southeast. Turning north, a single-track trail meets an old road, as you enjoy views of Spanish Springs Valley and the neighboring mountains. Pass by side trails providing access to the subdivision to the east on the way toward the next rock pile (Cairn 4) [9] in a low saddle. From there, a short and easy walk leads to the next rock pile (Cairn 5) [10] near the edge of a steep hill. A sweeping view from this point includes all of Spanish Springs Valley; the Pah Rah Range to the northeast, including 7,401-foot Spanish Springs Peak; the Sun Valley Hills to the northwest; and Peavine Peak to the west.

Make a stiff descent from Cairn 5 on the way downslope toward a set of power lines and a service road for a utility substation. Reaching the road [11], you turn left and head generally west, passing by another road on the right that follows alongside the Orr Ditch to Disc Drive. Walk past the substation and climb up the hillside onto gentler terrain, where you reach a junction [12].

Find a single-track section of trail heading south-southeast and begin a gentle traverse across the hillside, marked periodically by split-rail posts. Above the developed area of the park, several trails and old roads offer shortcuts back to the trailhead. However, you continue southeast across gentle terrain toward the west slope of Peak 4784 and a four-way junction [13].

Turn sharply left and make the very steep climb to the base of the rocks below the peak, where a short and easy scramble over the rocks leads to the summit [14] and a 360-degree view. A small-scale map covering a large enough area to include the mountains north of Spanish Springs and south to the end of the Carson Range would be helpful in identifying the numerous landmarks visible from this aerie. After thoroughly enjoying the view, retrace your steps to the junction.

At the four-way junction [13], turn left and walk a short distance to the close of the loop near Cairn 2 [7]. From there, simply retrace your steps to the trailhead [1].

ORR DITCH Similar to the other ditches in the Truckee Meadows, the Orr Ditch took water from the Truckee River and delivered it to thirsty agricultural properties, this time in Spanish Springs Valley. The ditch crossed right through the University of Nevada property and was eventually rerouted by use of an inverted siphon, which allowed expansion of the university. Later in 1911, Manzanita Lake was created when the ditch was dammed.

MILESTONES

1: Start at Fourth Street trailhead; 2: Turn right at junction; 3: View 1; 2: Turn right at junction; 4: Go straight at junction; 5: Veer left toward rock cairn; 6: Cairn 1; 7: Cairn 2; 8: Cairn 3; 9: Cairn 4; 10: Cairn 5; 11: Turn left at service road; 12: Turn left at junction; 13: Turn left at junction; 14: Top of Peak 4784; 13: Turn left at junction; 7: Return to trailhead.

GO GREEN I The City of Sparks: Parks and Recreation Department has an Adopt-A-Park program, where groups or individuals can donate their time to help support the parks. For more information, visit the City of Sparks website and follow the link for the Adopt-A-Park program, or contact the Parks Volunteer Coordinator at 775-353-2376.

The city of Sparks as seen from Wedekind Regional Park

OPTIONS ı So many old roads and trails crisscross the park that finding alternate routes is virtually unlimited. With two vehicles you could easily do a shuttle trip between the Fourth Street and Disc Drive trailheads.

24B ▪ View 2

LEVEL	Hike, intermediate
LENGTH	1.5 miles, out and back
TIME	1 hour
ELEVATION	+200'–50'
DIFFICULTY	Moderately strenuous
USERS	Hikers, runners, mountain bikers
DOGS	OK
SEASON	All year
BEST TIME	April to mid-May
FACILITIES	Port-a-potties
MAP	United States Geological Survey: *Vista*
MANAGEMENT	City of Sparks: Parks and Facilities at 775-691-9130, www.cityofsparks.us
HIGHLIGHTS	Views
LOWLIGHTS	Exposed to sun, traffic noise

TIP ı Pack water, as none is available at the park, and don't forget the sunscreen. Curiously, the photo-map at the trailhead is oriented with north heading down.

KID TIP | Although there's not much to engage young children along the way, the view from the top offers plenty of opportunities to identify points of interest. One way to make the trip more interesting for kids would be to create an activity using a GPS device. The Science Spot website (www.sciencespot .net/Pages/classgpslsn.html) is an excellent resource for such activities.

TRAILHEAD | 39°34.478′N, 119°44.620′W From Interstate 80, take Exit 18, head north on Pyramid Highway (SR 445) for 3.2 miles and then turn right at Disc Drive. After 0.3 mile, turn right and proceed to the Disc Drive trailhead for Wedekind Regional Park.

TRAIL | Similar to the Fourth Street trailhead, a variety of paths and roads head away from the parking area **[1B]**. From the trailhead, follow a short stretch of single-track trail uphill to the wide track of an old road **[2B]**. Head southeast on the road through open terrain on a gradual climb below the northeast flank of the unnamed peak above. Reach a pair of close junctions, where you bear to the right and almost immediately come to the second of these junctions **[3B]**, where a road heads east toward a substation and west toward Pyramid Highway. Turn right and follow the road westward toward a fence line paralleling the highway and a junction **[4B]** with a faint track on the right heading up the hillside.

Make a stiff climb up the open sagebrush scrub slope to where the route bends sharply to the right and follows an upward traverse across the south and east slopes of the knoll. Wrap around the hillside to the top, where a shade structure and pictorial map helps you identify a few of the major points of interest visible from View 2 **[5B]**. The extensive vista stretches south to the far end of the Truckee Meadows, bordered by the Virginia and Carson Ranges. After thoroughly enjoying the vista, retrace your steps back to the trailhead **[1B]**.

CHEATGRASS (*Bromus tectorum*) For much of Northern Nevada, the dominant vegetation carpeting the slopes of the hills is cheatgrass, a non-native plant from the Eurasian steppe. Overgrazing by sheep and cattle during the nineteenth century set the stage for this invasive species to take hold and expand, displacing much of the native sagebrush-grassland vegetation. One unfortunate consequence of this plant invasion is the highly flammable nature of dried cheatgrass contributing to an increase in rangeland wildfires. Because the seeds of cheatgrass germinate in autumn or early winter, it grows more quickly than native species and dries out and burns before the native vegetation has a chance to produce seeds, allowing cheatgrass to become more dominant with each passing season. Complicating matters even further, cheatgrass is nearly impossible to eradicate.

MILESTONES

1B: Start at Disc Drive trailhead; **2B:** Merge with old road; **3B:** Turn right at junction; **4B:** Turn right at junction; **5B:** View 2; **1B:** Return to trailhead.

GO GREEN | The City of Sparks: Parks and Recreation Department has an Adopt-A-Park program, where groups or individuals can donate their time to help support the parks. For more information, visit the City of Sparks website and follow the link for the Adopt-A-Park program, or contact the Parks Volunteer Coordinator at 775-353-2376.

OPTIONS | So many old roads and trails crisscross the park that finding alternate routes is virtually unlimited. With two vehicles you could easily do a shuttle trip between the Fourth Street and Disc Drive trailheads.

TRIP
25 | Alum Creek Loop

Although right on the very edge of civilization, the first part of this loop emits a feeling of remoteness thanks to infrequent use on an unmaintained route through the deep and narrow canyon of Alum Creek, where the sounds and sights of the city are muted by the gorge's high hills. The trip is especially fine in the spring when plenty of water fills the creek and a smattering of wildflowers adds scattered bursts of color to the slopes. Away from Alum Creek, the trip follows a steep and rocky section of Hunter Lake Road, which is open to motorized travel, but offers nice views along the way.

LEVEL	Hike, advanced
LENGTH	5.4 miles, loop
TIME	2 to 3 hours
ELEVATION	+1,325′–1,325′
DIFFICULTY	Moderately strenuous
USERS	Hikers, trail runners, mountain bikers, equestrians
DOGS	OK
SEASON	Late March to mid-November
BEST TIMES	Spring, fall
MAP	United States Geological Survey: *Mount Rose NE, Mount Rose NW*
MANAGEMENT	Humboldt-Toiyabe National Forest, Carson Ranger District at 775-882-2766, www.fs.usda.gov/htnf
HIGHLIGHTS	Forest, stream, views
LOWLIGHTS	Open to motorized vehicles; trail is not maintained, multiple roads and trails create navigational issues.

TIP | As part of this trip follows unofficial trail, visitors must have the ability to navigate with map and compass and/or GPS unit.

KID TIP | For the last couple of miles, this trip follows the course of Hunter Lake Road, which is a fairly well-used OHV route, requiring responsible adults to keep a close watch on any children.

TRAILHEAD | 39°28.807′N, 119°51.541′E Drive on McCarran Boulevard to the upper intersection with Caughlin Ranch Parkway and head southwest past a shopping center 0.3 mile to the second left-hand turn onto Village Green

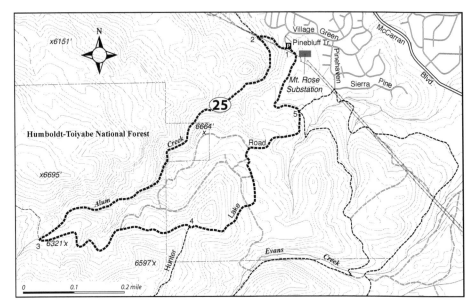

25. Alum Creek Loop

Parkway. Continue on Village Green for 0.3 mile and turn right onto Pinebluff Trail. Park your vehicle along the edge of the cul-de-sac as space allows.

TRAIL ǀ Begin the hike by following the closed power line road on the west side of the cul-de-sac (not Hunter Lake Road heading south) [1] as it descends steeply into the canyon of Alum Creek. At the bottom, reach a junction [2] with a road, where you angle back to the left and head upstream. If you continued downstream, you would reach the paved Caughlin Ranch path in about one-third mile (see Trip 6).

Heading up the canyon, the road soon narrows to a single-track trail. If not for the presence of rusting old automobiles pushed over the lip of the canyon by misguided thrill seekers, you might feel as though civilization was miles away at the bottom of this deep gorge. The trail follows the twists and bends of the canyon through Jeffrey pine forest with very little in the way of groundcover. Farther upstream the trail grows fainter until you intersect a jeep road [3] at 2.4 miles.

Turn left onto the jeep road and follow a general traverse around the folds and creases of the south side of the canyon through partially burned forest, moving farther away from the creek as you go. About a mile from the road/trail junction, reach a saddle on the ridge crest dividing the Alum Creek and Evans Creek drainages to meet the Hunter Lake Road [4].

Turn left and head east for a short while on a gently graded section of the Hunter Lake Road, which soon becomes steep and rocky. Leaving most of the forest behind, the road continues the stiff descent across a hillside

Foothills view from the Alum Creek Loop

and down to a flat, 4.8 miles from the start [5], where roads seem to come and go from all directions. Veer north to remain on Hunter Lake Road, which appears as the most well-traveled road in this maze of possible routes. The road veers east and then arcs around the hillside above a seasonal tributary before doubling back to the north-northwest toward the Mount Rose Substation. The grade eases on the way past some storage units before a short, steep descent leads to the end of the route at the cul-de-sac at the end of Pinebluff Trail [1].

> **SILVERY LUPINE** (*Lupinus argenteus*) This member of the pea family is a common wildflower within the Jeffrey pine forests of the Carson Range. Although occasionally producing white and yellow flowers, like most lupines this variety has mainly purple flowers. The species is named for the silvery hairs on the stem. Although attractive, plants and especially the seeds of lupines can be toxic to people and animals.

MILESTONES

1: Start at end of Pinebluff Trail; **2:** Turn left at junction; **3:** Turn left at jeep road; **4:** Turn left at Hunter Lake Road; **5:** Veer left at flat; **1:** End at Pinebluff Trail.

GO GREEN | As the route is not maintained, Good Samaritans can pack along a trash bag and pick up any debris found along the way. A helicopter with a trained pilot would be of great value hauling several old vehicles out of Alum Creek canyon.

OPTIONS | With so many jeep roads and dirt bike trails carpeting the hills in this section of the Carson Range, numerous alternative trips or extensions are possible for those with the requisite navigational or cross-country skills.

26 | Hunter Lake Road

Although somewhat popular with OHV users, the Hunter Lake Road provides a gateway into the heart of the mountains west of Reno. The rare sight of a Carson Range pond surrounded by lush meadows will reward those who travel all the way to Hunter Lake. Autumn is a particularly fine season to visit, as the copious amount of aspens and willows en route produces a vivid display of fall color.

LEVEL	Hike, moderate to advanced
LENGTH	Varies, up to 15 miles (out and back to Hunter Lake)
TIME	Half to full day
ELEVATION	+3,300′–350′ (to Hunter Lake)
DIFFICULTY	Strenuous
USERS	Hikers, trail runners, mountain bikers, equestrians
DOGS	OK
SEASON	June through October
BEST TIMES	June to early July, mid-October
FACILITIES	None
MAP	United States Geological Survey: *Mount Rose NE, Mount Rose NW*
MANAGEMENT	USFS: Humboldt-Toiyabe National Forest, Carson Ranger District at 775-882-2766, www.fs.usda.gov/htnf
HIGHLIGHTS	Autumn color, pond, views
LOWLIGHTS	Open to motorized vehicles; trail is not maintained, multiple roads and trails create navigational issues.

TIP | You can avoid some of the encounters with motorized vehicles by visiting this area on weekdays instead of weekends.

KID TIP | The long distance to the lake combined with OHV use on the Hunter Lake Road makes this trip unsuited for small children.

TRAILHEAD | 39°28.807′N, 119°51.541′E Drive on McCarran Boulevard to the upper intersection with Caughlin Ranch Parkway and head southwest past the shopping center 0.3 mile to the second left-hand turn onto Village Green Parkway. Continue on Village Green for 0.3 mile and turn right onto Pinebluff Trail. You can park along the edge of the cul-de-sac as space allows.

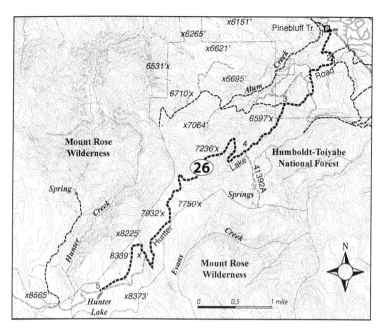

26. Hunter Lake Road

With a high-clearance vehicle, driving farther up the dirt-and-rock surface of Hunter Lake Road to a parking area just beyond the storage units is possible.

TRAIL | From the edge of the pavement [1], climb up Hunter Lake Road past the Mount Rose Substation and a storage facility and then bend around to a large flat [2], 0.6 mile from the end of Pinebluff Trail. The Hunter Lake Road, which always appears as the most well-traveled road, heads uphill to the right and climbs, steeply at times, to a saddle on a ridge crest separating the Alum Creek and Evans Creek drainages. A partially charred Jeffrey pine forest attests to the frequency of past fires in this area. Reach a junction [3] at 1.9 miles with the road to Alum Creek on the right.

Remaining on the Hunter Lake Road, head south-southwest on an upward traverse across the upper part of the canyon carrying the north branch of Evans Creek. Reach a T-junction, 2.4 miles from Pinebluff Trail, with a road heading off to the right. On the left-hand side is a relatively new signboard with a limited amount of information. Away from the junction, the grade eases and actually makes a slight descent before a gently rising path draws closer to the creek and the forest opens up a bit to allow views up the canyon. Soon the forest closes in again on the way to a trio of roads branching over toward the aspen-lined creek. The middle road [4], at 2.75 miles and signed 41392A, heads across the creek and continues south to some meadow-rimmed springs.

Continue ahead, climbing up the canyon via a couple of long-legged switchbacks on the way to a saddle southwest of Peak 7236. Away from the saddle, the ascent leads generally southwest through a mixture of conifer stands; copses of quaking aspens and willows; and drier slopes filled with currant, sagebrush, and tobacco brush. The open slopes offer grand views of the Truckee Meadows, bordered by peaks of the Virginia Range. Reach the crest of a ridge north of Peak 8339, 6.8 miles from Pinebluff Trail.

Enjoy the respite from the long stretch of climbing on a three-quarter-mile descent through lodgepole pine forest. Where the grade eases, you stroll across a good-sized meadow, eventually nearing the north shore of smallish, willow-lined Hunter Lake [5]. First-timers may be a bit disappointed in the "lake," which by most standards resembles a pond more than a bona fide lake. For anyone who doesn't mind the idea of lugging a pack all the way up here, a few pine-shaded campsites can be found near the meadow fringe and where the Hunter Lake Road crosses Hunter Creek farther west. The jeep road continues across the crest of the Carson Range, drops to the vicinity of Big Meadows, and then heads north toward Boomtown or southwest to the Truckee River Canyon. When your visit to Hunter Lake is over, retrace your steps to the trailhead [1].

> **HUNTER LAKE** Hunter Lake lies in a strip of land between the north and south sections of the Mount Rose Wilderness. Named for the operator of a toll bridge across the Truckee River, John M. Hunter, the tiny lake is one of a small number of lakes dotting the Carson Range. Unlike the characteristic granite basins near the main Sierra crest, water tends to percolate into the porous, volcanic soils of the Carson Range rather than collect into the granite bedrock above the opposite shore. Hunter Lake is a fairly popular destination for the OHV crowd and a routine watering hole for wildlife.

MILESTONES

1: Start at end of Pinebluff Trail; 2: Veer right on Hunter Lake Road; 3: Go straight ahead at junction with road to Alum Creek; 4: Go straight ahead at junction with FS Road 41392A; 5: Hunter Lake; 1: Return to Pinebluff Trail.

GO GREEN | As the route is not maintained, Good Samaritans can pack along a trash bag and pick up any debris found along the way.

OPTIONS | Areas around Hunter Lake are suitable for camping for groups who don't mind hauling a backpack all the way there.

TRIP
27 | Evans Creek

This trip is challenging, following a combination of unmaintained roads and trails, and the area has a feeling of remoteness for being so close to the edge of civilization. Starting out on Hunter Lake Road, you soon head south into the drainages of Evans Creek on the loop section. Autumn is a great time to visit, when aspens and willows lining the streams turn golden, and spring is also a good option, when the creeks are running full.

LEVEL	Hike, advanced
LENGTH	7.2 miles, semi-loop
TIME	Half day
ELEVATION	+1,100′–1,100′
DIFFICULTY	Moderately strenuous
USERS	Hikers, trail runners, mountain bikers, equestrians
DOGS	OK
SEASON	March to December
BEST TIMES	Spring, fall
FACILITIES	None
MAP	United States Geological Survey: *Mount Rose NE*
MANAGEMENT	USFS: Humboldt-Toiyabe National Forest, Carson Ranger District at 775-882-2766, www.fs.usda.gov/htnf
HIGHLIGHTS	Autumn color, canyon, stream, views
LOWLIGHTS	Open to motorized vehicles; trail is not maintained, multiple roads and trails create navigational issues.

TIP ǀ This is one trip where you don't want to be without a map and GPS unit or compass. Multiple roads and trails present themselves along the way and, since this route is not maintained, getting off route would be fairly easy. There are absolutely no trail signs to help guide the way.

KID TIP ǀ This trip is not the best route for small children, as the climb out of the north branch of Evans Creek canyon is very difficult and constant supervision may be necessary to avoid losing a curious kid who wanders off.

TRAILHEAD ǀ 39°28.807′N, 119°51.541′E Drive on McCarran Boulevard to the upper intersection with Caughlin Ranch Parkway and head southwest

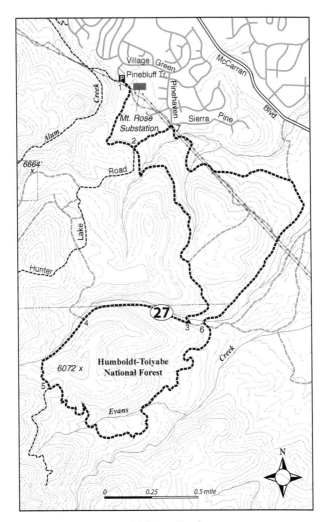

27. Evans Creek

past the shopping center 0.3 mile to the second left-hand turn onto Village Green Parkway. Continue on Village Green for 0.3 mile and turn right onto Pinebluff Trail. You can park along the edge of the cul-de-sac as space allows. With a high-clearance vehicle, driving farther up the dirt-and-rock surface of Hunter Lake Road to a parking area just beyond the storage units is possible.

TRAIL ı From the edge of the pavement [1], climb up Hunter Lake Road past the Mount Rose Substation and a storage facility and then bend around to a large flat [2], 0.6 mile from the end of Pinebluff Trail. The Hunter Lake Road heads uphill to the right, but you should follow the lower road (some maps refer to this as Cold Canyon Road) on an extended traverse headed generally south toward the Evans Creek drainage. Along the way, the old road passes through sagebrush scrub dotted with Jeffrey pines, vegetation typical of the east front of the Carson Range. At about 2 miles, you bend around and cross the north branch of Evans Creek and reach a road junction [3].

Turn right and head upstream above the creek on a stiff climb. At 2.4 miles is a Y-junction [4], where the right-hand road drops to a crossing of the stream and then climbs up the hillside, reaching the Hunter Lake Road in a half mile. This route would be a viable option for anyone interested in a shorter hike (4.5 miles)—simply turn right and follow the Hunter Lake Road back to the car.

Continue ahead from the Y-junction up the south side of the canyon into thicker Jeffrey pine forest, with a few firs lining the creek bottom and mountain mahoganies intermixing with the pines on the drier slopes. The road peters out at 2.75 miles, giving way to a somewhat indistinct section of loose, single-track trail that makes a very steep climb out of the canyon to the top the top of a knoll directly southwest of Peak 6072. On top of the knoll is a junction [5] with a better-defined stretch of trail. (A right-hand turn on this fairly good trail leads three-quarter mile into the main canyon of Evans Creek, where it abruptly ends.)

Turn left and begin a protracted descent that winds into the side canyon of a usually dry Evans Creek tributary. Breaking out of the forest, the trail continues downhill, recrossing the tributary after a half mile. A short climb out of the drainage is followed by another half-mile descent, where the trail intersects the road [6] and then bends west and heads up the north branch of Evans Creek. (A short distance up the road, a single-track trail veers away to the northeast, eventually providing a way back to Pinehaven Road but crosses a stretch of private property in the process.) Continue up the road, reaching a junction with another road. Proceeding ahead, you follow the road as it winds around toward the Sierra Pine Drive and Pinehaven Road intersection [7]. Veer to the left and head southwest toward Hunter Lake Road [2]. From there, retrace your steps one-third mile to Pinebluff Trail [1].

JEFFREY PINE (*Pinus jeffreyi*) The ubiquitous Jeffrey pine is a common sight at these elevations in the east front of the Carson Range. One of two three-needled pines found in the Sierra, Jeffrey pines differ from their ponderosa pine counterparts, with larger cones and reddish-brown bark that often emits a vanilla scent.

MILESTONES

1: Start at Pinebluff Trail; **2:** Proceed ahead on lower road; **3:** Turn right and head upstream; **4:** Proceed ahead at Y-junction; **5:** Turn left at junction; **6:** Turn right at junction; **7:** Turn left near intersection; **2:** Turn right at road junction; **1:** Return to Pinebluff Trail.

GO GREEN ∣ As the route is not maintained, Good Samaritans can pack along a trash bag and pick up any debris found along the way.

OPTIONS ∣ The cozy Lanna Thai Café (4786 Caughlin Parkway) dishes up some of the best Thai cuisine in the area and would be a great place to re-energize after your hike.

Ballardini Ranch Loop

One of the newer trails in the area, the Ballardini Ranch Loop follows a circuit through southwest Reno across mostly open sagebrush scrub with occasional forays to seasonal streams. The old ranch was previously a hotly contested site between developers wanting to build subdivisions and recreationists, who envisioned an entirely different use of the land as open space. A compromise between the City of Reno and the developer was eventually reached, which in part established this trailhead. The Great Recession temporarily brought the housing development to a halt, but a more favorable economic climate could renew such plans at any time.

LEVEL	Walk, moderate
LENGTH	2.0 miles, loop
TIME	1 hour
ELEVATION	+200′–200′
DIFFICULTY	Moderate
USERS	Hikers, trail runners, mountain bikers, equestrians
DOGS	On leash
SEASON	March through November
BEST TIME	Spring
FACILITIES	Picnic tables, vault toilet
MAP	None
MANAGEMENT	Washoe County Regional Parks and Open Space at 775-328-3600, www.washoecounty.us/parks
HIGHLIGHTS	Stream, views
LOWLIGHTS	The entire loop is without shade.

TIP | Get a very early start if you plan on doing this hike in the summer.

KID TIP | This short, relatively easy hike should be well suited for children of most ages, provided it's not a forced march during the scorching heat of an afternoon summer day. Without any shade, plenty of liquids and sunscreen should be readily available even in cooler seasons. In spring, the seasonal drainages should have enough water to provide areas of interesting exploration for youngsters.

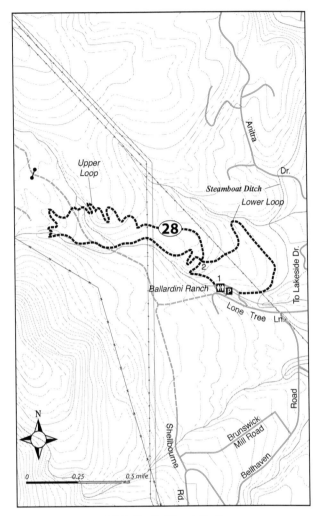

28. Ballardini Ranch Trail

TRAILHEAD | 39°20.944′N, 119°49.983′W From S. Virginia Street, head west on Holcomb Ranch Lane for 2.2 miles to where the road curves north and becomes Lakeside Drive. Continue another 0.2 miles and turn left onto Lone Tree Lane. Follow Lone Tree for 0.8 mile to the entrance into the parking area on the right.

TRAIL | From the trailhead [1], you follow the wide track of an old road up the hillside to a four-way junction [2] with the upper and lower loops near a power line.

Veer left and switchback up the hillside to where the grade eases on the way to a crossing of a seasonal stream. Across the drainage, you proceed

A grandparent and child examining a desert peach shrub
on the Ballardini Ranch Trail

generally west through open sagebrush scrub. Merge briefly with an old road and then veer left onto a lesser road that follows the streambed for a while, which is lined with cottonwoods, willows, and other riparian foliage. Eventually the trail leaves the stream and switchbacks up the hillside to where you veer to the right, where a road on the left continues west. Another switchback leads up to the crest of a low rise and across a major road. From there, you dip into another drainage, cross over a wooden bridge, and then climb up to the top of a knoll with a nice view of the Truckee Meadows and the Carson Range. Wind downslope for a while and then curve beneath the power line on the way back to the loop junction [2].

Unless you're in a hurry, take the left-hand path and follow the lower loop toward a gully carrying another seasonal tributary of Dry Creek. Once at the gully, the trail arcs above a section of the Steamboat Ditch before circling around to the parking area [1].

DESERT PEACH (*Prunus andersonii*) A deciduous shrub in the rose family, desert peach is a common plant in the sagebrush scrub community of the foothills. Growing to heights of over 6 feet, the plant is easily recognized in spring, when branches are full of small pink flowers. Mainly rodents eat the small apricot-colored fruits.

MILESTONES

1: Start at trailhead; **2:** Turn left at loop junction; **2:** Turn left at loop junction; **1:** Return to trailhead.

GO GREEN | Washoe County Regional Parks and Open Space has an Adopt-A-Park program, where volunteers can donate their time for working in the parks to keep them clean, attractive, and safe. The program is open to individuals and groups. For more information, visit their website at www .washoecounty.us/parks/volunteer_opportunities.php, or contact the Parks Volunteer Coordinator at 775-785-4512, ext. 107.

OPTIONS | A connection from the existing Ballardini Ranch Loop to the Thomas Creek Trail has been proposed, but time will tell if such a project ever materializes. If and when this trail becomes a reality, the options for further wanderings will be greatly enhanced, particularly for mountain bikers. In the meantime, there's not much in the way of additional recreational opportunities or amenities in the immediate area.

Coursing across the Huffaker Hills near the east side of the Truckee Meadows is a series of hiking trails with a touch of wildness. Built in the early 2000s by volunteers of the now apparently defunct Truckee Meadows Trail Association, three separate paths wander across the top of the hills, offering good views of the Truckee Meadows, Virginia Range, Carson Range, and a flood control reservoir nearby. The topography offers a sense of unexpected remoteness uncommon to a location so close to civilization. The description below combines the three trails into one semi-loop trip, but they can certainly be done separately.

Across the road from the Huffaker Hills trailhead sits a familiar landmark to residents of the Truckee Meadows: Rattlesnake Mountain. Despite the massive hulk's location almost in the middle of town near the south end of the airport, most residents haven't set foot on the peak. Following a steep and rocky jeep road over private land, the short climb is quite strenuous, but the view is an equitable reward for all the hard toil.

29A ▪ Huffaker Hills Loop

LEVEL	Hike, moderate
LENGTH	Varies to 3.2 total
TIME	1 to 2 hours
ELEVATION	+375′–375′
DIFFICULTY	Easy to moderate
USERS	Hikers, trail runners, mountain bikers
DOGS	On leash
SEASON	March through November
BEST TIMES	Spring, fall
FACILITIES	Interpretive signs, picnic tables, port-a-potty
MAP	United States Geological Survey: *Mount Rose NE*
MANAGEMENT	Washoe County Regional Parks and Open Space at 775-328-3600, www.washoecounty.us/parks
HIGHLIGHTS	Views
LOWLIGHTS	The entire loop is without shade.

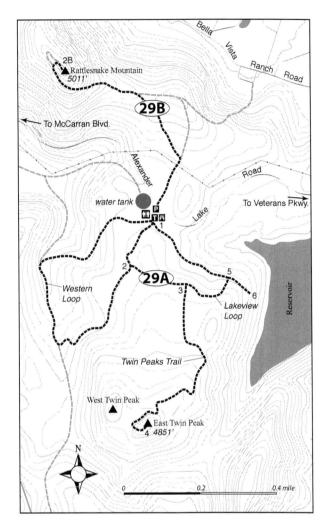

29. Huffaker Hills Loop and Rattlesnake Mountain

TIP I If you're not up for the full circuit, the trip can be shortened to a 1.8-mile, out-and-back hike to the top of East Twin Peak, a 1-mile journey along the Western Loop, or a 0.75-mile stroll on the Lakeview Loop.

KID TIP I The three variations offer adults the opportunity to tailor a hike to suit the ages and abilities of children. None of the climbs are particularly long or steep, but plenty of water and sunscreen should be available nonetheless.

TRAILHEAD I 39°28.001′N, 119°45.219′W A very short distance east of the S. McCarran Boulevard and Longley Lane intersection, turn right (south) onto Alexander Lake Road from eastbound McCarran. Follow this road on a winding climb for a mile to the Huffaker Hills trailhead parking lot on the right, which is just beyond a large water tank.

TRAIL | Leave the parking lot [1] and head southwest on a gently rising path across an open, sagebrush-scrub-covered slope to a three-way junction [2], 0.1 mile from the trailhead. This junction offers hikers a trio of alternatives. By continuing ahead, the one-mile Western Loop ducks behind hills to the west on a return to the trailhead. The left-hand trail provides access to both the out-and-back Twin Peaks Trail and the 0.75-mile Lakeview Loop back to the trailhead. The following description includes all three trails on a 3.2-mile circuit.

Turn left at the junction and head generally east-southeast for 0.2 mile to the Twin Peaks junction [3]. Turn right (south) and make a gently rising climb across more sagebrush scrub. After wet winters, spring hikers should see a smattering of colorful wildflowers, including balsamroot, daisy, phlox, and violet. Reach an interpretive sign and a view of the reservoir to the east, along with a portion of Alexander Lake below and the hills of the Virginia Range beyond. After a second interpretive sign, the grade increases on a sometimes-winding climb to the top of East Twin Peak [4], where a park bench beckons you to a lingering visit with a 360-degree vista. The wide-ranging view includes almost all of the Truckee Meadows, the Carson Range to the west, and the Virginia Range to the east. Over the years, visitors have constructed a large rock enclosure along the south edge of the peak.

After thoroughly enjoying the view, retrace your steps to the junction [3]. Just below the summit, a path branches west toward West Twin Peak but quickly dies out well below the top. The original plan was to continue the trail over to the west summit and then loop back to the trailhead. However, the Truckee Meadows Trail Association, a group of volunteers who built the original trails in Huffaker Hills, seems to have disbanded, which puts completion of that section in doubt.

Turn left at the junction between the Twin Peaks Trail and the Lakeview Loop and proceed eastbound, as the reservoir soon comes into view. A gently descending path arcs around the hillside on the way to a T-junction [5]. Turn right and walk a short distance to an overlook [6] of the reservoir, where a park bench affords a fine perch from which to sit and enjoy the view. After your stay, retrace your steps shortly back to the junction [5].

Continue ahead from the overlook junction and make a brief descent before beginning a moderate climb above the reservoir's fence. Soon you're back at the trailhead [1].

To complete the full circuit, proceed ahead from the trailhead briefly along a dirt road and then veer onto a single track. A moderately descending path heads down into a draw, where the surrounding hills block views of the

A mountain biker negotiates a turn in the Huffaker Hills.

city, making this section of the trip feel as though you've left civilization behind, if just for a moment. The trail winds across an old jeep road and ascends toward a fence line, where the route curves and continues climbing back toward the three-way junction [2]. From there, retrace your steps 0.1 mile to the parking lot [1].

COYOTE (*Canis latrans*) Perhaps no wild animal has adapted to the urbanization of the West better than this member of the dog family. Originally confined to the central United States and northern Mexico, coyotes have expanded their range all across the continent, due primarily to the eradication of their chief competitor, the wolf. Ranging from 20 to 40 pounds, they are opportunistic hunters in the wild, surviving primarily on rabbits, rodents, and carrion. Coyotes close to urban areas will raid garbage cans and prey on cats and small dogs when available. In contrast to legend, coyotes don't usually hunt in packs, preferring to hunt alone or with a mate. In urban settings, you're most likely to see an individual early in the morning or around sunset, whereas in the wild, they typically hunt during the day.

MILESTONES

1: Start at trailhead; 2: Turn left at junction; 3: Turn right at Lakeview junction; 4: Top of East Twin Peak; 3: Turn right at Lakeview Loop

junction; **5:** Turn right at Overlook junction; **6:** Overlook; **5:** Go straight
at Overlook junction; **1:** Trailhead/Go straight onto Western Loop;
2: Go straight at junction; **1:** Return to trailhead.

29B ▪ Rattlesnake Mountain

LEVEL	Hike, advanced
LENGTH	1.6 miles, out and back
TIME	1 to 2 hours
ELEVATION	+400′–400′
DIFFICULTY	Difficult
USERS	Hikers, trail runners, mountain bikers
DOGS	OK
SEASON	March through November
BEST TIMES	Spring, fall
FACILITIES	Interpretive signs, picnic tables, port-a-potty
MAP	United States Geological Survey: *Mount Rose NE*
MANAGEMENT	Private
HIGHLIGHTS	Views
LOWLIGHTS	The entire loop is without shade, steep, and on rocky ground.

TIP ǀ The climb is steep and can be brutal when the temperatures are warm.
Summer users should get a very early start.

KID TIP ǀ The steep and rocky jeep road to the top makes this trip ill suited for
young children. The nearby Huffaker Hills trails are much more kid friendly.

TRAILHEAD ǀ 39°28.001′N, 119°45.219′W A very short distance east of the
S. McCarran Boulevard and Longley Lane intersection, turn right (south)
onto Alexander Lake Road from eastbound McCarran. Follow this road on
a winding climb for a mile to the Huffaker Hills trailhead parking lot on the
right, which is just beyond a large water tank.

TRAIL ǀ From the Huffaker Hills trailhead [1], walk across Alexander Lake
Road to a gap in a fence and pick up the course of a jeep road climbing
north-northeast. After 0.2 mile, the road bends north-northwest and climbs
more steeply to the crest of the east ridge of Rattlesnake Mountain. Follow
the ridge to the base of the peak, pass around a steel gate, and climb steeply
up the road across the south flank of the mountain. Approaching the top, a
use trail angles up to the right prior to where the road makes a hairpin turn.
Follow this path to the top and proceed to the high point and the wide-
ranging view [2B].

MILESTONES

1: Start at Huffaker Hills trailhead; **2B:** Rattlesnake Mountain; **1:** Return to
trailhead.

Great Basin Rattlesnake (*Crotalus oreganus lutosus*) A subspecies of the western rattlesnake, the brownish-patterned Great Basin rattlesnake reaches 1.5 to 4 feet in length at maturity. They have a triangular-shaped head and the characteristic rattle at the tail. Their diet consists primarily of amphibians, reptiles, birds, eggs, and small mammals. Although their bites are poisonous to humans, these snakes are not aggressive and will preferentially flee the presence of humans unless all escape routes are blocked. Their first line of defense is to remain motionless in hopes their camouflage coloring will keep them from being detected. If humans come too close, they will oftentimes give an audible warning with their rattles. Reserving their venom for prey, rattlesnakes are reluctant to bite humans.

GO GREEN | Washoe County Regional Parks and Open Space has an Adopt-A-Park program, where volunteers can donate their time for working in the parks to keep them clean, attractive, and safe. The program is open to individuals and groups. For more information, visit their website at www .washoecounty.us/parks/volunteer_opportunities.php, or contact the Parks Volunteer Coordinator at 775-785-4512, ext. 107.

OPTIONS | Scattered around the McCarran Boulevard/Longley Lane intersection are several delis or fast-food franchises, where you could pick up a snack or a sandwich for the trail, or restaurants where you could enjoy a meal either pre- or post-hike.

TRIP

30 | Lower Whites Creek Trail

The Lower Whites Creek Trail offers a fine early season jaunt, when the Carson Range above is still locked in winter's deep freeze, or a late-season trip, when autumn color adorns the canyon. Whatever the season, visitors have the opportunity to experience the contrast between the lush riparian vegetation lining the creek and the drier sagebrush scrub of the slopes beyond.

LEVEL	Hike, intermediate
LENGTH	3.2 miles, shuttle; 6.4 miles, out and back
TIME	1½ to 2 hours (shuttle); 3 to 4 hours (out and back)
ELEVATION	+625'–0'; +625'–625'
DIFFICULTY	Moderate
USERS	Hikers, trail runners, mountain bikers, equestrians
DOGS	On leash
SEASON	Late March through November
BEST TIMES	Spring, fall
FACILITIES	Athletic field, picnic tables, playground, restrooms
MAP	United States Geological Survey: *Mount Rose NE*
MANAGEMENT	Washoe County Regional Parks and Open Space at 775-328-3600, www.washoecounty.us/parks
HIGHLIGHTS	Fall color, stream, views
LOWLIGHTS	Close to private homes

TIP | Since this trail receives a lot of use from dog walkers, joggers, and mountain bikers, using the trail early in the morning or late in the day will provide the best chance at minimizing the traffic. Summer users will definitely appreciate those times, as midday temperatures and a lack of shade combine to make this journey a particularly hot one.

KID TIP | Except during peak runoff, Whites Creek should be a fascinating place for kids to experience a natural watercourse. The full trip might be a bit long for smaller children, but a shorter trip is possible by parking a second vehicle at Thomas Creek Road (0.5 mile), or at Mountain Ranch Road (1.6 miles).

TRAILHEAD | 39°23.786'N, 119°47.008'W Take I-580 south to the Mount Rose Highway (SR 431) and proceed toward Lake Tahoe. At 0.6 mile past

145

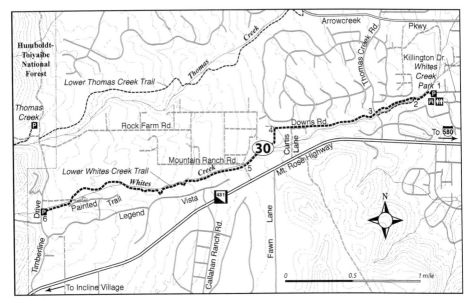

30. Lower Whites Creek Trail

the Wedge Parkway intersection, turn right onto Telluride Drive and travel 0.2 mile to Killington Drive. Turn left and follow Killington 0.2 mile to the entrance of Whites Creek Park. Continue past the athletic field to the parking area at the end of the road.

Shuttle users should continue on the Mount Rose Highway toward Lake Tahoe another 1.6 miles from the Wedge Parkway intersection to a right-hand turn onto Timberline Drive. After 0.6 mile, you pass Whites Creek Road on the left and shortly reach the bridge over the creek. Limited parking may be available on the right-hand shoulder just past the bridge. The trail is on the south side of the bridge (39°23.072′N, 119°50.268′W).

TRAIL | The trail begins by briefly following an old dirt road [1] before a single-track path rambles along the edge of sagebrush scrub and the riparian zone lining boisterous Whites Creek. A tangle of quaking aspens, willows, and alders thrives in the wet soils, as a couple of short paths lead over to the edge of the stream. Despite the modern homes on the rim of the canyon above, the initial stretch of trail through the bottom of the canyon feels quite wild and natural. Reach an unmarked junction [2] at 0.2 mile from the trailhead, where you can cross the creek on a wooden bridge and continue on the north side, or proceed ahead on the south side—both routes eventually lead out of the canyon bottom and up to Thomas Creek Road [3] at the 0.5-mile mark.

Cross Thomas Creek Road to the west side and locate the resumption of trail on the north side of the creek. Continue alongside the stream through dense foliage for another 0.5 mile to where private property forces the trail out of the canyon and away from the creek to temporarily follow the dirt surface of Downs Road. Where the road curves left and becomes Curtis Lane, you continue ahead onto a single-track trail. Follow a fence line past private homes for 0.1 mile to an unmarked, three-way junction [4].

Rather than continue ahead, veer left (south) and follow the trail for 0.1 mile back to Whites Creek. Soon you cross the creek on a wooden bridge and proceed upstream to a crossing of Mountain Ranch Road [5], 1.6 miles from the trailhead. A gravel area on the west side of the road (39°23.352′N, 119°48.592′W) offers parking for a second vehicle if you prefer a shorter trip option than the full route to Timberline Drive.

Away from the road the trail continues heading west, offering fine views from time to time of the Carson Range, including the summits of Mount Rose and Slide Mountain. Cross below a set of power lines after a half mile and continue through mostly open terrain, arcing around a couple of drainage areas on the way to a short wooden bridge across the creek, 2.8 miles from the trailhead. Now on the north side of Whites Creek, you continue toward the base of the Carson Range, passing a shady copse of aspens and willows before veering away from the creek for a while. Along this dry stretch, mountain mahogany shrubs become the dominant plant, the tiny flowers providing a burst of color to the high desert in spring. Sagebrush and ephedra fill the gaps between the mahoganies. Near the 3-mile mark, the trail bends back toward the creek and crosses a gravel emergency access road. A short distance farther, you cross the creek for the last time just downstream from a pretty cascade dumping into a small pool. The vegetation makes a dramatic change on the final section of the trail, as the appearance of Jeffrey pines heralds your arrival to upper Whites Creek canyon. Walk through an easement past some ranchettes to the end of the lower trail [6] at the edge of Timberline Drive. Without shuttle arrangements, you must retrace your steps 3.2 miles back to Whites Creek Park [1].

WILD ROSE (WOODS' ROSE) (*Rosa woodsii*) Easily recognizable by most passersby, the wild rose has the thorny stems, divided leaves, and pink flowers similar in appearance to the cultivated roses in our backyards. Found along many stream banks of northern Nevada, you should notice them where the trail closely follows Whites Creek. Unlike cultivated roses, the flowers of wild roses have only five petals, blooming for a short period in spring.

MILESTONES

1: Start at Whites Creek Park trailhead; 2: Turn right or go straight ahead at junction; 3: Cross Thomas Creek Road; 4: Turn left at junction; 5: Cross

Mountain Ranch Road; **6:** End at Timberline Drive trailhead (shuttle); **1:** Return to Whites Creek Park trailhead (out and back).

GO GREEN | Washoe County Parks and Open Space has an Adopt-A-Park program, where volunteers can donate their time for working in the parks to keep them clean, attractive, and safe. The program is open to individuals and groups. For more information, visit their website at www.washoecounty.us /parks/volunteer_opportunities.php, or contact the Parks Volunteer Coordinator at 775-785-4512, ext. 107.

OPTIONS | Although hiking the entire length of Whites Creek from where it dumps into Steamboat Creek in Damonte Ranch to its origin near the crest of the Carson Range is not entirely feasible, by combining this trip with Trip 40 (Whites Creek Trail), you could come away with a good understanding of the different ecological zones through which the stream passes.

31 | Lower Thomas Creek Trail

Another good early- or late-season option, the Lower Thomas Creek Trail travels along a section of Thomas Creek between Arrowcreek Park and Timberline Drive, exposing recreationists to a fine stretch of riparian foliage bordered by typical sagebrush scrub.

LEVEL	Hike, intermediate
LENGTH	2.6 miles, shuttle; 5.2 miles, out and back
TIME	1 to 2 hours (shuttle); 2 to 4 hours (out and back)
ELEVATION	+750′–0′; +750′–750′
DIFFICULTY	Moderate
USERS	Hikers, trail runners, mountain bikers, equestrians
DOGS	On leash
SEASON	Late March through November
BEST TIMES	Spring, fall
FACILITIES	Athletic field, picnic tables, playground, port-a-potty
MAP	United States Geological Survey: *Mount Rose NE*
MANAGEMENT	Washoe County Regional Parks and Open Space at 775-328-3600, www.washoecounty.us/parks
HIGHLIGHTS	Fall color, stream, views
LOWLIGHTS	Close to private homes

TIP ǀ Since this trail receives a lot of use from dog walkers, joggers, and mountain bikers, using the trail early in the morning or late in the day will provide the best chance at minimizing the traffic. Summer users will definitely appreciate those times, as midday temperatures and a lack of shade combine to make this journey a particularly hot one.

KID TIP ǀ Most kids should be fine with this relatively short trip. However, with plenty of side paths and roads in the area, young children should be well supervised to prevent them from wandering off the trail.

An autumn hike offers the opportunity for youngsters to collect different examples from the fallen leaves lining the trail and then identifying them at home. About Education's website (www.forestry.about.com/od /thecompletetree/a/Create_Your_Leaf_Collection.htm) is a good resource for guiding kids in preparing a leaf collection.

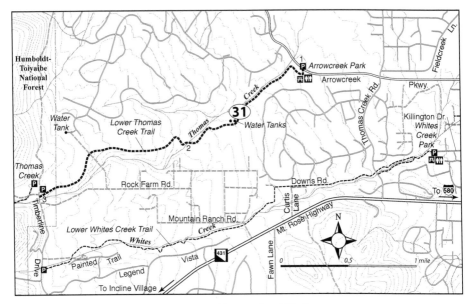

31. Lower Thomas Creek Trail

TRAILHEAD | 39°24.302′N, 119°48.093′W Take I-580 south to the Damonte Ranch Parkway exit (Exit 59) and turn right (west). Just past the S. Virginia Street intersection, veer left and follow Arrowcreek Parkway for 3 miles to Arrowcreek Park on the left, which is after the intersection of Thomas Creek Road and just before the entrance into the gated Arrowcreek community.

For the shuttle option, follow I-580 south to the Mount Rose Highway (Exit 56) and turn right toward Incline Village and Lake Tahoe. After 2 miles, turn right onto Timberline Drive and proceed 1 mile to a small, dirt parking area on the right, immediately after the bridge over Thomas Creek (39°23.529′N, 119°50.283′W). The Forest Service Thomas Creek trailhead is 0.1 mile farther up the road and has vault toilets, picnic tables, and an interpretive sign.

TRAIL | Find the start of the trail near the park entrance by a sign reading "EQUESTRIAN TRAIL, HIKERS WELCOME" [1] and head northwest paralleling Arrowcreek Parkway through sagebrush scrub for 0.1 mile to the canyon of Thomas Creek. Drop into the canyon and go upstream (southwest) along the edge of the riparian zone, where the banks are filled with the lush foliage of alders, cottonwoods, elderberries, quaking aspens, willows, and wild roses. Away from the riparian zone, the canyon slopes are covered with desert peach, mountain mahogany, rabbitbrush, sagebrush and non-native grasses. Climb moderately along the south bank of the creek on a well-used path, ignoring some lesser paths from above. On this initial stretch of trail, the canyon is deep enough to hide the surrounding development, lending a pleasant sense of wildness to the surroundings. In contrast, where you cross an old dirt road, you probably will notice an old vehicle rusting in a tangle of shrubs near the water. Beyond this eyesore, the trail leads out of the canyon and away from the creek, crosses a gravel road, and then passes around a pair of water tanks near the 0.75-mile mark.

Now in full view of the upscale homes of the Arrowcreek subdivision and the verdant fairways of the Arrowcreek Country Club, you continue generally southwest for a while, with a fine vista of the Carson Range along the way. At a signed junction at 0.9 mile, veer ahead to the left. Beyond the golf course and on the approach to some ranchettes, the trail angles toward Thomas Creek, merges very briefly with an old rocky road, and crosses to the far bank via a thick plank bridge, 1.25 miles from the trailhead [2]. The refreshing-looking stream provides a good turnaround point if you're interested in a shorter jaunt.

The grade increases a bit, as the trail moves away from the creek and ascends across open slopes of low sagebrush for the next mile. Good views of the Carson Range, including Mount Rose and Slide Mountain, are constant companions. Without the golf course and orderly Arrowcreek neighborhood, this section of the trail emits a more natural feel to the surroundings. Eventually the trail veers back toward the aspen-choked drainage of Thomas Creek and reaches a junction with an old jeep road on the right heading toward a water tank. Continue ahead on the main trail and follow the north bank of the creek into a light forest of aspens and scattered Jeffrey pines, which provides a marked contrast to the journey through sagebrush scrub you experienced previously. Soon after the single-track trail merges with an old road, you reach the upper trailhead at Timberline Drive [3].

Without shuttle arrangements, you'll need to retrace your steps 2.6 miles back to the Arrowcreek Park trailhead [1]. The Forest Service Thomas Creek trailhead lies 0.1 mile directly north, just off the road. If you wish to use the picnic area or vault toilets, simply walk west across Timberline onto Thomas Creek Road and proceed about 100 yards to a single-track trail heading north to the trailhead parking lot.

RUSSIAN THISTLE (TUMBLEWEED) (*Salsola tragus*) Almost as iconic to the American West as the cowboy himself is the sight of a tumbleweed rolling through a deserted frontier town in a western movie. Ironically, this noxious plant is not native to North America. Transported here from the Russian steppes, the bush is now widely distributed throughout the American West. This troublesome annual weed has spiny stems when green. After the plant dies, the dried plant detaches from the root system to tumble away in the wind.

MILESTONES

1: Start at Arrowcreek Park trailhead; **2:** Cross Thomas Creek; **3:** End at Timberline Road trailhead (shuttle); **1:** End at Arrowcreek Park trailhead (out and back).

GO GREEN | Washoe County Parks and Open Space has an Adopt-A-Park program, where volunteers can donate their time for working in the parks to keep them clean, attractive, and safe. The program is open to individuals and groups. For more information, visit their website at www.washoecounty.us /parks/volunteer_opportunities.php, or contact the Parks Volunteer Coordinator at 775-785-4512, ext. 107.

OPTIONS | Similar to Whites Creek, by combining the lower trail with a section of the upper Thomas Creek Trail (see Trips 32 and 42), you could experience nearly all of the ecological zones through which Thomas Creek travels, but that would make a very lengthy trip.

TRIP
32 | Lower Galena Creek Trail

Of all the creekside trails through the open slopes below the east front of the Carson Range, perhaps none provides such a contrast in scenery as the Lower Galena Creek Trail. Beginning at Callahan Park, the trail briefly travels through a natural environment before passing through an easement through Montreux, one of Reno's most upscale developments, where seemingly nary a pine needle is out of place. Beyond the manicured grounds of Montreux, the trail once again enters a more natural, forested environment on the way to the end near the Mount Rose Highway across from an entrance into Galena Creek Regional Park.

LEVEL Hike, intermediate

LENGTH 2.7 miles, shuttle; 5.4 miles, out and back

TIME 1 to 2 hours (shuttle); 2 to 4 hours (out and back)

ELEVATION +750'–0'; +750'–750'

DIFFICULTY Moderate

USERS Hikers, mountain bikers, equestrians

DOGS On leash

SEASON Late April through October

BEST TIMES Early summer, fall

FACILITIES Picnic tables, playground, restrooms

MAP United States Geological Survey: *Washoe City*

MANAGEMENT Washoe County Regional Parks and Open Space at 775-328-3600, www.washoecounty.us/parks

HIGHLIGHTS Autumn color, forest, stream

LOWLIGHTS Close to private homes

TIP | Unlike the lower trails along Whites and Thomas creeks, Lower Galena Creek has plenty of shade from a fairly dense forest.

KID TIP | The hike along tumbling Galena Creek should be a very fun one for kids of all ages. Very small children should be closely supervised in areas where the trail runs close to the creek.

TRAILHEAD | 39°21.777′N, 119°49.086′W Take I-580 south to the Mount Rose Highway (SR 431) and proceed toward Lake Tahoe. After about 3 miles, turn

153

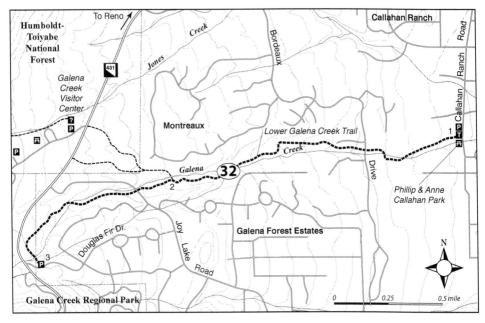

32. Lower Galena Creek Trail

left onto Callahan Ranch Road and continue 1.5 miles to Callahan Park. Park your vehicle in the gravel lot directly north of the main part of the park. The trail begins through an opening in the split-rail fence on the west edge of the parking area.

For the shuttle option, continue toward Lake Tahoe on the Mount Rose Highway another 3.2 miles past the turnoff for Callahan Ranch Road to Douglas Fir Drive (immediately south of the upper entrance to Galena Creek Park). Turn left onto Douglas Fir Drive and travel a very short distance to a gravel parking area on the left (39°21.272′N, 119°51.258′W).

TRAIL ⏐ Through a mixture of sagebrush scrub and Jeffrey pine forest, you follow a dirt path away from the trailhead [1] toward the north bank of Galena Creek. The stream is lined with typical riparian vegetation, including aspens, cottonwoods, willows, and wild roses. Steadily ascend for 0.3 mile to where the scenery takes a dramatic change, where the trail enters the very upscale Montreux development. For the next mile, you stroll alongside the verdant fairways of the championship golf course and past luxury homes. Immediately after entering the development, you cross the creek on a well-built bridge and proceed upstream along a fence for 0.1 mile to a second bridge. Pass below a couple of road bridges over Galena Creek and continue through the development, reaching a third bridge at 1.1 miles from the trailhead.

Lower Galena Creek

Beyond the third bridge, the surroundings revert to a more natural setting. Another 0.4 mile of steadily ascending trail leads to an obscure, unmarked junction [2] (39°21.604′N, 119°50.575′W) with a path on the right.
(Note: By following this trail, an alternate route leads shortly to a 2 × 4 plank
bridge across the creek, ascends steeply up the far bank, and then continues
climbing to a second junction near some Forest Service property signs. (The
trail ahead leads 0.4 mile to the Mount Rose Highway.) After turning right
at this junction, you step over a thin stream and head northwest, as the
trail merges into an old road and continues toward the Mount Rose Highway. You reach a closed steel gate across from the entrance into the Galena
Creek Visitor Center. Remaining on the main trail, you continue westbound
through the trees for another 0.2 mile to the Joy Lake Road bridge.)

Unless Galena Creek is raging, you should be able to pass below the
road bridge and then continue up the south bank. Along the way you'll see
some of the slightly less upscale homes of Galena Forest Estates perched
on the lip of the canyon. Aside from these houses, the drainage emits a very
natural ambiance. Occasional gaps in a light forest composed of Jeffrey pines
and aspen stands offer brief glimpses of Mount Rose above the treetops. At
2.3 miles from the trailhead, you cross the creek on a 2 × 4 plank bridge and
then follow the trail as it bends southwest, eventually drawing closer to the
highway. Soon the signs of civilization return in the form of a set of utility
lines and a pair of abandoned outhouses, apparently part of a former picnic

area or campground. Cross Galena Creek one last time on a flat-topped, fallen log and climb steeply up the far bank, soon reaching the ending trailhead [3] at a patch of gravel on the north shoulder of Douglas Fir Drive. Unless you're utilizing the shuttle option, retrace your steps 2.7 miles back to the trailhead [1].

> **WHITE FIR** (*Abies concolor*) More common at these elevations than red fir (*Abies magnifica*), white fir is a dominant member of the montane forest on the east side of the Carson Range. At first glance, distinguishing these two species from each other may be a bit difficult. However, closer inspection will reveal some subtle differences. The needles of white firs are yellowish-green and longer than the bluish-green needles of red firs. An easy way to tell these two trees apart is the needle test: if they are difficult to roll between your thumb and forefinger, it's a white fir, and if they roll easily, then it's a red fir.

MILESTONES

1: Start at Callahan Park trailhead; 2: Go straight at junction; 3: End at Douglas Fir Drive trailhead (shuttle); 1: End at Callahan Park trailhead (out and back).

GO GREEN | Washoe County Regional Parks and Open Space has an Adopt-A-Park program, where volunteers can donate their time for working in the parks to keep them clean, attractive, and safe. The program is open to individuals and groups. For more information, visit their website at www.washoecounty.us/parks/volunteer_opportunities.php, or contact the Parks Volunteer Coordinator at 775-785-4512, ext. 107.

OPTIONS | Within close proximity of Galena Creek Regional Park, you could easily arrange for a picnic lunch following the hike.

33 | Hidden Valley Regional Park

Hidden Valley Regional Park offers a trio of very easy, essentially flat, loop trails of varying length, well suited to the casual hiker, jogger, or dog walker. The shortest of the three at 1.0 mile is the Inner Loop Trail, situated in the middle of the park. The longest trail is the aptly named Perimeter Loop Trail, which makes a 2.4-mile circuit around nearly the entire length of the flat terrain of the park. The third trail, the Mia Vista Trail/South Park Loop follows a boot-shaped course for 1.3 miles across the gentle terrain at the south end of the park.

Intermediate hikers may find the Highland Loop Trail to be the best path the park has to offer. The 2.3-mile trail loops across the hilly terrain above the flat area of the park and is more defined than myriad routes crisscrossing the upper hills. Fine views across the Truckee Meadows and over to the Carson Range are frequent along the circuit.

Recreationists looking for a much more rugged adventure than the previously described trails within Hidden Valley Regional Park may enjoy the challenge of the unofficial loop of the Virginia Range Traverse, an oftentimes-strenuous endeavor requiring excellent route-finding abilities. Traveling through higher elevations above the park, the views are even more impressive than those on the Highland Loop.

33A ▪ Hidden Valley Loop Trails

LEVEL	Stroll, novice
LENGTH	Varies, 1.0 to 2.4 miles
TIME	½ to 1 hour
ELEVATION	Negligible
DIFFICULTY	Easy
USERS	Hikers
DOGS	On leash
SEASON	All year (occasional snow on trails during winter)
BEST TIMES	Spring, fall
FACILITIES	Dog Park, equestrian facilities, picnic area, sports fields, restrooms

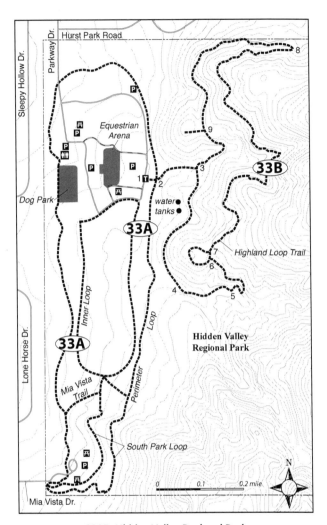

33AB. Hidden Valley Regional Park

MAP	Washoe County Parks: *Hidden Valley Regional Park Trails Map* (web-map at www.washoecounty.us/parks)
MANAGEMENT	Washoe County Regional Parks and Open Space at 775-328-3600, www.washoecounty.us/parks
HIGHLIGHTS	Child-friendly, flat trails
LOWLIGHTS	Hot in summer

TIP | A fair percentage of dog walkers seem to ignore the leash requirements, so be prepared if you bring Fido along.

KID TIP | These essentially level hikes are good ways to introduce little ones to the activity of hiking.

TRAILHEADS | (Inner Loop) 39°29.205′N, 119°42.663′W From McCarran Boulevard, turn east onto Pembroke Lane and proceed 1.8 miles to a right-hand turn onto Parkway Drive. Follow Parkway another 0.6 mile to the entrance into Hidden Valley Regional Park and continue ahead to a left-hand turn toward the Equestrian Arena. Follow the road around to the parking area on the right. The trail begins on the opposite side of the road.

(Perimeter Loop) From McCarran Boulevard, turn east onto Pembroke Lane and proceed 1.8 miles to a right-hand turn onto Parkway Drive. Follow Parkway another 0.6 mile to the entrance into Hidden Valley Regional Park and continue ahead toward the parking area near the restroom building.

(Mia Vista Trail/South Park Loop) From McCarran Boulevard, turn east onto Mira Loma Drive and proceed 1.8 miles to the intersection of West Hidden Valley Drive. Turn right, head south for 1.1 miles to Mia Vista Drive, and then turn left onto Mia Vista Drive. Follow Mia Vista to the south entrance of the park and continue to the parking area.

TRAILS | As the three trails in the lower park are straightforward, you should be able to navigate them without the aid of a detailed description.

33B ▪ Highland Loop Trail

LEVEL	Hike, intermediate
LENGTH	2.3 miles, loop
TIME	1 to 2 hours
ELEVATION	+325′–325′
DIFFICULTY	Moderate
USERS	Hikers, trail runners, mountain bikers, equestrians
DOGS	On leash
SEASON	March through November
BEST TIME	April
FACILITIES	Dog park, equestrian facilities, picnic area, sports fields, restrooms
MAP	Washoe County Parks: *Hidden Valley Regional Park Trails Map* (web-map at www.washoecounty.us/parks)
MANAGEMENT	Washoe County Regional Parks and Open Space at 775-828-6612, www.washoecounty.us/parks
HIGHLIGHTS	Views
LOWLIGHTS	Myriad unmarked roads and paths crisscross the trail. The trail is hot and exposed in the summer.

TIP | The upper slopes of Hidden Valley Regional Park are crisscrossed by numerous social trails. When in doubt about the correct route of the Highland Trail, look for periodically placed 4 × 4 posts, which should help to keep you on the right path.

Twilight brings out a deer at Hidden Valley Regional Park.

KID TIP | With so many directions kids could wander, adults should make sure young children are always in sight.

TRAILHEAD | 39°29.205'N, 119°42.663'W From McCarran Boulevard, turn east onto Pembroke Lane and proceed 1.8 miles to a right-hand turn onto Parkway Drive. Follow Parkway another 0.6 mile to the entrance into Hidden Valley Regional Park and continue ahead to a left-hand turn toward the Equestrian Arena. Follow the road around to the parking area on the right. The trail begins on the opposite side of the road.

TRAIL | From the equestrian parking lot above the arena, head east across the access road and onto a single-track trail [1] that immediately climbs up and over the old roadbed that is the current route of the Perimeter Loop Trail [2]. Continue on the path ahead angling slightly left and uphill toward a gate in a wire fence. Pass through the gate, making sure to close it behind you, and make a short, moderate climb through sagebrush scrub to the loop junction [3].

Turn right at the junction to begin a counterclockwise circuit on the Highland Loop Trail. Soon pass above a pair of water tanks surrounded by a fence topped with razor wire and then follow a general traverse toward the south. Above the second tank you'll encounter the first of many social trails crisscrossing the park and the surrounding BLM lands. When in doubt about which trail to take, look for periodically placed 4 × 4 posts delineating the correct path of the maintained Highland Loop. Follow a wire fence briefly on the way to an unmarked Y-junction, where the right-hand path heads south and descends into the canyon of a seasonal stream. Continue on the left-hand trail, soon dropping into the dry wash to an unsigned junction [4] with an old road that you follow on the far side up the canyon a short way to an unsigned junction [5].

At the junction, you leave the road, cross back over the wash, and start climbing steeply up the hillside, which will constitute most of the trip's 350-foot elevation gain. Wind up the hillside toward the top of a rise and meet a junction [6] with a trail on the left, which travels shortly to a viewpoint and then loops back to the main trail [7]. This brief diversion is well worth the little time involved for the fine vista of the Truckee Meadows, bordered by the tall peaks of the Carson Range.

Back on the main trail, you continue northbound on a general traverse, passing well above the water tanks and crossing more social trails heading upslope. The trail bends into and out of a small side canyon, where scattered pinyon pines join the typical sagebrush scrub vegetation.

Out of the small canyon, you continue toward the north boundary of the park, where the trail bends east into a more pronounced canyon and pinyon pines once again dot the slopes above the drainage. Continue up the canyon above a recent subdivision to a 4 × 4 post [8], which marks a rather inauspicious point where the trail angles sharply back to the west. By all appearances on the ground, the path continues straight ahead but this is the route of the Virginia Range Traverse heading up the canyon; the Highland Loop Trail doubles back and eventually arcs out of the canyon before heading south. Reach another 4 × 4 post, just prior to where a short side path [9] heads west to the top of a knoll with a lone pinyon pine and another fine view of the valley and the mountains.

Away from the side path junction, continue ahead and drop into and across a wash. Turn down the wash and proceed toward the loop junction [3]. From there, retrace your steps to the trailhead and the parking area [1].

SINGLE-LEAF PINYON PINE (*Pinus monophylla*) The original state tree of Nevada, the single-leaf pinyon pine is one of the most widely distributed pines in the state, along with Utah juniper. This drought-tolerant tree spans a wide range of elevations across the Great Basin. Many animals depend on this conifer for a food source, as did the Native Americans who used pine nuts as a staple of their diet. During the mining boom, Euro-Americans used the wood as the main source of charcoal for smelting silver ore. Today, pine nuts have become a gourmet food item.

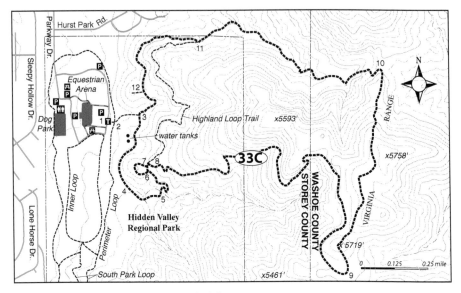

33C. Virginia Range Traverse

MILESTONES
1: Start at trailhead; 2: Go straight at Perimeter Loop junction; 3: Turn right at Highland Loop junction; 4: Merge with old road; 5: Turn left at single-track trail junction; 6: South junction with viewpoint loop; 7: North junction with viewpoint loop; 8: Turn left at 4 × 4 post; 9: Go straight at viewpoint junction; 3: Turn right at Highland Loop junction; 2: Straight at Perimeter Loop junction; 1: Return to trailhead.

33C · Virginia Range Traverse

LEVEL	Hike, advanced
LENGTH	5.2 miles, loop
TIME	2 to 4 hours
ELEVATION	+1,225′–1,225′
DIFFICULTY	Strenuous
USERS	Hikers, trail runners, mountain bikers, equestrians
DOGS	On leash (in park)
SEASON	March through November
BEST TIME	April
FACILITIES	Dog park, equestrian facilities, picnic area, sports fields, restrooms
MAP	Washoe County Parks: *Hidden Valley Regional Park Trails Map* (web-map at www.washoecounty.us/parks)

MANAGEMENT Washoe County Regional Parks and Open Space at
775-328-3600, www.washoecounty.us/parks

HIGHLIGHTS Views

LOWLIGHTS Myriad unmarked roads and paths crisscross the trail. The
trail is hot and exposed in the summer. There are sections of
steep, rough, and poor trail.

TIP | Bring plenty of water on this hike, as the route is steep and exposed. So
many paths, dirt-bike trails, and jeep roads crisscross this area that following the description may be challenging. However, the terrain is open and
straightforward for anyone with fair navigational skills. Don't fret if following alternate directions becomes necessary.

KID TIP | The strenuous and difficult nature of the trail makes this trip is ill
suited to children.

TRAILHEAD | 39°29.205′N, 119°42.663′W From McCarran Boulevard, turn
east onto Pembroke Lane and proceed 1.8 miles to a right-hand turn onto
Parkway Drive. Follow Parkway another 0.6 mile to the entrance into Hid-
den Valley Regional Park and continue ahead to a left-hand turn toward the
Horsemen's Arena. Follow the road around to the parking area on the right.
The trail begins on the opposite side of the road.

TRAIL | From the equestrian parking lot above the arena, head east across
the access road and onto a single-track trail [1] that immediately climbs up
and over the old roadbed that is the current route of the Perimeter Loop
Trail [2]. Continue on the path ahead angling slightly left and uphill toward
a gate in a wire fence. Pass through the gate, making sure to close it behind
you, and make a short moderate climb through sagebrush scrub to the loop
junction [3].

Turn right at the junction to begin a counterclockwise circuit on the
Highland Loop Trail. Soon pass above a pair of water tanks surrounded by a
fence topped with razor wire and then follow a general traverse toward the
south. Above the second tank you'll encounter the first of many social trails
crisscrossing the park and the surrounding BLM lands. When in doubt about
which trail to take, look for periodically placed 4 × 4 posts delineating the
correct path of the maintained Highland Loop. Follow a wire fence briefly
on the way to an unmarked Y-junction, where the right-hand path heads
south and descends into the canyon of a seasonal stream. Continue on the
left-hand trail, soon dropping into the dry wash to an unsigned junction [4]
with an old road that you follow on the far side up the canyon a short way to
another unsigned junction [5].

At this junction, you leave the road, cross back over the wash, and start
climbing steeply up the hillside. Wind up the hillside toward the top of a rise
and meet the south junction [6] with a trail on the left headed to a viewpoint

on the edge of a bluff. This brief diversion is well worth the little time involved for the fine vista of the Truckee Meadows, bordered by the tall peaks of the Carson Range. From the viewpoint, the trail loops around to rejoin the Highland Trail at the north junction [7].

Rather than continue on the Highland Loop, head straight uphill to the right and proceed shortly to an unmarked Y-junction [8]. Take the right-hand branch and sweep around a hill via a couple of switchbacks. As you continue stiffly uphill, views improve out to the Carson Range and pinyon pines start to appear in some of the drainages. Longer-legged switchbacks lead above a draw to where the grade eases a bit and the trail makes an ascending traverse through widely scattered pinyon pines. After winding around a bit, another long ascending traverse heads south toward the crest of the range. Reach a saddle [9] at the top where jeep roads come up from the east.

Heading north along the crest, you follow a well-traveled road and trails along the undulating ridge over Point 5758 and down to another saddle [10] at the head of a canyon to the west, not quite a mile from the previous saddle.

Drop steeply into the canyon and follow a single-track trail down through the gorge of a usually dry seasonal stream. Approaching the subdivision at the base of the canyon, follow single-track to the left uphill for a short distance to the crest of a hill. Watch for a 4 × 4 post [11] designating the route of the Highland Loop at a switchback.

From the post, follow the lower trail, which eventually arcs out of the canyon and then heads south. Reach another 4 × 4 post, just prior to where a short side path [12] heads west to the top of a knoll with a lone pinyon pine and another fine view of the valley and the mountains.

Away from the side path junction, continue ahead and drop into and across a wash. Turn down the wash and proceed toward the Highland Loop junction [3]. From there, retrace your steps to the trailhead and the parking area [1].

MUSTANGS (WILD HORSES) In the hills of the Virginia Range are herds of free-roaming horses, or mustangs. In 1971 Congress passed legislation giving this species a level of protection as important symbols of the American West. The protection and management of these animals falls under the purview primarily of the Bureau of Land Management (BLM). Controversy has swirled around the management of the mustangs for decades. In areas where their predators have been severely reduced or eliminated altogether, overpopulation occurs. So far, management practices appear to have been somewhat inadequate to deal with the situation to the satisfaction of all parties involved.

MILESTONES

1: Start at trailhead; **2:** Go straight at Perimeter Loop junction; **3:** Turn right at Highland Loop junction; **4:** Merge with old road; **5:** Turn left at single-track trail junction; **6:** South Junction with viewpoint loop; **7:** Turn right at North Junction with viewpoint loop; **8:** Turn right at Y-junction; **9:** Turn left at first saddle; **10:** Turn left at second saddle; **11:** Turn right at 4 × 4 post; **12:** Go straight at viewpoint junction; **3:** Turn right at Highland Loop junction; **2:** Go straight at Perimeter Loop junction; **1:** Return to trailhead.

GO GREEN | Washoe County Regional Parks and Open Space has an Adopt-A-Park program, where volunteers can donate their time for working in the parks to keep them clean, attractive, and safe. The program is open to individuals and groups. For more information, visit their website at www.washoecounty.us/parks/volunteer_opportunities.php, or contact the Parks Volunteer Coordinator at 775-785-4512, ext. 107.

OPTIONS | With so many paths and roads littering the upper slopes of the Virginia Range, numerous options present themselves for wandering these hills. You could probably spend a couple of weeks here and still not have walked them all.

Additional Trips

VALLEY WOOD TRAILS | 39°31.983′N, 119°53.495′W Paved paths that follow a pair of Chalk Creek tributaries through narrow strips of wetlands sandwiched between housing developments in northwest Reno make up the Valley Wood Trails. Adding a mile-plus-long stroll along the sidewalks of Robb Drive, Las Brisas Avenue, and Avenida De Landa, creates a 3.75-mile loop trip with periodic views of Peavine Peak, a portion of the Truckee Meadows, and the north end of the Carson Range.

CHAPTER FIVE

THE MOUNTAINS

One can't ignore the topography surrounding Reno and the Truckee Meadows, as mountains rise up from the plain on nearly every side. The two most prominent ranges include the brown hills of the Virginia Range to the east, and the higher, greenish-tinged Carson Range, a spur of the mighty Sierra Nevada, to the west. This chapter also includes the most dominant mountain in the immediate vicinity, Peavine Peak, just northwest of downtown Reno. Much of the land within the Carson Range belongs to the public, administered by the Carson Ranger District of the Humboldt-Toiyabe National Forest. Consequently, a bounty of hiking trails is available for residents and visitors to explore. Access to the Virginia Range is much more limited, due to a patchwork of private and public land. Primarily the Bureau of Land Management administers the public land in the Virginia Range, where developed trails are almost nonexistent and OHVs dominate the terrain.

34 | Poeville and Peavine Peak

Hikers not up to the challenge of scaling Peavine Peak can choose to go about half way to Poeville, the site of John Poe's former mining town that, although hard to believe these days, once housed hundreds of residents. Along the way, at 1.4 miles, is a murky green settling pond used during the mining heyday, now a favored haunt of target shooters, evidenced by thousands of spent shells littering the shoreline. From there, the route winds up to the yellow tailing piles of the old Golden Fleece Mine and the Poeville townsite a short way farther.

Many hikers may balk at the prospect of walking along a long, steep, and rough jeep road frequented by OHVs, and passing through occasional litter-strewn areas—as well they should. However, the mere physical challenge of hiking (or running or biking) to the top of 8,266-foot-high Peavine Peak will be enough attraction for the physically fit, and the lofty view from the summit is certainly an enticement as well (although driving to the top with any modern sedan is possible via the Peavine Peak Road). While most human-powered recreation on Peavine is confined to vehicle-banned areas on the southeast flank, this route begins near the edge of the North Valleys area and follows an eastside canyon to the old townsite of Poeville as described in trip 34A. Beyond Poeville, the route becomes a lot steeper, gaining the southeast ridge and then following the ridge to the top. The twin-topped summit is covered with a preponderance of communication towers and associated buildings. However, the 360-degree view should be a fine reward for the extreme effort involved in getting there.

34A ▪ Poeville

LEVEL	Walk, intermediate
LENGTH	5.6 miles, out and back
TIME	2 to 3 hours
ELEVATION	+1,050′–0′
DIFFICULTY	Moderate
USERS	Hikers, trail runners, mountain bikers, equestrians
DOGS	OK
SEASON	Late March to Late November

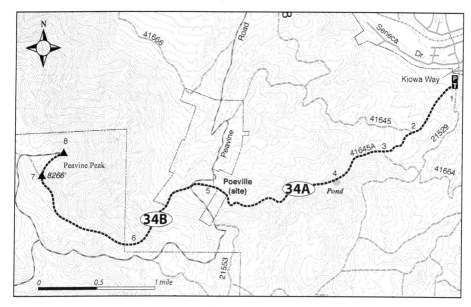

34. Poeville and Peavine Peak

BEST TIME	April
FACILITIES	None
MAP	United States Geological Survey: *Verdi*
MANAGEMENT	USFS Humboldt-Toiyabe National Forest, Carson Ranger District at 775-882-2766, www.fs.usda.gov/htnf
HIGHLIGHTS	History, views
LOWLIGHTS	Open to motorized vehicles, rough and rocky trail

TIP | Visit the area on a weekday or during the off-season to minimize encounters with OHVs.

KID TIP | The short and relatively easy trip to Poeville may be appealing to the younger crowd, but adults must supervise small children at all times for encounters with OHVs, as well as around the settling pond.

TRAILHEAD | 39°35.868′N, 119°51.989′W From Reno, head northbound on US 395 to Exit 74 for Lemmon Drive, turn left and head southwest a half mile to N. Virginia Street. Turn right and follow N. Virginia Street northwest for a half mile to Seneca Drive and turn left. Follow Seneca Drive for a half mile and turn left onto Kiowa Way. Proceed shortly to the end of the pavement and a graveled parking area just beyond.

TRAIL | From the parking area [1], follow FS Road 41645 generally southwest through typical sagebrush-scrub vegetation on a moderate ascent toward the mouth of a canyon that carries a seasonal stream. After about a half mile is a Y-intersection [2], where FS Road 41645 angles away to the right, but you proceed ahead, now on FS Road 41645A. Continue a quarter mile farther to another junction [3] near where the road approaches the streambed. Here FS Road 41664 heads across the streambed and continues generally southeast. Continue up the narrowing and deepening canyon, the lusher streamside foliage of willows and cottonwoods testifying to the presence of life-giving moisture in the soils. After 1.4 miles, the steady climb leads to the deep hole of a settling pond [4] once used by the miners associated with the mines around Poeville farther upstream. The green, slimy water in the pond is further marred by the presence of numerous spent shells littering the ground nearby, as the area is a favorite site for target practice. The good news is that only a relatively small number of vehicles travel beyond the settling pond.

You continue climbing up the cleft of the canyon, winding around past a side canyon on the left before wrapping around to the yellowish tailing piles of the Golden Fleece Mine and the former site of the town of Poeville [5]. Following your visit to Poeville, retrace your steps to the trailhead [1].

POEVILLE This old mining town once boasted three hotels, a few bars, and a post office, reaching its population zenith of several hundred people in the mid-1870s. The mine, although founded on the prospect of reaping gold and silver, produced mostly copper and was quickly played out, ceasing operations by 1880, when only fifteen people remained in town. Today there is very little evidence that the town ever existed and even envisioning where one would have been located in this steep topography is a bit difficult. The town site, 2.8 miles from the parking area, is a good turnaround point for a moderate, half-day hike.

MILESTONES

1: Start at parking area; **2:** Junction with FS Road 41645; **3:** Junction with FS Road 41664; **4:** Settling pond; **5:** Poeville; **1:** Return to parking area.

34B ▪ Peavine Peak

LEVEL	Hike, advanced
LENGTH	10.4 miles, out and back
TIME	Full day
ELEVATION	+2,660′–70′
DIFFICULTY	Very strenuous
USERS	Hikers, trail runners, mountain bikers, equestrians
DOGS	OK
SEASON	Late May to mid-October
BEST TIME	June
FACILITIES	None
MAP	United States Geological Survey: *Verdi*

Wildflowers near the historic townsite of Poeville

MANAGEMENT USFS Humboldt-Toiyabe National Forest, Carson Ranger District at 775-882-2766, www.fs.usda.gov/htnf

HIGHLIGHTS History, views

LOWLIGHTS Open to motorized vehicles, rough and rocky trail

TIP Visit the area on a weekday or during the off-season to minimize encounters with OHVs.

KID TIP The long, steep climb to the summit of Peavine on sometimes-rough trail is ill suited for young children. The shorter and easier trip to Poeville (see Trip 34A) should be more appealing for the younger crowd.

TRAILHEAD 39°35.868′N, 119°51.989′W From Reno, head northbound on US 395 to Exit 74 for Lemmon Drive, turn left and head southwest a half mile to N. Virginia Street. Turn right and follow N. Virginia Street northwest for a half mile to Seneca Drive and turn left. Follow Seneca Drive for a half mile and turn left onto Kiowa Way. Proceed shortly to the end of the pavement and a graveled parking area just beyond.

TRAIL | Follow the description above past the yellowish tailing piles of the Golden Fleece Mine and continue to the former site of the town of Poeville [5].

From Poeville, your route soon crosses the main road for access to the communication equipment on top of Peavine Peak, ascends and then drops around a hillside to a steep jeep road that follows a set of power lines up to the top of a ridge. Along the way, scattered pinyon pines herald your arrival into the higher elevations, where melting winter snows provide just enough moisture for the single-needled pines to eke out an existence. Gain the crest of the ridge [6] near an array of communication equipment, 4 miles from the parking area.

Turning northwest, you climb steeply along the ridge, with short intermittent stretches where the grade briefly eases. Sweeping views along the way hint at the expansive vista awaiting at the top. A rugged mile of stiff ascent on a sometimes-rocky trail along old jeep roads leads to the south summit [7], which is covered with communication towers and associated small structures. You'll have to move about the fringe of the broad top in order to fully enjoy the 360-degree view. On exceptionally clear days, Lassen Peak is visible to the northwest; the serrated summits of Sierra Buttes are typically the farthest landmark in that direction during normal atmospheric conditions. Immediately west is Dog Valley and the Junction House Range. Farther west is the spine of the northern Sierra. Gazing southwest, you get an uncommon, linear view of the eastern front of the Carson Range. As expected, the Truckee Meadows dominates the immediate view to the south, bordered on the east by the peaks of the Virginia Range.

For those with a bit of extra energy, gaining the north summit [8] is a straightforward, 0.3-mile walk along the well-graded service road, offering a less cluttered view to the northeast. After fully admiring the views, retrace your steps to the trailhead.

AMERICAN VETCH (*Vicia americana*) Peavine Peak was so named for the wild peas growing on the mountain near springs. Although present in most of North America, early settlers must have been somewhat surprised by their presence here. The plant produces flowers in lavender and fuchsia shades and fruits of hairless pods, usually containing a pair of light brown peas. Prior to the Comstock Lode, the slopes of Peavine Peak were once covered with a light forest.

MILESTONES

1: Start at parking area; **2:** Junction with FS Road 41645; **3:** Junction with FS Road 41664; **4:** Settling pond; **5:** Poeville; **6:** Southeast ridge; **7:** South summit; **8:** North summit; **1:** Return to parking area.

GO GREEN ǀ Good Samaritans can take along a garbage bag and pick up some of the trash along the way. The Poedunks is a local mountain bike club dedicated to planning, designing, building, and maintaining single-track trails on and around Peavine Peak. Their projects have included Keystone Canyon and the Halo Trail. One of their ultimate goals is to build single-track to the top of Peavine. For more information, or to donate funds, consult their website at www.poedunk.org.

OPTIONS ǀ There's not much in the immediate area to recommend. However, you could plan a pre- or post-trip visit to the Nevada Historical Society Museum at the north end of the UNR campus. Spanning a period from prehistoric times to the present, the museum showcases the state's mining history. For more information, visit the website at www.museums.nevadaculture.org.

TRIP

35 | Hunter Creek Trail

The journey along the Hunter Creek Trail is a fascinating romp through the transition between drought-tolerant, sagebrush-scrub-covered slopes of the lower canyon, pinyon and juniper woodland in the middle, and damp and lush montane forest in the upper canyon. To see such a dramatic shift in plant communities in the course of just a few miles is quite remarkable. A significant waterfall at the end of maintained trail is the icing on the cake. For being located so close to town, the away-from-it-all feeling one has on the trail after the first half mile or so is also noteworthy.

LEVEL Hike, intermediate

LENGTH 7.0 miles, out and back

TIME Half day

ELEVATION +1,450′−150′

DIFFICULTY Moderate

USERS Hikers, trail runners, equestrians

DOGS On leash (first mile)

SEASON Mid-April to late October

BEST TIME May

FACILITIES Interpretive signs, picnic tables, vault toilets

MAP United States Forest Service: *Mount Rose Wilderness*;
United States Geological Survey: *Mount Rose*

MANAGEMENT USFS Humboldt-Toiyabe National Forest, Carson Ranger District at 775-882-2766, www.fs.usda.gov/htnf;
Trailhead: Washoe County Regional Parks and Open Space at 775-328-3600, www.washoecounty.us/parks

HIGHLIGHTS Canyon, forest, stream, waterfall

LOWLIGHTS Sections of poor trail

TIP | A use trail once led beyond the waterfall on Hunter Creek over a steep hill to a large meadow, but a forest fire damaged much of that route. With some effort, you should be able to find your way farther up canyon to the meadow, but most hikers will be satisfied with the waterfall as their ultimate destination. The idea of the Hunter Creek Trail leading to Hunter Lake seems to be a popular local myth. While such a cross-country route is

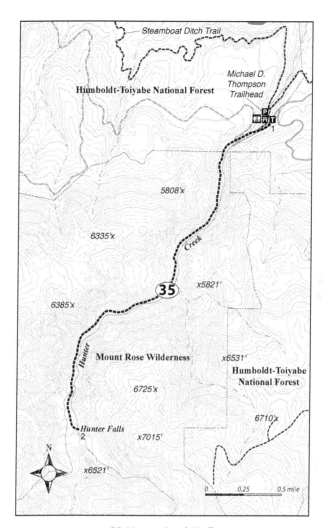

35. Hunter Creek Trail

possible, the rugged off-trail journey through upper Hunter Creek canyon, followed by the steep climb out of the canyon to the Hunter Lake Road, requires difficult route finding, extreme stamina, and determination way beyond the desires of the average hiker.

KID TIP | The steep topography combined with sections of poor trail makes this trip ill suited for families with small children. Bigger kids should certainly find the creek and especially the waterfall to be quite interesting.

TRAILHEAD | 39°29.581′N, 119°53.678′W From the Caughlin Parkway/Plumb Lane/McCarran Boulevard intersection in west Reno, head west on Caughlin

Hunter Creek

Parkway for 1.2 miles and then turn left onto Plateau Road. After 0.6 mile, make another left onto Woodchuck and follow this road 0.8 mile to the signed Michael D. Thompson trailhead.

TRAIL | Follow an old jeep road away from the trailhead [1] for 0.2 mile to a crossing of Hunter Creek—an easy affair when the stream is shallow. During periods of higher water, look for a narrow plank bridge just above the crossing. Continue upstream noting the difference between the lush riparian vegetation along the creek and the sagebrush scrub carpeting the usually dry hillsides. Early-season visitors may see a smattering of colorful wildflowers, especially following particularly wet winters or springs. Proceed to the vicinity of a gauging station, where the road ends and single-track trail enters the signed Mount Rose Wilderness.

The trail follows a rising, but slightly undulating, course well above the west bank of the creek, slicing across the steep canyon wall. Rocky cliffs and occasional washouts in this section should create enough difficulty to dissuade anyone from bringing very young children on this hike. As you continue, a smattering of Jeffrey pines and mountain mahoganies provide a subtle clue to the more dense forest waiting farther up the canyon. The thick riparian foliage along the creek includes such species as cottonwood, elderberry, quaking aspen, and willow.

Around the 2-mile mark, the tree cover increases dramatically, with ponderosa pines, white firs, and incense cedar creating a dense canopy that shades a lush forest floor carpeted with ferns and other shade-loving plants. You cross three tiny rivulets on your way through this verdant grotto, which seems a bit out of place so far east of the Sierra crest. Along with the main branch of Hunter Creek, these rivulets keep the area well watered and the associated plants flourishing. This enchanted woodland is interrupted briefly at a grassy clearing, beyond which the trail reenters forest and then drops down to a crossing of Hunter Creek on a large fallen log. On the far side of the creek is a small flat and the scenic waterfall nearby [2], a silvery ribbon of water plunging across a dark rock face. The waterfall is quite dramatic in spring, when snowmelt from farther up the canyon swells the creek.

After thoroughly enjoying the beauty of the waterfall, retrace your steps back 3.5 miles back to the Michael D. Thompson trailhead [1].

MILESTONES
1: Start at Michael D. Thompson trailhead; 2: Hunter Falls;
1: Return to trailhead.

INCENSE CEDAR (*Calocedrus decurrens*) While not entirely rare, incense cedars are not commonly seen to a great extent on the eastern slopes of the Carson Range. Where they do appear is usually in the drainages of perennial streams, taking root in soils damp enough to provide plenty of extra moisture. While hiking the Hunter Creek Trail, watch for these trees, with flat, lacey foliage, in the forest beyond the 2-mile mark. To the untrained eye, these red-barked trees are often mistaken for redwoods, conifers naturally nonexistent on this side of the Sierra.

GO GREEN | Friends of Nevada Wilderness have been quite active within the Mount Rose Wilderness with such projects as eradicating non-native weeds and reseeding the area burned by the 2014 Hunter Falls Fire. Check out their website at www.nevadawilderness.org.

OPTIONS | Before or after you hike, Walden's Coffeehouse in Mayberry Landing (3940 Mayberry Drive) is the place to grab a cup of specialty coffee or tea, or to enjoy breakfast (served all day) or lunch. On Friday nights, Walden's stays open past the typical 5:00 PM close (3:00 PM on Sundays) for live music.

TRIP

36 | Galena Creek Regional Park

The Galena Creek Nature Trail inside the regional park offers a journey of discovery for young and old alike. After crossing a bridge over the creek, a downloadable brochure keyed to eighteen numbered posts guides you along a loop circuit through a section of forest representative of the flora on the east front of the Carson Range. With a 1-mile or three-quarter-mile option, you can tailor the trip to fit the needs of your party. The nearby creek provides an additional opportunity to explore a typical riparian environment.

The Bitterbrush Trail is used mainly as a connector between the south and north parts of the park, suitable for an easy stroll or for just walking the dog. Connections to other trails in the area are possible.

36A ▪ Nature Trail

LEVEL	Walk, novice
LENGTH	0.75 mile or 1 mile, loop
TIME	½ hour
ELEVATION	+150′–150′
DIFFICULTY	Easy
USERS	Hikers
DOGS	On leash
SEASON	May to December
BEST TIME	May to June
FACILITIES	Picnic tables, restrooms
MAP	Humboldt-Toiyabe National Forest: *Jones/Whites/Thomas Creeks Trail System* (web-map at www.fs.usda.gov/Internet/FSE_DOCUMENTS/stelprdb5275045.pdf)
MANAGEMENT	Washoe County Regional Parks and Open Space at 775-328-3600, www.washoecounty.us/parks
HIGHLIGHTS	Forest, interpretive brochure, stream
LOWLIGHTS	None

TIP ⏐ The Nature Trail provides a wonderful experience just about anytime of year, but spring is when Galena Creek puts on a show.

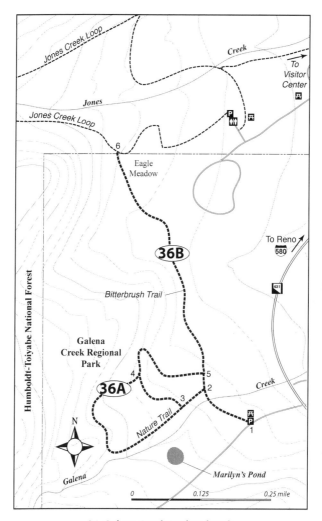

36. Galena Creek Regional Park

KID TIP | With brochure in hand, adults can impart interesting facts to inquisitive children, primarily about the natural history with a couple of human history tidbits as well. The relatively short distance should keep young ones engaged for the entire circuit, but the 0.75-mile option provides a quick escape for the ones who may start to become restless. A promise of an after-hike picnic in the nearby picnic area may be an effective carrot. When not roaring with snowmelt, Galena Creek provides a great place for children to experience a stream environment with appropriate supervision. Nearby Marilyn's Pond offers the opportunity for fishing.

TRAILHEAD | 39°21.234'N, 119°51.449'W From Reno, drive southbound on I-580 to the Mount Rose Highway Exit 56 and then head southwest on State Route 431 toward Incline Village and Lake Tahoe. After 6.3 miles, turn right into the south entrance of Galena Creek Regional Park, drive a short distance up the access road and park your vehicle in the lot near Galena Creek.

TRAIL | From the parking lot [1], follow a short section of trail over to a stout bridge across tumbling Galena Creek and then continue on the wide, gravel surface of an old, boulder-lined road, now known as the Bitterbrush Trail, soon coming to the signed junction [2] with the Nature Trail on the left.

Turn left and follow a slightly winding path upstream along the north bank of Galena Creek, soon passing the indistinct junction with the shortcut for the 0.75-mile option on the right. Continue ahead and at about one-third mile into the hike, the trail veers away from the creek and ascends north deeper into the forest to the top of a rise, which is the high point of the loop. A short descent leads to an unmarked junction with a lightly used path on the left, which is an unmaintained, semi-cross-country route up Black's Canyon. Remaining on the Nature Trail, you continue ahead, as the path continues to descend and arcs around to the northeast. In the midst of the descent, you reach a large, granodiorite boulder split into two pieces near post 14. Nearby is the somewhat indistinct junction [3] where the two loops of the Nature Trail diverge.

SHORT LOOP | To continue with the brochure and the remaining four posts, you must turn right at the split boulder, passing between the two pieces of rock and heading southeast from the junction on a more defined trail. The short, winding path eventually reconnects with the previously hiked section of the Nature Trail at a junction [4] just above post 5. From there, turn left to retrace your steps to the south junction [2] with the Bitterbrush Trail, where a right turn leads across the bridge over Galena Creek and back to the parking lot [1].

LONG LOOP | To follow the long loop option, continue ahead from the split boulder junction near post 14 and resume the descent. Reach a switchback and then proceed to the unmarked north junction [5] with the Bitterbrush Trail. Turn right to follow the wide, gravel track of an old road to the south junction [2] and then retrace your steps over the bridge and back to the parking lot [1].

MILESTONES

SHORT LOOP | 1: Start at Galena Creek trailhead; 2: Turn left at south Nature Trail junction; 3: Turn right at split boulder junction; 4: Turn left at junction at loop junction; 2: Turn right at south junction; 1: Return to trailhead.

LONG LOOP | **1:** Start at Galena Creek trailhead; **2:** Turn left at south Nature Trail junction; **3:** Go straight at junction; **4:** Go straight at split boulder junction; **5:** Turn right at north Nature Trail junction; **2:** Go straight at south junction; **1:** Return to trailhead.

36B ▪ Bitterbrush Trail

TYPE	Walk, novice
LENGTH	0.4 mile, point to point
TIME	15 minutes
ELEVATION	Negligible
DIFFICULTY	Easy
USERS	Hikers
DOGS	On leash
SEASON	Mid-April to November
BEST TIME	May
FACILITIES	Picnic tables, restrooms
MAP	Humboldt-Toiyabe National Forest: *Jones/Whites/Thomas Creeks Trail System* (web-map at www.fs.usda.gov/Internet /FSE_DOCUMENTS/stelprdb5275045.pdf)
MANAGEMENT	Washoe County Regional Parks and Open Space at 775-328-3600, www.washoecounty.us/parks
HIGHLIGHTS	Forest
LOWLIGHTS	No prominent destination

TIP | The Bitterbrush Trail is primarily used as a connector between the north and south parts of Galena Creek Park, so combining this path with some of the other trails in the area will make for a more interesting hike.

KID TIP | Other than the surrounding forest, there's not much to capture the attention of children. However, the short and easy trail won't tax their stamina.

TRAILHEAD | 39°21.234′N, 119°51.449′W From Reno, drive southbound on I-580 to the Mount Rose Highway Exit 56 and then head southwest on State Route 431 toward Incline Village and Lake Tahoe. After 6.3 miles, turn right into the south entrance of Galena Creek Regional Park, drive a short distance up the access road and park your vehicle in the lot near Galena Creek.

TRAIL | From the parking lot [1], follow a short section of trail over to a bridge over tumbling Galena Creek and then continue on the wide, gravel surface of an old, boulder-lined road, soon coming to the first, signed south junction [2] and then the second, unsigned north junction [5] of the Galena Creek Nature Trail. Continue ahead through scattered, primarily Jeffrey pine forest with an understory of manzanita and the namesake bitterbrush. Pass by a grass-covered, fenced area known as Eagle Meadow, which the park uses for occasional presentations. At the far end of the meadow is a junction [6], where the trail ahead goes 0.2 mile to a junction with the Jones Creek Loop, and a right turn leads shortly to the Galena Visitor Center access road and the Jones Creek and Whites Creek Loop trailhead.

> **BITTERBRUSH** (*Purshia tridentata*) A member of the rose family, bitter-brush is a dominant shrub within the sagebrush-scrub community. At-taining heights of 1 to 3 feet, foliage is comprised of small, three-lobed, wedge-shaped, green leaves. Numerous small, pale-yellow flowers ap-pear in spring and early summer. Within the Carson Range, the leaves of bitterbrush are major forage for mule deer, while ants, birds, and rodents eat the seeds.

MILESTONES

1: Start at Galena Creek trailhead; **2:** Go straight at south junction with the Galena Creek Nature Trail; **5:** Go straight at north junction with the Galena Creek Nature Trail; **6:** Junction to Jones Creek Loop and Jones Creek and Whites Creek Loop trailhead.

GO GREEN | The Great Basin Institute at Galena has been involved in outdoor education, primarily for students but with the desire to expand their adult programs. You can volunteer for service projects or make donations through www.galenacreekvisitorcenter.org.

OPTIONS | Bring a picnic lunch to enjoy in the nearby picnic area. The Raley's on Wedge Parkway is a full-service grocery store on the way up the Mount Rose Highway if you need any last-minute supplies.

TRIP 37 | Jones Creek Loop

Those searching for a short and relatively easy trip through the Jeffrey pine forest on the east side of the Carson Range should look no further than the Jones Creek Loop, a less than 2-mile circuit with an elevation gain of only 275 feet.

LEVEL	Walk, novice
LENGTH	1.7 miles, loop
TIME	1 to 1½ hours
ELEVATION	+275′–275′
DIFFICULTY	Easy
USERS	Hikers, trail runners, mountain bikers
DOGS	On leash
SEASON	Mid-April to November
BEST TIME	May
FACILITIES	Picnic tables, vault toilets (Galena Creek Visitor Center nearby)
MAP	Humboldt-Toiyabe National Forest: *Jones/Whites/Thomas Creeks Trail System* (web-map at www.fs.usda.gov/Internet /FSE_DOCUMENTS/stelprdb5275045.pdf)
MANAGEMENT	USFS Humboldt-Toiyabe Forest, Carson Ranger District at 775-882-2766, www.fs.usda.gov/htnf
HIGHLIGHTS	Forest, stream
LOWLIGHTS	Of the handful of streams in the area, Jones has the lowest flows and is often dry by mid or late summer.

TIP ǀ For a hike in the mountains, this trip is at lower elevations than many in the Galena/Mount Rose area, making for an excellent early-season ramble when the high country is still buried in snow.

KID TIP ǀ At less than 2 miles, this loop is a great option for small children ready to hike under their own power. When seasonal Jones Creek has water, the stream is a relatively safe playground for supervised small children.

TRAILHEAD ǀ 39°21.738′N, 119°51.457′W From Reno, drive southbound on I-580 to the Mount Rose Highway Exit 56 and then head southwest on

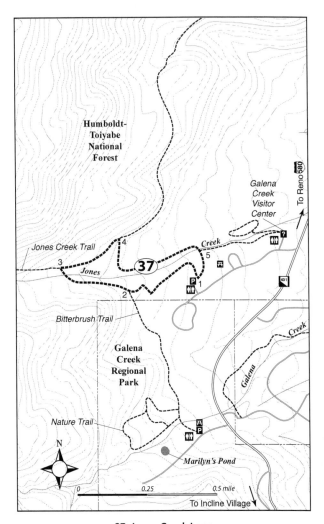

37. Jones Creek Loop

State Route 431 toward Incline Village and Lake Tahoe. After 5.6 miles, turn right toward the Galena Creek Visitor Center. Following signs marked TRAILHEAD," head past the visitor center and group picnic areas to a right-hand turn into the Jones Creek trailhead parking lot. Hikers and mountain bikers should park in the paved area, while equestrians should use the gravel lot.

TRAIL | From the paved parking area, walk through the graveled equestrian parking lot to the signed trailhead on the west side [1]. On a mild to moderate ascent, you weave through widely scattered Jeffrey pines with a patchy understory of mainly manzanita bushes with lesser amounts of bitter-brush and tobacco brush. In years of sufficient moisture, you may also see a sprinkling of colorful wildflowers alongside the trail in spring and early summer. Reach a T-junction [2] after 0.3 mile, where the left-hand path heads south into Galena Creek Regional Park and a connection with the Bitterbrush Trail.

Turn right at the junction and climb a bit more steeply through denser forest cover on the way to the next junction [3]. Just before this junction is a crossing of the thin ribbon of aspen-lined Jones Creek. Except in early season, you should be able to jump this narrow rivulet quite easily, other-wise a bridge of small-diameter logs should provide a dry passage (usually the seasonal creek dries up by late summer, but sometimes earlier following winters of less than average snowfall). Above the far bank is a three-way junction with the Jones Creek and Whites Creek Loop Trail, 0.6 mile from the trailhead.

You turn right (east) and head away from the junction and the high point of the circuit on a gently graded descent through light forest. Reach the next junction [4] after 0.5 mile of pleasant walking.

Leaving the Jones Creek and Whites Creek Loop, you angle sharply back to the right and head downhill through Jeffrey pine forest. Eventually, the trail switchbacks and comes alongside a white fir–shaded section of Jones Creek. Farther downstream, the forest opens up a bit, allowing enough sun-light for alders to flourish along the banks. At 0.5 mile from the previous junction, the trail crosses the creek above a culvert and comes to a junction [5] with a side path that continues downstream to the Galena Creek Visitor Center.

Proceeding ahead (south) on the Jones Creek Loop, you travel 0.1 mile past picnic tables to the trailhead on the east side of the parking lot [1] near the vault toilet.

RED-TAILED HAWK (*Buteo jamaicenses*) If you don't see a red-tailed hawk soaring above the stream canyons on the east side of the Carson Range, you may hear their characteristic high-pitched, descending screech echoing through the forest. In flight, its rust-colored tail easily identifies this large raptor.

MILESTONES

1: Start at Jones Creek trailhead; **2:** Go straight at junction of Bitterbrush Connector; **3:** Turn right at Jones Creek and Whites Creek Loop junction; **4:** Turn right at Jones Creek Loop junction; **5:** Go straight ahead at junction with trail to visitor center; **1:** Return to Jones Creek trailhead.

GO GREEN | The Nevada All-State Trail Riders, in conjunction with the Forest Service, provide annual maintenance on the Jones Creek and Whites Creek Loop, which occurs on National Trails Day (the first Saturday in June). For more information, check out their website at www.nastr.org.

OPTIONS | Picnic tables spread around the area near the trailhead offer the opportunity to enjoy a meal before or after your hike. The Galena Creek Visitor Center is definitely worth a visit as well.

38 Jones Creek to Church's Pond

In early season, Church's Pond is a picturesque body of water at the north base of Chocolate Peak. Without an inlet, the water level shrinks over the course of the summer, reducing its attractiveness a bit by late season. A stiff climb up the canyon of Jones Creek is required to get to the pond, but the scenery in the canyon is quite nice and the views from the open ridge above are excellent. The fall color in the upper canyon is superb at its peak.

LEVEL	Hike, moderate
LENGTH	7 miles, out and back
TIME	Half day
ELEVATION	+2,150′−0′
DIFFICULTY	Strenuous
USERS	Hikers, trail runners, equestrians
DOGS	On leash (first mile)
SEASON	Mid-May to November
BEST TIMES	Late May to late June, mid-October
FACILITIES	Picnic tables, vault toilets
MAPS	United States Geological Survey: *Washoe City, Mount Rose*; Humboldt-Toiyabe National Forest: *Jones/Whites/Thomas Creeks Trail System* (web-map at www.fs.usda.gov/Internet /FSE_DOCUMENTS/stelprdb5275045.pdf)
MANAGEMENT	USFS Humboldt-Toiyabe Forest, Carson Ranger District at 775-882-2766, www.fs.usda.gov/htnf
HIGHLIGHTS	Autumn color, forest, pond, stream, views
LOWLIGHTS	Church's Pond tends to shrink in size as the summer progresses.

TIP | Due to the south-facing exposure, the Jones Creek Trail is usually snow-free to the Whites Creek junction sooner than the surrounding trails, which can make the first 2.8 miles of the trip a good early-season option. However, the trail beyond the junction to Church's Pond typically holds onto its snow a good deal longer.

KID TIP | Many small children will find the steep sections of the trail to be quite taxing, making this a trip for older kids in good physical condition.

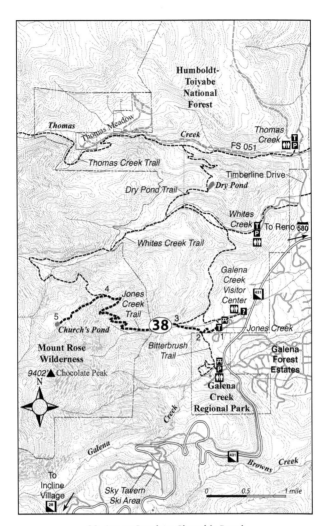

38. Jones Creek to Church's Pond

TRAILHEAD | 39°21.738′N, 119°51.457′W From Reno, drive southbound on I-580 to the Mount Rose Highway Exit 56 and then head southwest on State Route 431 toward Incline Village and Lake Tahoe. After 5.6 miles, turn right toward the Galena Creek Visitor Center. Following signs marked "TRAIL-HEAD," head past the visitor center and group picnic areas to a right-hand turn into the Jones Creek Trail trailhead parking lot. Hikers and mountain bikers should park in the paved area, while equestrians should use the gravel lot.

TRAIL | From the paved parking area, walk through the graveled equestrian parking lot to the signed trailhead on the west side [1]. On a mild to

Hikers descending the Jones Creek Trail

moderate ascent, you weave through widely scattered Jeffrey pines with a patchy understory of mainly manzanita bushes with lesser amounts of bitterbrush and tobacco brush. In years of sufficient moisture, you may also see a sprinkling of colorful wildflowers alongside the trail in spring and early summer. Reach a T-junction [2] after 0.3 mile, where the left-hand path heads south into Galena Creek Regional Park and a connection with the Bitterbrush Trail.

Turn right at the junction and climb a bit more steeply through denser forest cover on the way to the next junction [3]. Just before the junction is a crossing of the thin ribbon of aspen-lined Jones Creek. Except in early season, you should be able to jump this narrow rivulet, otherwise a bridge of small-diameter logs should provide a dry passage. Usually, the seasonal creek dries up by late summer, but sometimes earlier following dry winters. Above the far bank is a three-way junction with the Jones Creek and Whites Creek Loop trail, 0.6 mile from the trailhead.

Continue ahead from the junction up the canyon of Jones Creek, climbing more steeply on the way to the signed Mount Rose Wilderness boundary. The banks of the creek below are lined by a prolific stand of quaking aspen, which provides a stunning display of color during autumn. Farther up the canyon, the height of the walls seems quite imposing, requiring a series of long-legged switchbacks in order to gain the northern lip. The steady ascent is eventually rewarded at the top of the divide between Jones Creek and Whites Creek with a wide-ranging view of the surrounding terrain. A short way beyond this view-packed aerie is a junction [4] between the continuation of the Jones Creek and Whites Creek Loop on the right and the side path to Church's Pond ahead, 2.8 miles from the trailhead.

The trail to the pond continues climbing along the mostly open, sun-baked ridge, offering more excellent views along the way. After a switchback, the path dips behind the ridge crest and enters a stand of aspen. As the grade eases, you emerge from the trees and cross a slope covered with sagebrush scrub before dropping to the shore of Church's Pond [5].

The pond fills a shallow depression ringed by the tall summits of Chocolate Peak, Mount Rose, Church Peak, and a pair of unnamed high points, where about 2,500 feet of relief occurs between the pond and the top of Mount Rose. Since Church's Pond is dependent upon the collection of snowmelt for its existence, the water level fluctuates through the course of the season. Widely scattered pines and small stands of aspen line the far shore, which is otherwise surrounded by sagebrush scrub.

When ready, retrace your steps back to the Jones Creek Trail trailhead [1].

JAMES E. CHURCH, PhD (1869–1959) Church's Pond was named for a University of Nevada, Reno, (UNR) professor, who helped found the Mount Rose Weather Observatory in 1906. The first European American to make a winter ascent of Mount Rose, he made repeated climbs over the course of his career to make snow and weather observations. In 1906 Church developed the Mount Rose Snow Sampler, the first scientific instrument to measure the water content of snow. In addition to the pond, his name was affixed to the 10,601-foot peak immediately north-northwest of Mount Rose. A dedicated supporter of the arts, his name was also given to the Church Fine Arts Building on the UNR campus.

MILESTONES

1: Start at Jones Creek trailhead; **2:** Go straight ahead at junction of Bitterbrush Connector; **3:** Go straight ahead at Jones Creek and Whites Creek Loop lower junction; **4:** Go straight ahead at Jones Creek and Whites Creek Loop upper junction; **5:** Church's Pond; **1:** Return to Jones Creek trailhead.

GO GREEN | The Nevada All-State Trail Riders, in conjunction with the Forest Service, provide annual maintenance on the Jones Creek and Whites Creek Loop, which occurs on National Trails Day (the first Saturday in June). For more information, check out their website at www.nastr.org.

OPTIONS | Picnic tables spread around the area near the trailhead offer the opportunity to enjoy a meal before or after your hike. The Galena Creek Visitor Center is definitely worth a visit as well.

Jones Creek and
Whites Creek Loop

Some may consider this loop to be the premier hike in the area, especially when the extra trip to Church's Pond (see Trip 38) is added. The scenery is certainly outstanding, with a pair of beautiful stream canyons, dense forests, and exceptional views. Fall visitors will be thrilled by the autumn color in the aspen-filled canyons.

LEVEL	Hike, advanced
LENGTH	9.5 miles, loop
TIME	Full day
ELEVATION	+2,525'–2,525'
DIFFICULTY	Strenuous
USERS	Hikers, trail runners, equestrians
DOGS	On leash (first mile)
SEASON	Late May to November
BEST TIMES	June, mid-October
FACILITIES	Picnic tables, vault toilets
MAPS	United States Geological Survey: *Washoe City, Mount Rose, Mount Rose NW, Mount Rose NE*; Humboldt-Toiyabe National Forest: *Jones/Whites/Thomas Creeks Trail System* (web-map at www.fs.usda.gov/Internet/FSE_DOCUMENTS/stelprdb 5275045.pdf); Humboldt-Toiyabe National Forest: *Mount Rose Wilderness*
MANAGEMENT	USFS Humboldt-Toiyabe Forest, Carson Ranger District at 775-882-2766, www.fs.usda.gov/htnf
HIGHLIGHTS	Autumn color, forest, stream, views
LOWLIGHTS	None

TIP | If you wish to visit Church's Pond, add 1.4 mile to the mileage listed above (see Trip 38).

KID TIP | Many small children will find the steep sections and length of this trail to be quite taxing, making this a trip for older kids in good physical condition only.

TRAILHEAD | 39°21.738'N, 119°51.457'W From Reno, drive southbound on I-580 to the Mount Rose Highway Exit 56 and then head southwest on State

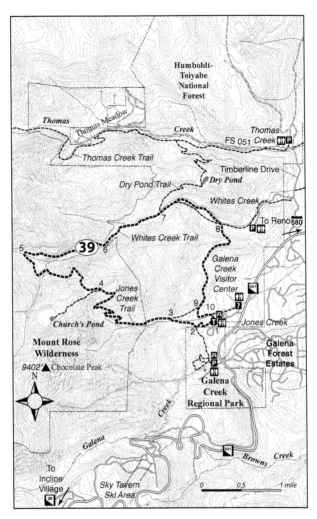

39. Jones Creek and Whites Creek Loop

Route 431 toward Incline Village and Lake Tahoe. After 5.6 miles, turn right toward the Galena Creek Visitor Center. Following signs marked "TRAIL-HEAD," head past the visitor center and group picnic areas to a right-hand turn into the Jones Creek Trail trailhead parking lot. Hikers and mountain bikers should park in the paved area, while equestrians should use the gravel lot.

TRAIL | From the paved parking area, walk through the graveled equestrian parking lot to the signed trailhead on the west side [1]. On a mild to moderate ascent, you weave through widely scattered Jeffrey pines with a patchy understory of mainly manzanita bushes with lesser amounts of bitterbrush and tobacco brush. In years of sufficient moisture, you may also see a sprinkling of colorful wildflowers alongside the trail in spring and early summer. Reach a T-junction [2] after 0.3 mile, where the left-hand path heads south into Galena Creek Regional Park and a connection with the Bitterbrush Trail.

Turn right at the junction and climb a bit more steeply through denser forest cover on the way to the next junction [3]. Just before the junction is a crossing of the thin ribbon of aspen-lined Jones Creek. Except in early season, you should be able to jump this narrow rivulet, otherwise a bridge of small-diameter logs should provide a dry passage. Usually the seasonal creek dries up by late summer, but sometimes earlier, following dry winters. Above the far bank is a three-way junction with the Jones Creek and Whites Creek Loop Trail, 0.6 mile from the trailhead.

Continue ahead from the junction up the canyon of Jones Creek, climbing more steeply on the way to the signed Mount Rose Wilderness boundary. The banks of the creek below are lined by a prolific stand of quaking aspen, which provides a stunning display of color during autumn. Farther up the canyon, the height of the walls seem quite imposing, requiring a series of long-legged switchbacks in order to gain the northern lip. The steady ascent is eventually rewarded at the top of the divide between Jones Creek and Whites Creek with a wide-ranging view of the surrounding terrain, including Mount Rose and Slide Mountain. A short way beyond this view-packed aerie, the trail dips slightly to a junction [4] between the continuation of the Jones Creek and Whites Creek Loop on the right and the side path to Church's Pond ahead, 2.8 miles from the trailhead (for a side trip to the pond, see Trip 38).

Turn right and begin a long descent into the canyon of Whites Creek, initially passing through aspen groves and open areas filled with grasses and scattered wildflowers in season. Soon the north-facing slope is covered with white fir forest, as you weave your way down to a bridged crossing of a Whites Creek tributary, about a mile from the junction. Climb briefly away from the creek, traverse across the forested hillside for a bit, and then resume the descent toward the floor of the canyon. Reach the main stem of perennially flowing Whites Creek [5], 1.5 miles from the Church's Pond junction, where small-diameter logs should provide a straightforward crossing to the far bank (following winters of heavy snowfall, this crossing may be difficult in early season).

The trail follows the creek downstream well above the south-facing bank, where Jeffrey pines and a groundcover of sagebrush and grasses have replaced the white fir forest previously seen on the descent of the north-facing wall of the canyon. However, white firs, aspens, and moisture-loving plants thrive in the moist soils immediately adjacent to the creek. At 1.3 miles from

View of the Mount Rose area from the Jones Creek and Whites Creek Loop.

the upstream crossing of Whites Creek, the trail bends sharply down into a shallow ravine and over to a boulder hop of the creek. Beyond the crossing, you ascend the south bank, merge with the old Whites Creek Road, and soon reach the Mount Rose Wilderness boundary [6].

Away from the wilderness boundary, the route continues down the old road through the trees for another 0.8 mile to a junction [7] with the Dry Pond Trail on the left.

Proceed ahead from the Dry Pond junction on the old road for a short distance until you reach a 4 × 4 post marking the separation of the equestrian route, which continues down the old road, and a single-track trail for hikers and mountain bikers on the left. After a 0.7-mile descent down the trail, you reach a three-way junction [8] between the Whites Creek Trail ahead and the continuation of the Jones Creek and Whites Creek Loop on the right.

Turning right (south), you immediately cross the old Whites Creek jeep road and begin a stiff climb across a Jeffrey pine–covered slope toward the top of the ridge dividing the drainages of Whites Creek and Jones Creek. Beyond, the vegetation switches to open slopes of sagebrush scrub allowing excellent views of the Carson Range summits of Slide Mountain and Mount Rose to the southwest, as well as Washoe Valley backed by the Virginia Range to the southeast. Early-season visitors may have the added bonus of mule's ears adding bursts of brilliant yellow flowers to the vista.

From the saddle, an angling descent slices across the hillside offering more excellent views of the surrounding terrain. Eventually, the forest cover returns on the way to the bottom of a dry canyon. A short climb over a minor ridge lined with mountain mahogany is followed by a general descent through Jeffrey pine forest on the way to a junction [9] with the Jones Creek Loop, 1.5 miles from the Whites Creek Trail junction.

Leaving the official Jones Creek and Whites Creek Loop, you veer left at the junction and head downhill through Jeffrey pine forest. Eventually, the trail switchbacks and comes alongside a white fir–shaded section of Jones Creek. Farther downstream, the forest opens up a bit, allowing enough sunlight for alders to flourish along the banks. At 0.5 mile from the previous junction, the trail crosses the creek above a culvert and comes to a junction [10] with a side path that continues downstream to the Galena Creek Visitor Center.

Proceeding ahead (south) on the Jones Creek Loop, you travel 0.1 mile past picnic tables to the trailhead on the east side of the parking lot [1] near the vault toilet.

CURL-LEAF MOUNTAIN MAHOGANY (*Cercocarpus ledifolius*) Common to the Carson Range, mountain mahogany appears extensively within the pinyon and juniper woodland and also on the dry slopes of the Jeffrey pine forest. Unrelated to the tropical mahoganies, this evergreen is classified within the rose family. Rarely attaining heights of up to 30 feet, they often appear more like a large shrub than a bona fide tree. Early residents commonly used the wood for making charcoal.

MILESTONES

1: Start at Jones Creek Trailhead; **2:** Go straight ahead at Junction of Bitterbrush Connector; **3:** Go straight ahead at Jones Creek and Whites Creek Loop lower junction; **4:** Turn right at Jones Creek and Whites Creek Loop upper junction; **5:** Upper crossing of Whites Creek; **6:** Lower crossing of Whites Creek and wilderness boundary; **7:** Go straight ahead at Dry Pond Loop junction; **8:** Turn right at Whites Creek Trail junction; **9:** Turn left at Jones Creek Trail junction; **10:** Turn right at junction with trail to visitor center; **1:** Return to Jones Creek Trailhead.

GO GREEN | The Nevada All-State Trail Riders, in conjunction with the Forest Service, provide annual maintenance on the Jones Creek and Whites Creek Loop, which occurs on National Trails Day (the first Saturday in June). For more information, check out their website at www.nastr.org.

OPTIONS | Picnic tables spread around the area near the trailhead offer the opportunity to enjoy a meal before or after your hike. The Galena Creek Visitor Center is definitely worth a visit as well.

Upper Whites Creek flows through a forested canyon offering a shady environment for a morning or afternoon hike that eventually leads into the Mount Rose Wilderness (no bikes).

LEVEL	Hike
LENGTH	7 miles, out and back
TIME	Half day
ELEVATION	+1,300'–0'
DIFFICULTY	Moderate
USERS	Hikers, trail runners, equestrians
DOGS	On leash (first mile)
SEASON	May to Late October
BEST TIME	Mid-May through June
FACILITIES	Picnic tables, vault toilets
MAP	United States Geological Survey: *Mount Rose NE*; Humboldt-Toiyabe National Forest: *Jones/Whites/Thomas Creeks Trail System* (web-map at www.fs.usda.gov/Internet/FSE_DOCU MENTS/stelprdb5275045.pdf); Humboldt-Toiyabe National Forest: *Mount Rose Wilderness*
MANAGEMENT	USFS Humboldt-Toiyabe Forest, Carson Ranger District at 775-882-2766, www.fs.usda.gov/htnf
HIGHLIGHTS	Autumn color, forest, stream
LOWLIGHTS	None

TIP I This trail is quite popular with dog walkers. Make sure you pick up after Fido if you plan on bringing along a dog.

KID TIP I The trip up Whites Creek is at a moderate grade and should not be too taxing for the little ones. The trail is usually not far from the creek, which would be an interesting diversion for kids, although please obey the "Closed for Restoration" signs where they occur.

Younger kids may enjoy the opportunity to pan for gold in the creek. The Reno Prospecting & Detecting Club may be a good resource for more information (renoprospectinganddetecting.com).

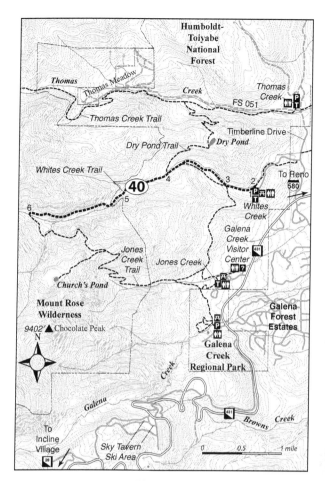

40. Whites Creek Trail

TRAILHEAD | 39°22.679′N, 119°50.884′W From Reno, drive southbound on I-580 to the Mount Rose Highway Exit 56 and then head southwest on State Route 431 toward Incline Village and Lake Tahoe. After 0.6 mile, turn left and follow Whites Creek Road for 0.5 mile to the trailhead.

TRAIL | From the parking area [1], cross the road and proceed northwest on a stretch of single-track trail toward the creek, soon reaching a junction [2] marked by a 4×4 post. Turn left and head up Whites Creek through Jeffrey pine forest, intermixed with lesser amounts of white fir and mountain mahogany. Pockets of aspen provide golden color in autumn. Continue upstream where a less used trail comes in from the right. Reach another junction [3] marked by a 4×4 post, 0.4 mile from the trailhead, where a connector trail on the left heads toward Jones Creek as part of the Jones Creek and Whites Creek Loop (see Trip 39).

Traveling straight ahead from the junction, you follow the tumbling course of Whites Creek through shady, mixed forest. At 1.2 miles from the trailhead and 0.8 mile from the previous junction, reach the marked junction [4] of the Dry Pond Loop (see Trip 41) on the right.

Remaining on the Whites Creek Trail, you proceed up the south bank of the stream through the moderately forested canyon. Around a half mile from the previous junction, the path merges with a piece of the old Whites Creek jeep road, which you follow for a short distance to the signed Mount Rose Wilderness boundary (mountain bikers are not allowed past this point). From there, the trail bends sharply downhill to a crossing of vigorous Whites Creek [5], a usually straightforward boulder hop, unless the stream is full of snowmelt.

Head up the north bank on a steady climb through the trees. Technically, the Whites Creek Trail ends [6] at 3.5 miles from the trailhead, where the Jones Creek and Whites Creek Loop trail continues across the creek via some logs and then climbs stiffly up the south wall of the canyon to the top of the ridge dividing the two watersheds. Competent cross-country hikers can travel farther up Whites Creek to the remains of an old cabin.

At the conclusion of your journey, retrace your steps back to the Whites Creek trailhead [1].

STELLER'S JAY (*Cyanocitta stelleri*) One can't travel for very long through the forests of the Carson Range without seeing one of these blue-and-black jays hopping along the forest floor, or hearing its harsh cackle. These jays are also capable of imitating the screams of hawks, so oftentimes visual recognition is necessary to identify between the two. Away from their nest, these jays can be quite noisy and they can become very bold when accustomed to humans.

MILESTONES

1: Start at Whites Creek trailhead; 2: Turn left at junction; 3: Go straight at Jones Creek and Whites Creek Loop junction; 4: Go straight at Dry Pond junction; 5: Cross Whites Creek; 6: End of Whites Creek Trail; 1: Return to trailhead.

GO GREEN | The Nevada All-State Trail Riders, in conjunction with the Forest Service, provide annual maintenance on the Jones Creek and Whites Creek Loop, which occurs on National Trails Day (the first Saturday in June). For more information, check out their website at www.nastr.org.

OPTIONS | Picnic tables spread around the area near the trailhead offer the opportunity to enjoy a meal before or after your hike.

The Galena Creek Visitor Center is definitely worth a visit before or after your hike.

Dry Pond Loop

The Dry Pond Loop offers a pleasant circuit along the eastern edge of the Carson Range, passing through the lower sections of the upper canyons of Thomas Creek and Whites Creek with a stop at ephemeral Dry Pond in between. Except during drought periods or after midseason, the pond is usually a picturesque mirror for the summits of Slide Mountain and Mount Rose, as well as a temporary haven for waterfowl. As summer progresses, the pond steadily shrinks, eventually becoming a grass-tinged meadow. Lower in elevation than many of the surrounding trails, the Dry Pond Loop has a correspondingly extended season, which makes the trip a fine spring or fall option.

LEVEL	Hike, intermediate
LENGTH	4.5 miles, shuttle; 6.3 miles, loop
TIME	Half day
ELEVATION	+1,000′–750′ (shuttle); +1,100′–1,100′ (loop)
DIFFICULTY	Moderate
USERS	Hikers, trail runners, mountain bikers, equestrians
DOGS	On leash (first mile)
SEASON	May to Late October
BEST TIME	Mid-May through June
FACILITIES	Picnic tables, vault toilets
MAP	United States Geological Survey: *Mount Rose NE*; Humboldt-Toiyabe National Forest: *Jones/Whites/Thomas Creeks Trail System* (web-map at www.fs.usda.gov/Internet/FSE_DOCU MENTS/stelprdb5275045.pdf); Humboldt-Toiyabe National Forest: *Mount Rose Wilderness*
MANAGEMENT	USFS Humboldt-Toiyabe Forest, Carson Ranger District at 775-882-2766, www.fs.usda.gov/htnf
HIGHLIGHTS	Forest, pond, stream, views
LOWLIGHTS	Dry Pond usually lives up to its name by midsummer. Without shuttle arrangements, completing the loop requires walking on roads. The trail is exceedingly popular on weekends, so don't expect much solitude.

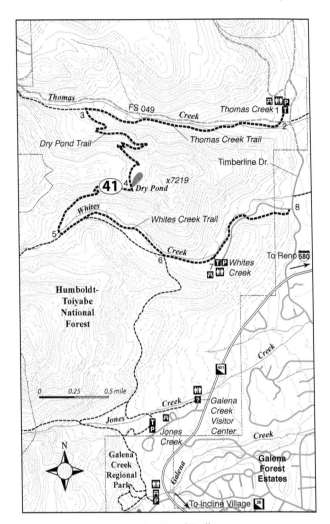

41. Dry Pond Trail

TIP | With shuttle arrangements you can lop off 1.8 miles of mostly road travel between the Thomas Creek and Whites Creek trailheads.

KID TIP | The shuttle version of this trip should be well suited to children who have been out of the child carrier for a while and are ready to don their own packs and go for a real hike. The short climb from Thomas Creek up to Dry Pond may be challenging, but should be quickly forgotten once they see the waterfowl on the pond's surface (provided you are early in the season).

TRAILHEAD | 39°23.625′N, 119°50.292′W From Reno, drive southbound on I-580 to the Mount Rose Highway Exit 56 and then head southwest on State Route 431 toward Incline Village and Lake Tahoe. After 2 miles, turn right

Dry Pond in spring

onto Timberline Drive and proceed 1.1 mile to the left-hand entry into the Thomas Creek trailhead parking area, crossing short bridges over Whites Creek and Thomas Creek on the way.

For the shuttle option, leave a vehicle at the Whites Creek trailhead by following Timberline Drive for 0.6 mile from the Mount Rose Highway and turning left onto Whites Creek Road. The trailhead is 0.5 mile up the road (39°22.679′N, 119°50.884′W).

TRAIL | From the southwest edge of the parking area [1], follow single-track trail through sagebrush scrub below scattered pinyon and Jeffrey pines to a crossing of Thomas Creek Road [2]. Across the road, turn up the canyon and walk through a dirt parking area to the beginning of single-track trail, which shortly leads to a bridge over Thomas Creek. Beyond the crossing the trail heads upstream along a riparian zone shaded by aspens, cottonwoods, Jeffrey pines, and white firs. Periodic openings in the forest are filled with sagebrush, bitterbrush, and purple lupines in the spring and early summer. After 1.5-mile of a gently ascending path, you reach a junction [3] marked by a 4 × 4 post.

Leaving the Thomas Creek Trail, you turn left at the junction and follow the Dry Pond Loop on a moderate climb up a wooded slope, soon zigzagging up the south side of the canyon via a set of long-legged switchbacks. Gaining the crest of the ridge dividing the drainages of Thomas Creek and Whites Creek, the trail bends toward a large, flat clearing. Early in the season the grass-fringed clearing is filled with the shallow waters of Dry Pond [4], with a small flock of ducks usually paddling across the surface near the far shore.

By midsummer the water has disappeared, hence the name. A sign requests that visitors stay on the trail and off of the usually squishy pond bottom to avoid environmental degradation. The view across Dry Pond includes Mount Rose and Slide Mountain to the southwest. The trail passes beneath the trees at the edge of the forest, arcing around the clearing to the lip of Whites Creek canyon. By heading cross-country east from there, you can ascend an old firebreak to the top of Peak 7219 for a superb view of the surrounding terrain.

Plunging toward the bottom of Whites Creek canyon, the trail switchbacks down a mostly open, south-facing hillside with good views of the Carson Range, at least until the descent leads back under forest cover near the floor of the canyon. Follow the trail through the trees and over to a bridge across the creek. Above the far side of the creek is a junction [5] near a 4 × 4 post with the old Whites Creek jeep road.

Turn left and head downstream on the road, which at one time conveyed motorized transport up the length of the canyon. Nowadays, except for brief multi-use stretches like this one, the old road is a designated equestrian route. After a brief walk, single-track trail veers left away from the road and continues downstream through mixed forest. The trail is never far from tumbling Whites Creek and occasionally is right next to this perennial stream. About three-quarter mile from the crossing of Whites Creek, you reach a three-way junction [6] marked by a 4 × 4 post, where the right-hand trail heads up the south side of the canyon and into the Jones Creek drainage as part of the Jones Creek and Whites Creek Loop (see Trip 39).

Proceed ahead from the junction, soon reaching a small flat next to the creek. Beyond the flat, mountain mahoganies join the mixed forest. Farther down the canyon you may notice numerous mahogany stumps, the result of a thinning and controlled burn program administered by the Forest Service in an attempt to reduce the fuels and prevent a major forest fire from erupting so close to the urban fringe. At 1.25 miles from the Whites Creek crossing is an unmarked junction between two parallel paths, a little-used path that closely follows the creek and the well-used main trail that follows the lip of the drainage (the creek path rejoins the main trail just prior to the crossing of the Whites Creek Road). After a short distance, the right-hand main trail leads to another junction [7], this one also marked by a 4 × 4 post, where the trail ahead goes shortly to the Whites Creek trailhead parking area (take this path if you're utilizing the shuttle option).

To complete the full loop, proceed down the canyon on the left-hand trail, which moves away from the creek and closer to Whites Creek Road, traveling through a drier section of forest. After a while, the trail crosses the road and continues down the canyon. Upon reaching the end of the trail, you must walk down the paved road a short distance to Timberline Drive [8].

To return to the Thomas Creek trailhead, turn left and follow Timberline Drive across the bridge over Whites Creek and proceed another 0.6 mile to the Thomas Creek bridge and the Thomas Creek Road immediately beyond. Continue ahead past the road for another 0.1 mile to the entrance into the Thomas Creek trailhead parking area [1] and the close of the loop.

BROOK TROUT (*Salvelinus fontinalis*) Although not particularly abundant in number or size, brook trout have found a home in Whites Creek and Thomas Creek. Planted in the streams from the 1950s through the early 1970s, their population is now self-sustaining. The only other species of trout present is rainbow, 1,000 of which continue to be stocked each spring in both creeks. Brook trout tend to be darker on top and do not have the characteristic red or pink streak on their sides, as do rainbow trout. Anglers are limited to a catch of five fish per day.

MILESTONES

1: Start at Thomas Creek trailhead; **2:** Cross Thomas Creek Road; **3:** Turn left at Dry Pond junction; **4:** Dry Pond; **5:** Turn left at Whites Creek junction; **6:** Jones Creek junction; **7:** Go straight ahead at Whites Creek trailhead junction; **8:** Turn left at Timberline Drive; **1:** End at Thomas Creek trailhead.

GO GREEN | Friends of Nevada Wilderness have been quite active within the Mount Rose Wilderness with such projects as eradicating non-native weeds and reseeding areas burned by forest fires. Check out their website at www .nevadawilderness.org.

OPTIONS | Picnic tables spread around the area near both the Whites Creek and Thomas Creek trailheads offer the opportunity to enjoy a meal before or after your hike. The Galena Creek Visitor Center is definitely worth a visit as well.

Anglers who wish to fish in the creeks can stop in at the Reno Fly Shop for fishing reports, information on tying flies, or guided trips. Visit their website at www.renoflyshop.com.

42 | Upper Thomas Creek Loop

By just about any standard, this strip is long and strenuous from either the upper or lower trailheads. Hikers must be in excellent shape and should get an early start to allow for plenty of daylight hours in order to complete the trip. The rewards for such a strenuous endeavor are excellent, including beautiful scenery, expansive vistas, and lots of solitude. Autumn visitors should be amazed at the widespread color in upper Thomas Creek canyon.

LEVEL Hike, advanced

LENGTH 22.8 miles, lollipop loop (lower trailhead); 16.4 miles, lollipop loop (upper trailhead)

TIME Full day

ELEVATION +4,475'–4,475' (lower trailhead); +3,375'–3,375' (upper trailhead)

DIFFICULTY Very strenuous

USERS Hikers, trail runners, equestrians

DOGS On leash (first mile)

SEASON July to Mid-October

BEST TIMES Mid-July to early August, mid-October

FACILITIES Interpretive sign, picnic tables, vault toilets

MAP United States Geological Survey: *Mount Rose NE, Mount Rose NW* (trail not shown on 1982 maps); Humboldt-Toiyabe National Forest: *Mount Rose Wilderness* (trail not shown on 2009 map)

MANAGEMENT USFS Humboldt-Toiyabe Forest, Carson Ranger District at 775-882-2766, www.fs.usda.gov/htnf

HIGHLIGHTS Autumn color, forest, streams, views

LOWLIGHTS Stretch of poor trail from crest of Carson Range into Thomas Creek canyon

TIP | Although the stiff climb out of Thomas Creek canyon is the most strenuous part of the trip, the descent from the crest of the Carson Range back into the canyon is on a poor and steep trail, so don't expect clear sailing until just before the close of the loop section.

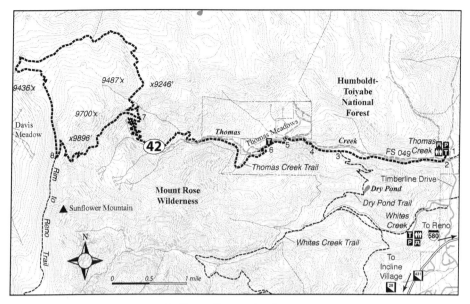

42. Upper Thomas Creek Loop

KID TIP | Find another trail (although the first couple of miles from the upper trailhead might make for a kid-friendly day hike).

LOWER TRAILHEAD | 39°23.625′N, 119°50.292′W From Reno, drive southbound on I-580 to the Mount Rose Highway Exit 56 and then head southwest on State Route 431 toward Incline Village and Lake Tahoe. After 2 miles, turn right onto Timberline Drive and proceed 1 mile to Thomas Creek Road, crossing short bridges over Whites Creek and Thomas Creek on the way. Continue ahead another 0.1 mile to the left-hand entry into the Thomas Creek trailhead parking area.

UPPER TRAILHEAD | 39°23.661′N, 119°53.107′W *Note: A high-clearance vehicle will be necessary to reach the upper trailhead.* Follow the directions above to Thomas Creek Road. Rather than continue ahead to the lower trailhead parking area, turn left and follow Thomas Creek Road (FS 049) west for 2.2 miles to an intersection with a private, gated road on the right, which leads to several homes around Thomas Meadows. Veer left at the intersection and descend for 0.1 mile on a narrow jeep road to a crossing of Thomas Creek (may be difficult in early season). Continue past the creek crossing for another 0.3 mile to a small dirt parking area on the left just below a closed steel gate. The trail begins near the signboard at the edge of the parking area.

TRAIL FROM LOWER TRAILHEAD | From the southwest edge of the lower Thomas Creek trailhead parking area [1], follow single-track trail through sagebrush scrub below scattered pinyon and Jeffrey pines to a crossing of Thomas

Creek Road [2]. Across the road, turn up the canyon and walk through a dirt parking area to the beginning of single-track trail, which shortly leads to a bridge over Thomas Creek. Beyond the crossing the trail heads upstream along a riparian zone shaded by aspens, cottonwoods, Jeffrey pines, and white firs. Periodic openings in the forest are filled with sagebrush, bitter-brush, and purple lupines in the spring and early summer. After 1.5-mile of a gently ascending path, you reach a junction [3] with the Dry Pond Trail marked by a 4 × 4 post.

Go straight ahead, remaining on the Thomas Creek Trail, continuing the steady climb along the edge of the riparian zone lining the creek and the mostly Jeffrey pine forest on the slopes above. The trail weaves back and forth to the south bank a few times before bending over to cross the creek on a plank bridge [4] at 0.5 mile from the Dry Pond junction. Don't take the path continuing ahead above the crossing, as the tread soon disappears. Beyond the crossing the trail intersects Thomas Creek Road, where you turn up the canyon and follow the road 100 yards along a curve to the resumption of single-track trail at a small sign.

Climb stiffly away from the road for a bit before the grade returns to a more moderate ascent, passing through a more open area across from some interesting-looking cliffs on the south side of the canyon. Lying in the brush near the stream is an old rusted automobile, which you may not notice on the way up, but is painfully obvious on the return. About a half mile from the creek crossing, a side trail dives down next to a scenic stretch of the stream. The main trail continues up the canyon through a stand of aspen, which provides some welcome shade after the previously exposed section. Farther on, the forest opens up briefly, allowing your first view of the ridge above the upper canyon. The trail merges with the road again, which soon bends toward a crossing [5] of the twin-branched creek. Except during periods of high water, the boulder hops should be easily accomplished.

Where the road bends back up the canyon, you follow single-track trail above the road through scattered forest, with occasional views of Thomas Meadows to the north. Head back under thicker forest cover and continue to the small, dirt parking area at the upper trailhead [6], 3.2 miles from the lower trailhead.

TRAIL FROM UPPER TRAILHEAD I The trail continues away from the upper trail-head on a switchbacking climb up the south wall of the canyon through predominantly Jeffrey pine forest, a necessary diversion to avoid crossing some of the private property surrounding Thomas Meadows. At the top of the switchbacks, a mildly descending traverse heads across the shady, pine-studded hillside. A half mile from the upper trailhead, you bend around a side drainage, cross an old jeep road, and then descend back toward the creek. The trail merges with a section of the old Thomas Creek Road and then ascends for a short while until single-track trail bends away to the left (equestrians should continue up the old road). Walk a short distance to a ford of Thomas Creek, 1.6 miles from the parking area, an easy crossing except when the creek is running high with snowmelt.

Proceed up the north side of the creek through more open forest. The trail merges with the old road once more, crosses the signed Mount Rose Wilderness boundary, and then passes through a lush grove of aspens. About 2 miles from the upper trailhead, the route veers away from the old road and the vicinity of the creek to ascend single-track trail north into the forest. Soon the trail bends west and continues to the crossing of a small, but usually vigorous, side stream, where once again the equestrian and hiker routes part ways. Nearing the main branch of the creek again, you travel through open terrain, which permits fine views up the canyon, including a prominent rock face above the south side of Thomas Creek. Continuing, a few short-legged switchbacks offer a warm-up for the stiff climb waiting ahead, followed by a moderate ascent up a manzanita-covered hillside.

Follow a set of long-legged switchbacks up a steep slope carpeted with rabbitbrush, sagebrush, mountain mahogany, and an occasional Jeffrey pine, enjoying a fine view of the upper canyon on the way. After a dozen switchbacks, you stand on the crest of the north ridge of the canyon, where the view expands to include the Truckee Meadows to the northeast and Sunflower Mountain, Alpine Walk Peak, Church Peak, Chocolate Peak, and Mount Rose to the south. You climb along the top of the ridge a short way to the loop junction [7], 4.4 miles from the upper trailhead.

Turn right and follow a counterclockwise circuit, continuing to climb through mostly open terrain until entering a mostly lodgepole pine forest. A couple of switchbacks lead higher up the slope and then across a usually dry tributary of Thomas Creek. Not far beyond, you come to a saddle between Peaks 9487 and 9246 and then begin a gentle, moderately forested, somewhat-winding descent to the north-northwest. After the stiff climb out of Thomas Creek canyon, walking on the gently graded trail can be quite pleasant. Without much groundcover, this slope stands in stark contrast to the lush vegetation previously seen along Thomas Creek. Other than circumventing the edge around a couple of boulder fields, the lodgepole pine forest remains constant, sprinkled with an occasional associate of whitebark pine or mountain hemlock. About a mile and a half from the loop junction, the gentle descent comes to a conclusion.

Shortly after, an extended climb begins and just beyond some switchbacks is a rock knob with a view of the distant Truckee Meadows. Rising trail leads to another rock knob after a bit, with views north toward Peavine Peak and the much closer upper canyon of a Hunter Creek tributary below. Continue climbing, soon traversing across a rocky trail below an

Rock formation in upper Thomas Creek Canyon

interesting-looking rock outcrop. Heading back into lodgepole pine forest, you make a long, gently rising ascent until reaching another rock knob at 7.5 miles from the upper trailhead. Here a fine view unfolds: Big Meadow and Deep Canyon are in the immediate foreground, while Peavine Peak, the Verdi Range, Stampede Reservoir, Mount Lola, and Sierra Buttes are some of the more distant highlights. Beyond a short climb over a saddle near Peak 9436, the grade mellows a bit on a wandering route through the forest. Farther on, the grade increases as the trail make an angling, mile-long, ascending traverse below the west side of the Carson Range crest. Where the path crosses a rockslide, views open up temporarily of the surrounding terrain. Reach a junction [8] near a 4 × 4 post, 5.9 miles from the loop junction, where the Rim to Reno Trail continues ahead (south).

Turn left (northeast) at the junction and follow a half-mile, moderate, switchbacking climb to the crest of the Carson Range. From the crest a scramble along the ridge to the top of either Peak 9896 (north) or 9890 (south) offers superb views of the surrounding terrain for anyone with enough extra energy.

The trail drops rather steeply away from the crest back into the Thomas Creek drainage (you'll more than likely be glad not to have climbed up this way), switchbacking down the steep hillside for nearly a mile before reaching a more pleasantly graded traverse across the upper canyon. The mile-long traverse eventually leads back to the loop junction [7] at 1.7 miles from the Rim to Reno junction. From there, retrace your steps 4.4 miles to the parking area at the upper trailhead [6], or 7.6 miles to the lower trailhead [1].

QUAKING ASPEN (*Populus tremuloides*) Perhaps no autumn sight in the eastern Sierra is more scintillating than a canyon filled with a stand of quaking aspen, when the yellow-green, spade-shaped leaves of summer turn a brilliant orange-gold. Even before they turn, a multitude of leaves that tremble in the mildest of breezes is quite stunning. Although growing from seeds is possible, most aspens sprout from the spreading roots of a single parent, amazingly resulting in stands of genetically identical individuals.

MILESTONES

1: Start at lower Thomas Creek trailhead; **2:** Cross Thomas Creek Road; **3:** Go straight at Dry Pond junction; **4:** Cross Thomas Creek; **5:** Cross Thomas Creek; **6:** Upper Thomas Creek trailhead; **7:** Turn right at loop junction; **8:** Turn left at Rim to Reno junction; **7:** Turn right at loop junction; **1:** Return to lower Thomas Creek trailhead.

GO GREEN | Friends of Nevada Wilderness have been quite active within the Mount Rose Wilderness with such projects as eradicating non-native weeds and reseeding areas burned by forest fires. Check out their website at www .nevadawilderness.org.

OPTIONS | More than likely you'll be pooped after this trip, wishing you had a hot tub waiting at home to comfort your tired muscles. Disheveled hikers could find comfort in a cold brew and pub food at Bully's (18156 Wedge Parkway), located in the Raley's shopping center at the northeast corner of the Mount Rose Highway and Wedge Parkway.

43 | Browns Creek Trail

The Browns Creek Trail offers a couple of options for hikers searching for a short or moderate trip. The short version climbs less than 1.5 miles to an excellent viewpoint of the Virginia Range and Washoe and Pleasant Valleys. Shortly beyond the viewpoint, the longer loop portion travels along a stretch of Browns Creek and a seasonal tributary, both lined with lush riparian foliage. The loop provides good views along the way as well.

LEVEL	Hike, intermediate
LENGTH	4.9 miles, lollipop loop
TIME	Half day
ELEVATION	+1,000′–1,000′
DIFFICULTY	Moderate
USERS	Hikers, trail runners, mountain bikers, equestrians
DOGS	On leash (first mile)
SEASON	Late May to November
BEST TIME	June through July
FACILITIES	None
MAP:	Washoe County Parks: *Brown's Creek Trail Map* (web-map at www.washoecounty.us/parks); United States Geological Survey: *Washoe City* (trail not shown on 1994 map); Humboldt-Toiyabe National Forest: *Mount Rose Wilderness* (trail not shown on 2009 map)
MANAGEMENT	Washoe County Regional Parks and Open Space at 775-328-3600, www.washoecounty.us/parks
HIGHLIGHTS	Forest, interpretive sign, stream, views
LOWLIGHTS	The south tributary of Browns Creek usually dries up by midsummer.

TIP ⏐ The park bench at the viewpoint is a pleasant lunch spot.

KID TIP ⏐ The really interesting parts of this trip occur after the first 1.3 miles of rather mundane scenery, so make sure any children along are in for the long haul.

TRAILHEAD ⏐ 39°20.944′N, 119°49.983′W From Reno, drive southbound on I-580 to the Mount Rose Highway Exit 56 and then head southwest on State

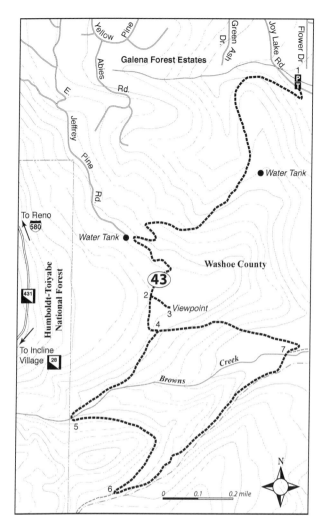

43. Browns Creek Trail

Route 431 toward North Lake Tahoe. After 6 miles, 0.3 mile past the turn-off for the Galena Visitor Center, turn left onto Joy Lake Road and travel 1.5 miles to the gravel trailhead parking lot on the left-hand shoulder. (The creek next to the parking area is not Browns Creek but a tributary of Galena Creek.)

TRAIL | The signed trail [1] begins across Joy Lake Road from the parking area and follows a moderate ascent up the hillside through light Jeffrey pine and mountain mahogany forest with an understory of manzanita and bitter-brush. The trail switchbacks and continues climbing, the grade easing a bit where you bend south into a usually dry side canyon. Pass over the trace of a pine-needle-covered old road and keep climbing to the crossing of a more defined jeep road at 0.5 mile from the trailhead. Above this second road, near the crest of the ridge, is a water tank, one of two tanks serving the adjacent subdivisions you will see along this route. Farther on, approaching the second water tank, the trail starts switchbacking up the slope and then winds up across the broad crest of a ridge, which affords filtered views to the east of the Virginia Range and northeast of the Steamboat Hills. At the far side of the ridge, 1.25 miles from the trailhead, is a signed junction [2] with a short side path to a viewpoint.

A short and easy stroll leads about 125 yards to a fine view [3] with a park bench and an interpretive sign about Sundown Town, an old Wild West attraction near Joy Lake. For those seeking a shorter trip than the full 5-mile circuit, this is a good turnaround point. After thoroughly enjoying the view, simply retrace your steps back to the junction.

Away from the vista junction, the trail descends off the ridge and down to the loop junction at 1.3 miles from the trailhead [4].

Turning right to follow a counterclockwise circuit around the loop, you make an angling descent toward the floor of Browns Creek canyon through the arid terrain typical of a south-facing slope on the east side of the Carson Range. The open topography allows for fine views up the canyon to the hulk of Slide Mountain and the ski runs of Mount Rose Ski Tahoe. Drawing closer to Browns Creek, the healthy riparian vegetation in the drainage seems a welcome sight following the dry conditions on the hillside. Soon after reaching the floor of the canyon and heading upstream, a switchback leads shortly to a 2 × 6 plank bridge spanning the creek [5].

Away from the creek the trail follows a gently rising traverse across the north-facing slope of Peak 6450 through Jeffrey pines and a healthy understory of manzanita. At 0.4 mile from the bridge, the trail rounds the nose of the ridge and traverses across the hillside toward the bottom of a canyon carrying a seasonal tributary of Browns Creek. Nearing the creek, you come to a signed junction [6] with a trail continuing upstream onto Forest Service land after 0.2 mile.

Turning left at the junction, the Browns Creek Loop descends for 0.6 mile along the north side of the tributary stream. Soon after a pair of short-legged switchbacks, the sound of tumbling water from the main fork of Browns Creek returns and then you make a pair of crossings over twin channels of the stream, the first on a pair of worn boards and the second on a 2 × 6 plank bridge [7]. A short way past the bridge is an unmarked junction with a path headed downstream onto the private property of St. James Village.

Away from the creek the trail starts to regain all of the previously lost elevation. Initially, you make an angling ascent northeast across the hillside to a switchback, and then follow a lengthy, moderate climb generally west across an open slope of sagebrush scrub offering good views of Slide Mountain and the surrounding terrain. Upon reaching the close of the loop [4], retrace your steps 1.3 miles back to the trailhead.

BLACK BEAR (*Ursus americanus*) The only species of bear found in Nevada, black bears are confined to the hills of the eastern Sierra as part of the Sierra Nevada population, which is estimated to include 10,000 to 15,000 individuals. Despite the name, these omnivores can also be shades of brown, blond, and cinnamon. Some males can reach up to 600 pounds but the average size is between 300 and 350 pounds. These fascinating mammals have rather poor eyesight, but their hearing is good and they have an excellent sense of smell. Black bears are very fast, attaining speeds up to 15 miles per hour. They are also good tree climbers.

MILESTONES

1: Start at Browns Creek trailhead; **2:** Turn left at vista junction; **3:** Vista; **2:** Return to vista junction; **4:** Turn right at loop junction; **5:** West Bridge over Browns Creek; **6:** Turn left at Forest Service junction; **7:** East Bridge over Browns Creek; **4:** Turn right at loop junction; **1:** Return to Browns Creek trailhead.

GO GREEN ǀ Although the Browns Creek Trail is not a park per se, Washoe County Regional Parks and Open Space has an Adopt-A-Park program, where volunteers can donate their time for working in the parks to keep them clean, attractive, and safe. The program is open to individuals and groups. For more information, visit their website at www.washoecounty.us/parks/volunteer_opportunities.php, or contact the Parks Volunteer Coordinator at 775-785-4512, ext. 107.

OPTIONS ǀ There's not much in the way of commercial enterprises in the immediate vicinity of the trailhead. As mentioned above, you could enjoy a picnic lunch while enjoying the view from the park bench at the vista point, 1.3 miles from the trailhead.

From junction **6**, a trail, used primarily by mountain bikers, continues southwest up the drainage and eventually intersects a dirt fire road. Turning north, this road can be followed for a half mile to where steep single-track climbs along the south rim of the main canyon of Browns Creek up to East Bowl Road (SR 878), the access road to the Slide side of Mount Rose Ski Tahoe. Continuing north on the fire road all the way to the Mount Rose Highway is also possible.

44 | Mount Rose Trail

A pleasant early or mid-July day is an excellent time for a hike to the waterfall on an upper branch of Galena Creek, when, unless the previous winter's snowpack was dismally below average, the waterfall should be flowing at full force and the neighboring wildflowers should be achieving peak bloom. Trails in the area allow you to see the waterfall from the base and the top, providing two different yet complementary perspectives of this watery wonder. Bonus views of Lake Tahoe occur within the first half mile of trail and Mount Rose is never out of sight for very long. The lovely scenery combined with a relatively short trail and modest elevation gain makes the trip to the waterfall quite popular with casual and serious hikers alike, especially on weekends.

Imagining a more popular path than the Mount Rose Trail is difficult, as seemingly every summer day the parking lot is jammed full of cars belonging to day trippers bound for the waterfall, hikers attempting to complete a section of the Tahoe Rim Trail, or hopeful summiteers hoping to stand on top of the Tahoe Basin's third highest summit (10,776′). Ask anyone who's attempted to hike at least one trail in the Reno-Tahoe area what his or her favorite trail is and the answer will invariably be the Mount Rose Trail. This popularity is definitely justified, as the scenery is excellent, the views stunning, the wildflowers dazzling, and the ascent challenging. Along the way you'll experience picturesque views of Lake Tahoe, a beautiful waterfall, colorful wildflowers along Galena Creek, one of the Tahoe Basin's few alpine zones, and a sweeping vista from the top of the mountain. The 2,100-foot climb, most of which occurs on the second half of the route, will tax most hikers and should only be attempted by those in good physical condition.

44A ▪ The Waterfall

LEVEL	Hike, intermediate
LENGTH	4.6 miles, out and back
TIME	Half day
ELEVATION	+325′–225′; +225′–325′
DIFFICULTY	Moderate

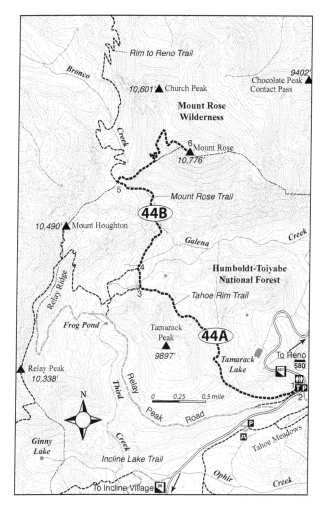

44. Mount Rose Trail

USERS Hikers, trail runners

DOGS On leash (first mile)

SEASON July to mid-October

BEST TIME Early to mid-July

FACILITIES Interpretive signs, vault toilets, (campground nearby)

MAP United States Geological Survey: *Mount Rose*; Humboldt-Toiyabe National Forest: *Mount Rose Wilderness*

MANAGEMENT USFS Humboldt-Toiyabe Forest, Carson Ranger District at 775-882-2766, www.fs.usda.gov/htnf

HIGHLIGHTS Forest, waterfall, wildflowers

LOWLIGHTS Popular trail

Galena Falls on the Mount Rose Trail

TIP | Plan your hike for a weekday or get an early start on weekends to beat the crowds.

KID TIP | As many parents can attest, the generally mildly graded trip to the waterfall and back makes a great family trip, as any relatively easy hike to a dramatic waterfall would.

TRAILHEAD | 39°18.744′N, 119°53.846′W From Reno, drive southbound on I-580 to the Mount Rose Highway Exit 56 and then head southwest on State Route 431 toward North Lake Tahoe. After 15 miles you reach the large parking lot for the Mount Rose trailhead on the right, near the high point of the highway (8,911 feet), which is the highest road summit open all year in the Sierra Nevada.

TRAIL | Find the start of the trail behind the restroom building [1] and very soon reach a junction [2], where mountain bikers are directed onto the lower trail leading a half mile to the Relay Peak Road. Hikers follow the upper trail on an ascending traverse across the hillside below Peak 9201, which is covered with sagebrush scrub and dotted with lodgepole and whitebark pines. Clumps of purple lupine and yellow mule's ears add splashes of color from early to midsummer, highlighting the view of Tahoe Meadows below and Lake Tahoe farther afield. The rising, half-mile-plus climb leads to a saddle between Peak 9201 and the southeast ridge of 9,897-foot Tamarack Peak.

Leaving the views behind, the trail begins a forested traverse, which now includes the drooping tips of mountain hemlocks, across the east slope of

Tamarack Peak. Farther on, intermittent breaks allow for brief glimpses of Tamarack Lake below, encircled by lush green meadows. The hiking is quite pleasant along this stretch of trail, gaining a slight bit of elevation along the way to the lip of the canyon above Galena Creek. At 1.5 miles, the trail bends west and begins a mild descent toward the creek, slicing across steep hillsides on the north side of Tamarack Peak along the way. Eventually, you'll hear the roar of the waterfall before arriving at its base, 2.3 miles from the parking lot. Just before the fall is a junction [3] where the Mount Rose Trail continues ahead and the Tahoe Rim Trail switchbacks up the slope directly left of the waterfall (a short but steep hike up the Tahoe Rim Trail offers a view of Galena Creek from the top of the waterfall). A side trail leads very shortly to the base and a view of the waterfall's silvery strand of water cascading across the dark volcanic rock. Bordering wildflowers enhance the lovely scenery through midsummer.

At the conclusion of your stay, retrace your steps 2.3 miles back to the trailhead.

MOUNTAIN MULE'S EARS (*Wyethia mollis*) Many open, dry slopes in the Carson Range are covered by a blanket of mule's ears in early summer. The abundance of this opportunistic wildflower, which thrives in disturbed areas, is attributed to overgrazing by sheep in the early 1900s. Mule's ears have long, oblong, whitish-green leaves and bright, 3-inch wide, golden yellow flowers. Both members of the sunflower family, mule's ears are often mistaken for arrowleaf balsamroot (*Balsamorhiza sagittata*). The easiest way to distinguish between the two plants is by the height of the flowers—mule's ears flowers and oblong leaves are similar in height, while the flowers of balsamroot rise well above the arrow-shaped leaves.

MILESTONES

1: Start at Mount Rose trailhead parking lot; **2:** Veer right at junction with side path to Relay Peak Road; **3:** Junction of Tahoe Rim Trail and Mount Rose Trail/Galena Creek Waterfall; **1:** Return to trailhead.

44B ▪ The Summit

LEVEL	Hike, advanced
LENGTH	9.8 miles, out and back
TIME	Full day
ELEVATION	+2,100′–325′
DIFFICULTY	Strenuous
USERS	Hikers, trail runners

DOGS	On leash (first mile)
SEASON	July to mid-October
BEST TIME	Mid-July
FACILITIES	Interpretive signs, vault toilets (campground nearby)
MAPS	Humboldt-Toiyabe National Forest: *Mount Rose Wilderness*; United States Geological Survey: *Mount Rose*
MANAGEMENT	USFS Humboldt-Toiyabe Forest, Carson Ranger District at 775-882-2766, www.fs.usda.gov/htnf
HIGHLIGHTS	Forest, stream, summit, views, waterfall, wildflowers
LOWLIGHTS	Popular. Summit can be quite windy at times.

TIPS | Plan your hike for a weekday or get an early start on weekends to beat the crowds. Pack plenty of layers, as the conditions can change radically between the trailhead and the usually windy summit.

KID TIPS | The climb of Mount Rose is usually a bit too much of a physical effort for most small children; many families go no farther than the much easier 2.3 miles to the waterfall as described in the previous trip. Older children attempting to go all the way to the top should be physically active and in good shape. Responsible adults should closely monitor their fluid intake and energy levels, particularly on the more rigorous second half of the ascent. Plenty of warm clothing should be stowed in packs, as conditions at the summit may be quite different than those at the trailhead. Any groups with children should get an early start in order to deal with any unexpected difficulties on the way and still have plenty of time to complete the trip before sunset.

TRAILHEAD | 39°18.744'N, 119°53.846'W From Reno, drive southbound on I-580 to the Mount Rose Highway Exit 56 and then head southwest on State Route 431 toward North Lake Tahoe. After 15 miles you reach the large parking lot for the Mount Rose trailhead on the right, near the high point of the highway (8,911 feet), which is the highest road summit open all year in the Sierra Nevada.

TRAIL | From the trailhead [1], hike to the junction [3] of the Tahoe Rim and Mount Rose Trails near the waterfall as described above.

Proceeding ahead at the junction, fairly easy hiking on the Mount Rose Trail continues past the crossing of the stream below the waterfall, where the path skirts a lush meadow bordering the creek. However, beyond the meadow the trail forsakes its gentle ways for the duration of the trip, climbing moderately, crossing a branch of Galena Creek, and then reaching a junction [4] with an old jeep road. Before the previous section of trail was constructed, this road was the route of the old Mount Rose Trail, connecting to the Relay Peak Road near Frog Pond (named for the prolific Pacific tree frogs) to the southwest. The inferior route of the old road, now used mainly by mountain bikers, bypassed the scenic waterfall and was a bit longer than the realigned trail.

Continue ahead from the junction, soon crossing a spring-fed branch of Galena Creek (which usually is the last reliable water). The midsummer floral display here is jaw dropping, including abundant amounts of angelica, corn lily, larkspur, lupine, and monkeyflower. Away from this verdant oasis, the trail makes a stiff rising traverse across dry, sagebrush-scrub slopes on the way into a steep side canyon, where the grade unmercifully increases. Except for early in the season, or after a particularly snowy winter, the seasonal streambed you cross twice in this narrow ravine will more than likely be dry. Arriving at the whitebark pine–dotted ridge above the ravine, the trail enters the signed Mount Rose Wilderness and reaches a junction [5] with the newly constructed Rim to Reno Trail, 3.6 miles from the trailhead.

Turn sharply northeast (right) and follow the pine-dotted ridge on a moderate climb toward the dark, looming hulk of Mount Rose's volcanic summit. Where the ridge melds into the upper mountain, five switchbacks lead farther upslope. Beyond the switchbacks, the trail breaks out of the stunted and diminishing whitebark pines on an angling climb headed toward a saddle between Mount Rose and Church Peak. Before heading out onto the exposed, windswept slopes of the upper mountain, take a moment to check the current conditions. If thunderheads are developing, turn around and make a hasty descent to more hospitable climes. In addition to the threat of lightning, high winds can make the temperature feel bitterly cold at the upper elevations—a hasty retreat is equally advisable if you're not equipped with the proper clothing to handle the windchill.

Continuing the climb, the trail enters one of the rare alpine zones spread about the very upper reaches of the Tahoe basin. Alpine plants face harsh conditions at these elevations, which include a short growing season, intense sunlight, strong winds, and cold nighttime temperatures. Plants suitably adapted to these stressors are compact and low-growing perennials with tiny leaves. Their flowers, which, unlike the host plant, only grow for a brief time, may oftentimes be quite large and showy in comparison. While scaling the upper slope of the mountain, look for alpine cryptantha, alpine gold, cut-leaved daisy, dwarf alpine daisy, showy polemonium, and spreading phlox.

Before reaching the saddle between Mount Rose and Church Peak, the trail switchbacks and then winds steeply up the rocky northwest summit ridge. Eventually, the top is gained [6], where a sweeping view unfolds. Over the years some of the thousands of trekkers who reach the summit each year have built a series of rock walls, attempting to thwart the persistent winds—count sunny and warm days with little or no wind as a blessing. Those wishing to record their achievement should locate the container with

Wildflowers and Mount Rose

the summit register in the highest of these rock-walled aeries. A map of the surrounding area will be very helpful in identifying myriad peaks, lakes, and other significant features visible from this lofty perch.

At the conclusion of your stay, retrace your steps 4.9 miles back to the trailhead [1].

LAKE TAHOE DRABA (*Draba asterophora*) A small but significant alpine zone occurs on a handful of the Lake Tahoe Basin's highest peaks, including Mount Rose. Within a subarea of this alpine zone is a rare flowering plant called Lake Tahoe Draba, which grows within the basin only on the upper slopes of Mount Rose, Monument Peak, and Freel Peak. This alpine plant has small, yellow flowers above a mat of dark-green leaves. Since 2009, the Forest Service has been monitoring the status of this rare plant. Stay on the trail at all times to avoid trampling this fragile plant.

MILESTONES

1: Start at Mount Rose trailhead parking lot; **2:** Turn right at junction with side path to Relay Peak Road; **3:** Go straight at Tahoe Rim Trail and Mount Rose junction; **4:** Turn right at jeep road junction (old Mount Rose Trail); **5:** Turn right at Rim to Reno junction; **6:** Summit of Mount Rose; **1:** Return to trailhead.

GO GREEN | Friends of Nevada Wilderness have been quite active within the Mount Rose Wilderness with such projects as eradicating non-native weeds and reseeding areas burned by forest fires. Check out their website at www.nevadawilderness.org.

OPTIONS | Most wanderers will find the trip to the top of Mount Rose to be a strenuous, full-day activity. The Sunrise Café (18603 Wedge Parkway) is a fine place to get revved up with a hearty breakfast before the hike. If you prefer to pick up a sandwich for lunch, Jimmy Johns in the same complex, or Port of Subs across the highway, can fill that bill. Also across the Mount Rose Highway (18144 Wedge Parkway) is Raley's, a full-service grocery store with deli and liquor department for those planning a picnic lunch.

Hardy adventurers may opt for a full-moon hike to the summit of Mount Rose. Another celestial event when Mount Rose offers a fine observation point is the Perseids meteor shower, the zenith usually occurring during the nights leading up to the middle of August. Those who choose either of these options should bring plenty of warm clothing and those who pack a sleeping bag will probably be glad they did.

Rim to Reno Trail

One of the newer additions to the trail network in the area, the Rim to Reno Trail connects the Tahoe Rim, Mount Rose, and Thomas Creek trails to form an 18- or 21-mile journey across a remote section of the Carson Range. Starting on the very popular route to Mount Rose, the trail forsakes the summit in favor of a descent into and out of the little-used Bronco Creek drainage, followed by an extended traverse across the even less visited west side of the Carson Range. After climbing to the crest, the final section drops into Thomas Creek canyon and heads downstream to a pair of trailheads.

This is a long hike by just about anyone's standards, requiring a full day to complete by hikers in top physical condition. Between Bronco and Thomas creeks, water is nonexistent, so plan accordingly. Backpackers can do the trip as an overnighter by establishing a camp near Bronco Creek. For those up to the task, fine, rarely seen views and plenty of midtrip solitude are the rewards.

LEVEL	Hike, advanced
LENGTH	18.0 miles (to upper trailhead); 20.8 miles (to lower trailhead), shuttle
TIME	Full day
ELEVATION	+2,250′–4,075′ (to upper trailhead); +2,250′–5,200′ (to lower trailhead)
DIFFICULTY	Very strenuous
USERS	Hikers, backpackers, trail runners, equestrians
DOGS	On leash (first mile)
SEASON	July to early October
BEST TIME	Mid-July to mid-August
FACILITIES	Interpretive signs, vault toilets (campground nearby)
MAPS	Humboldt-Toiyabe National Forest: *Mount Rose Wilderness*; United States Geological Survey: *Mount Rose, Mount Rose NW*
MANAGEMENT	USFS Humboldt-Toiyabe National Forest, Carson Ranger District at 775-882-2766, www.fs.usda.gov/htnf
HIGHLIGHTS	Forest, streams, views, waterfall, wildflowers
LOWLIGHTS	Distance

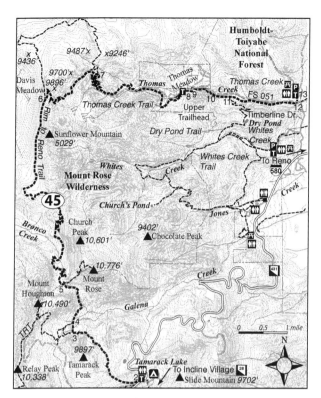

45. Rim to Reno Trail

TIP | Get an early start when doing this trip as a day hike and mentally prepare for a very long day.

KID TIP | The 18- to 21-mile-long distance makes this trip unsuitable for children.

TRAILHEAD START | 39°18.744′N, 119°53.846′W To reach the starting trailhead, drive southbound from Reno on I-580 to the Mount Rose Highway Exit 56 and then head southwest on State Route 431 toward North Lake Tahoe. After 15 miles you reach the large parking lot for the Mount Rose trailhead on the right, near the high point of the highway (8,911 feet), which is the highest road summit open all year in the Sierra Nevada.

END | There are two possible ending points for this hike. Without a high-clearance vehicle, you must park at the lower Thomas Creek trailhead just off Timberline Drive. With a high-clearance vehicle, you can shave off almost three miles by parking at the upper trailhead.

LOWER TRAILHEAD | 39°23.625′N, 119°50.292′W From Reno, drive southbound on I-580 to the Mount Rose Highway Exit 56 and then head southwest on State Route 431 toward Incline Village and Lake Tahoe. After 2 miles, turn right onto Timberline Drive and proceed 1 mile to Thomas Creek Road, crossing short bridges over Whites Creek and Thomas Creek on the way. Continue ahead another 0.1 mile to the left-hand entry into the Thomas Creek trailhead parking area.

UPPER TRAILHEAD | 39°23.661′N, 119°53.107′W *Note: A high-clearance vehicle will be necessary to reach the upper trailhead.* Follow the directions above to Thomas Creek Road. Rather than continue ahead to the lower trailhead parking area, turn left and follow Thomas Creek Road (FS 049) west for 2.2 miles to an intersection with a private, gated road on the right, which leads to several homes around Thomas Meadows. Veer left at the intersection and descend for 0.1 mile on a narrow jeep road to a crossing of Thomas Creek (may be difficult in early season). Continue past the creek crossing for another 0.3 mile to a small dirt parking area on the left just below a closed steel gate. The trail begins near the signboard at the edge of the parking area.

TRAIL | Find the start of the trail behind the restroom building [1] and very soon reach a junction [2], where mountain bikers are directed onto the lower trail leading a half mile to the Relay Peak Road. Hikers follow the upper trail on an ascending traverse across the hillside below Peak 9201, which is covered with sagebrush scrub and dotted with lodgepole and whitebark pines. Clumps of purple lupine and yellow mule's ears add splashes of color from early to midsummer, highlighting the view of Tahoe Meadows below and Lake Tahoe farther afield. The rising, half-mile-plus climb leads to a saddle between Peak 9201 and the southeast ridge of 9,897-foot Tamarack Peak.

Leaving the views behind, the trail enters the forest and follows a traverse across the east slope of Tamarack Peak, as the drooping tips of mountain hemlocks intermix with the more dominant lodgepole pines. Farther on, intermittent breaks in the conifers allow brief glimpses of Tamarack Lake encircled by lush green meadows below, and occasionally out to the southern Truckee Meadows. The hiking is quite pleasant along this stretch of trail, gaining a slight bit of elevation along the way to the canyon of Galena Creek. At 1.5 miles, the trail bends west and begins a mild descent toward the creek, slicing across steep hillsides on the north side of Tamarack Peak. Eventually, you'll hear the roar of the waterfall before arriving at the base, 2.3 miles from the parking lot. Just before the waterfall is a junction [3], where the Tahoe Rim Trail switchbacks up the slope directly to the left of this pretty cascade, while the Mount Rose Trail continues ahead (north). The silvery strand of water cascading across the dark volcanic rock makes a fine destination for many hikers setting out from the Mount Rose trailhead.

Fairly easy hiking on the Mount Rose Trail continues past the crossing of the stream below the waterfall, where the path skirts a lush meadow bordering the creek. However, beyond the meadow the trail forsakes its gentle ways for the duration of the trip, climbing moderately, crossing a branch of

Galena Creek, and then reaching a junction [4] with an old jeep road. Before the previous section of trail was constructed, this road was the route of the old Mount Rose Trail, connecting to the Relay Peak Road near Frog Pond (named for the prolific Pacific tree frogs) to the southwest. The inferior route of the old road, now used mainly by mountain bikers, bypassed the scenic waterfall and was a bit longer than the realigned trail.

Continue ahead from the junction, soon crossing a spring-fed branch of Galena Creek (which usually is the last reliable water). The midsummer floral display here is jaw dropping, including abundant amounts of angelica, corn lily, larkspur, lupine, and monkeyflower. Away from this verdant oasis, the trail makes a stiff rising traverse across dry, sagebrush-scrub slopes on the way into a steep side canyon, where the grade unmercifully increases. Except for early in the season, or after a particularly snowy winter, the seasonal streambed you cross twice in this narrow ravine will more than likely be dry. Arriving at the whitebark pine–dotted ridge above the ravine, the trail enters the signed Mount Rose Wilderness and reaches a junction [5] between the continuation of the Mount Rose Trail on the right and the newly constructed section of the Rim to Reno Trail straight ahead, 3.6 miles from the trailhead.

Drop off the ridge and descend into the drainage of Bronco Creek, passing through flower-sprinkled meadows and pockets of mixed forest. The trail winds across the nascent creek a couple of times, which may be dry at this elevation as the summer wanes. Continue the winding descent into light forest to where the grade mellows near a crossing of Bronco Creek [6], which should have a reliable flow throughout the hiking season—fill up your containers here as this is the last source of water until Thomas Creek.

Easier hiking leads shortly to a forested flat, where backpackers can spend the night, about the only place to camp close to a water supply for miles. Away from the flat, follow an arcing course around the east side of Bronco Creek canyon. The Rim to Reno Trail makes a prolonged ascent with the aid of some switchbacks beneath a band of rocky cliffs below Peak 9610. The long, steep climb leads to a bench with excellent views of the Bronco Creek drainage and the Carson Range peaks of Mount Houghton and Church Peak. Beyond the bench, fine vistas continue of the surrounding terrain along a curving, gentle traverse across the slopes of Peak 10083 on the way to a tree-covered outcrop that offers intermittent views.

Bending around the edge of the outcrop, you follow the trail as it turns north and makes a two-mile, gently graded journey through mixed forest, passing below Sunflower Mountain along the way. Easy hiking leads through the trees without much in the way of views during this stretch of trail. After a couple of miles, you reach a junction [7] with the North Loop of the Upper Thomas Creek Trail.

Veer to the right at the junction and make a moderate climb via switchbacks for a half mile to a 9,780-foot saddle [8] on the Carson Range crest. A short scramble along the ridge to either the north or south leads to excellent vistas of the surrounding terrain.

An older section of trail leads steeply downslope from the saddle and into the Thomas Creek drainage on short and steep switchbacks. The mile-long descent is a bit tedious on a poor trail but eventually leads to more agreeable hiking on a gently graded traverse across the slopes of the upper canyon. A mile of pleasant walking leads to the Thomas Creek Loop junction [9], 12.3 miles from the trailhead.

Follow the top of the north lip of Thomas Creek canyon for a while until the trail follows a series of long-legged switchbacks across open slopes down to the creek. Head downstream through aspens and water-loving shrubs for a while, followed by a stretch of trail through Jeffrey pine forest. Cross a usually vigorous tributary of Thomas Creek and follow the trail back toward the main branch, merging briefly with a section of the old Thomas Creek Road. After crossing the main creek, single-track trail makes a short climb through mixed forest of Jeffrey pines, white firs, and mountain mahoganies alternating with aspen stands. As the descent resumes, cross the track of an old road and proceed to where four switchbacks lead down to the upper Thomas Creek trailhead [10]. If you have a car parked here, or have arranged for pickup, your 18-mile journey is over.

To continue to the lower trailhead, head downstream for a short time to where the trail merges with the Thomas Creek Road and reaches a ford of the creek and a seasonal tributary at 0.3 mile from the upper trailhead. Follow the road downstream for about 150 yards to the resumption of single-track trail on the right. Farther down the canyon, the narrow walls force the trail to merge with the road for a short stretch once again. Back on the trail, you follow the stream down to a junction [11] with the Dry Pond Trail.

Go straight at the junction and walk through the forest for about a mile to a footbridge across the creek. Proceed through a dirt parking area, cross Thomas Creek Road [12], and then follow a short section of single-track trail to the lower Thomas Creek trailhead [13].

YELLOW-BELLIED MARMOT (*Marmota flaviventris*) The rock slopes within the Carson Range create a fine habitat for this member of the squirrel family. These 4- to 11-pound rodents dig their burrows underneath rocky slopes to avoid predators, which include coyotes and golden eagles in western Nevada. Marmots spend a large percentage of time in their burrows, hibernating during winter and escaping the midday heat of summer. The best opportunities to observe them are typically while sunning themselves in the morning or foraging in late afternoon. However, the chances of hearing their characteristic whistle of alarm are probably greater than actually seeing one of these usually chubby-looking rodents up close.

MILESTONES

1: Start at Mount Rose trailhead parking lot; **2:** Turn right at junction with side path to Relay Peak Road; **3:** Go straight at Tahoe Rim Trail and Mount Rose junction; **4:** Turn right at jeep road junction (old Mount Rose Trail); **5:** Turn right at Rim to Reno junction; **6:** Bronco Creek; **7:** Turn right at junction with North Loop of Upper Thomas Creek Trail; **8:** Carson Range Saddle; **9:** Turn right at Thomas Creek Loop junction; **10:** Upper Thomas Creek trailhead; **11:** Go straight at Dry Pond Trail junction; **12:** Cross Thomas Creek Road; **13:** End at Lower Thomas Creek trailhead.

GO GREEN | Friends of Nevada Wilderness have been quite active within the Mount Rose Wilderness with such projects as eradicating non-native weeds and reseeding areas burned by forest fires. Check out their website at www .nevadawilderness.org.

OPTIONS | For an even greater challenge, the direction of the trip can be reversed by starting at Thomas Creek and ending at the Mount Rose trailhead.

Tahoe Rim Trail: Mount Rose Trailhead to Relay Peak and Mount Houghton

A newer section of the Tahoe Rim Trail provides a much nicer approach to Relay Peak than hiking on the old service road around Tamarack Peak that climbs steeply up to the communication-littered top of Relay Ridge. The initial segment of the new route follows the same course as Trip 45 to the waterfall on Galena Creek, but then veers away from the highly popular Mount Rose Trail on a stiff climb on a section of the Tahoe Rim Trail to the back side of Relay Ridge and then up to the 10,338-foot summit of Relay Peak (highest point along the entire Tahoe Rim Trail). Successful summiteers will enjoy a sweeping view of the northern Sierra, as well as on clear days a glimpse of the Cascade Range volcano of Lassen Peak. Avoiding the redundancy of a simple out-and-back trip, you can loop back to the trailhead via the Relay Peak Road (see Options below).

Completed in 2014 by volunteers of the Tahoe Rim Trail Association, a 0.7-mile side path from the Tahoe Rim Trail provides summiteers with an additional option for peak bagging in the Mount Rose area. Sharing the trail to Relay Peak for most of the distance, the route ultimately veers away from the Tahoe Rim Trail on a short, winding ascent up the south ridge to the summit of Mount Houghton. Similar to its associates, Relay Peak and Mount Rose, the top of Mount Houghton offers supreme views of the Tahoe Sierra and more distant points of interest.

LEVEL Hike, advanced
LENGTH 12.0 miles, out and back to Relay Peak, plus 1.4-mile side trip to Mount Houghton
TIME Full day
ELEVATION +2,000′–750′
DIFFICULTY Strenuous
USERS Hikers, trail runners
DOGS On leash (first mile)
SEASON July to mid-October
BEST TIME Mid- to late July
FACILITIES Interpretive signs, vault toilets (campground nearby)
MAP United States Forest Service: *Mount Rose Wilderness*; United States Geological Survey: *Mount Rose*

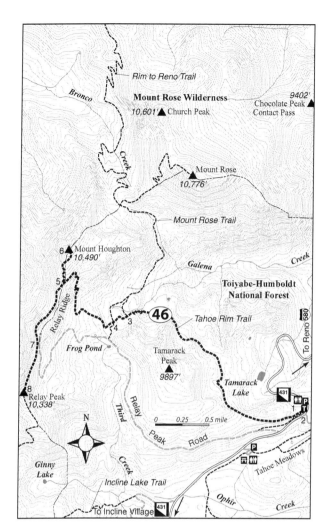

46. Tahoe Rim Trail: Mount Rose Trailhead to Mount Houghton and Relay Peak

MANAGEMENT USFS Humboldt-Toiyabe National Forest, Carson Ranger
District at 775-882-2766, www.fs.usda.gov/htnf

HIGHLIGHTS Forest, summit, stream, views, waterfall, wildflowers

LOWLIGHTS Popular trail to waterfall; summit can be quite windy.

TIP | Plan your hike for a weekday or get an early start on weekends to beat
the crowds. Pack plenty of layers, as the conditions can change radically
between the trailhead and the oftentimes-windy summit. Although you'll
undoubtedly see lots of people on the way to the waterfall on Galena Creek,
the section of the Tahoe Rim Trail beyond there to Relay Peak sees far fewer
visitors.

KID TIP | The climbs of Relay Peak and Mount Houghton are usually a bit too much of a physical effort for most small children; many families go no farther than the much easier 2.3 miles to the waterfall as described in Trip 45. Older children attempting to go all the way to the top should be physically active and in good shape. Responsible adults should closely monitor their fluid intake and energy levels, particularly on the more rigorous second half of the ascent. Plenty of warm clothing should be stowed in packs, as conditions at the summit may be quite different than those at the trailhead. Any groups with children should get an early start in order to deal with any unexpected difficulties on the way and still have plenty of time to complete the trip before sunset.

TRAILHEAD | 39°18.744′N, 119°53.846′W From Reno, drive southbound on I-580 to the Mount Rose Highway Exit 56 and then head southwest on State Route 431 toward North Lake Tahoe. After 15 miles you reach the large parking lot for the Mount Rose trailhead on the right, near the high point of the highway (8,911 feet), which is the highest road summit open all year in the Sierra Nevada.

TRAIL | Find the start of the trail behind the restroom building [1] and very soon reach a junction [2], where mountain bikers are directed onto the lower trail leading a half mile to the Relay Peak Road. Hikers follow the upper trail on an ascending traverse across the hillside below Peak 9201, which is covered with sagebrush scrub and dotted with lodgepole and whitebark pines. Clumps of purple lupine and yellow mule's ears add splashes of color from early to midsummer, highlighting the view of Tahoe Meadows below and Lake Tahoe farther afield. The rising, half-mile-plus climb leads to a saddle between Peak 9201 and the southeast ridge of 9,897-foot Tamarack Peak.

Leaving the views behind, the trail begins a forested traverse, which now includes the drooping tips of mountain hemlocks, across the east slope of Tamarack Peak. Farther on, intermittent breaks allow for brief glimpses of Tamarack Lake below, encircled by lush green meadows. The hiking is quite pleasant along this stretch of trail, gaining a slight bit of elevation along the way to the canyon of Galena Creek. At 1.5 miles, the trail bends west and begins a mild descent toward the creek, slicing across steep hillsides on the north side of Tamarack Peak along the way. Eventually, you'll hear the roar of the waterfall before arriving at its base, 2.3 miles from the parking lot. Just before the waterfall is a junction [3] between the Tahoe Rim Trail and Mount Rose Trail.

Turn left and follow the Tahoe Rim Trail on a switchbacking climb to the top of the waterfall, from where you enjoy a nice view not only of the waterfall but of the upper Galena Creek drainage and the dark hulk of Mount Rose as well. Away from the top of the waterfall, the trail continues to wind up the slope through scattered forest to the crossing of an old jeep road [4], a half

Equestrians on the Tahoe Rim Trail

mile from the junction (this road once served as the route of the Mount Rose Trail before the newer section to the waterfall was constructed).

Cross the road and continue the ascent through scattered-to-light lodgepole pine forest above sparse groundcover. You pass beneath a utility line and continue upslope on a winding climb toward Relay Ridge. Higher up the hillside, whitebark pines begin to replace the lodgepoles as the dominant conifer, diminishing in stature as you near the top. After gaining the ridge, the trail enters the Mount Rose Wilderness and encounters a junction [5] with the side path to the summit of Mount Houghton.

SIDE TRIP TO MOUNT HOUGHTON | Turn right (north) and climb moderately along the south ridge of Mount Houghton. A number of switchbacks lead you along the east and west sides and occasionally right on top of the ridge through dwarf whitebark pines. A final set of three short-legged switchbacks gets you to the top [6] and a superb view, including the peaks of the Sierra crest and much of the Carson Range, with Lake Tahoe as the lovely centerpiece. Clear days allow views to the northwest of Sierra Buttes and the oftentimes snow-covered slopes of Lassen Peak beyond. Closer at hand is the Truckee area, surrounded by Donner Lake and Stampede, Boca, and Prosser reservoirs. After thoroughly enjoying the view, retrace your steps back to the Tahoe Rim Trail junction [5].

Veer right at the junction, cross to the west side, and begin a rising traverse below Relay Ridge and the preponderance of communication equipment littering the top. Beyond the electronic debris, the Tahoe Rim Trail reaches the apex of the ridge and a junction [7] with a very short path connecting to the Relay Peak Road. From there, continue ahead on single-track trail and follow the moderately steep spine of Relay Peak's north ridge to the 10,338-foot summit [8].

The view from the highest point on the Tahoe Rim Trail circuit is expansive, including the peaks of the Sierra crest and much of the Carson Range. Other notable summits include the dark ramparts of Sierra Buttes to the northwest, and snow-covered Lassen Peak farther afield, the southernmost significant volcanic peak in the Cascade Range. Nearer at hand are Donner Lake and Stampede, Boca, and Prosser reservoirs.

After thoroughly enjoying the view, you can retrace your steps back to the Mount Rose trailhead [1], or return via the alternate route described below in Options.

WHITEBARK PINE (*Pinus albicaulis*) and **CLARK'S NUTCRACKER** (*Nucifraga columbiana*) This five-needled member of the pine family is found in the high, subalpine elevations of the Carson Range. On exposed ridge tops, like Relay Ridge, trees may be dwarfed and multitrunked, sometimes forming shrubby mats called *krummholz*. When present, distinctive purplish cones easily identify the tree, but they tend to crumble on the branches, if not eaten by Clark's nutcrackers, pale, gray birds with black wings similar in size to jays but with a shape more like crows. They are birds of the high mountains, and the purple cones of whitebark pines are a staple of their diet. Spike-like bills allow them to pick seeds out of the cones, some of which are consumed immediately and others stored in the ground for later use. Unused seeds replenish the whitebark pine forest. Dubbed "camp robbers" by backpackers, Clark's nutcrackers can sometimes be quite aggressive in their attempts to steal food at campsites.

MILESTONES

1: Start at Mount Rose trailhead; **2:** Go straight at junction with side path to Relay Peak Road; **3:** Turn left at Tahoe Rim Trail and Mount Rose junction; **4:** Go straight at jeep road junction (old Mount Rose Trail); **5:** Turn right at Mount Houghton and Tahoe Rim Trail junction; **6:** Top of Mount Houghton; **5:** Turn right at Mount Houghton and Tahoe Rim Trail junction; **7:** Go straight at junction with side path to Relay Peak Road; **8:** Summit of Relay Peak; **1:** Return to trailhead.

GO GREEN | Friends of Nevada Wilderness have been quite active within the Mount Rose Wilderness with such projects as eradicating non-native weeds and reseeding areas burned by forest fires. Check out their website at www.nevadawilderness.org.

OPTIONS | To avoid simply backtracking via the same route to the trailhead, you can shorten the return by a mile by following the Relay Peak Road. Simply return to junction 7 on Relay Ridge and then follow the road downslope to the head of the Third Creek drainage. Continue on the road, arcing around the west and south slopes of Tamarack Peak. Before reaching the Mount Rose Highway, reach a signed junction on the left with single-track trail leading a half mile back to the trailhead parking area [1].

47 | Incline Lake Trail to Gray Lake

Since 2008, the previously private Incline Lake property has been available to the public, with a trail providing a short but steep climb into a portion of the Mount Rose Wilderness, a connection to the Tahoe Rim Trail, and from there a straightforward route to tiny and shallow Gray Lake. Although steep at times, the climb is mostly shaded by pleasant forest, with fine views of Lake Tahoe and the surrounding terrain at the top. Gray Lake is a serene pond in the heart of the Mount Rose Wilderness, which, despite its proximity to the Tahoe Rim Trail, doesn't receive as many visitors as the picturesque setting warrants. Midsummer wildflowers around the lake's inlet and along a tributary of Third Creek are fine complements to the lovely scenery.

LEVEL	Hike, advanced
LENGTH	8.0 miles, lollipop loop
TIME	Three-quarter day
ELEVATION	+2,050′−2,050′
DIFFICULTY	Moderate to strenuous
USERS	Hikers, trail runners
DOGS	OK
SEASON	July to mid-October
BEST TIME	Mid-July
FACILITIES	None
MAP	Humboldt-Toiyabe National Forest: *Mount Rose Wilderness*; United States Geological Survey: *Mount Rose*
MANAGEMENT	USFS Lake Tahoe Basin Management Unit at 530-543-2600, www.fs.usda.gov/ltbmu
HIGHLIGHTS	Forest, lake, views, wildflowers
LOWLIGHTS	Trail is not signed or maintained.

TIP ⏐ This trail has been in existence since the Incline Lake property was in private hands. Now transferred to the Forest Service, the trail is unmaintained (although the trail is generally in good shape) and not signed at either the trailhead, or at the junctions with the access road and the Tahoe Rim Trail. You must have the skills to read a map and find your own way on the lower section.

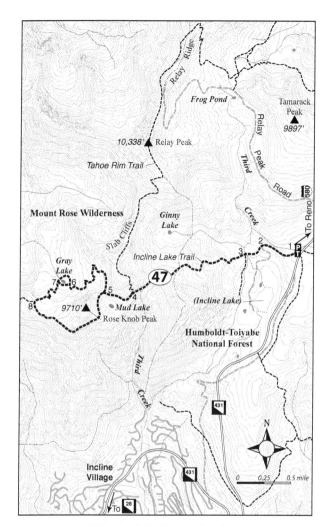

47. Incline Lake Trail to Gray Lake

KID TIP ǀ The stiff climb will be unappealing to most youngsters. Walking the road to the site of the old lake is probably a better alternative.

TRAILHEAD ǀ 39°18.040′N, 119°55.252′W From Reno, drive southbound on I-580 to the Mount Rose Highway Exit 56 and then head southwest on State Route 431 toward North Lake Tahoe. After 15 miles you pass the large parking lot for the Mount Rose trailhead on the right, near the high point of the highway (8,911 feet), which is the highest road summit open all year in the Sierra Nevada. Continue toward Incline Village to the far end of Tahoe Meadows on the left, reaching Incline Lake Road on the right, 1.5 miles from the highway summit. Park your vehicle off the highway and along the edge of the road, being careful not to block the closed gate nearby.

TRAIL | From the parking area [1], walk around the closed steel gate and proceed along the dirt surface of Incline Lake Road on a moderate descent through lodgepole pine forest. Ignore a side trail on the left about 0.15 mile from the gate and continue to follow the main road. In areas of ample groundwater, aspen stands and lush vegetation, including a smattering of colorful wildflowers in early season, line the road farther away from the trailhead. About 0.4 mile from the gate, the road makes a horseshoe bend. Near the far end of this bend, your unmarked, single-track trail [2] on the right veers southwest and drops toward a crossing of Third Creek. This junction is easily missed by first-timers—look for the path between two twin-trunked pines with red reflectors nailed to their trunks. If you come to a "15 MPH" sign, you've gone too far.

A short descent leads to the gurgling creek, which is bordered by a verdant display of foliage. When necessary, a pair of wood planks provides a straightforward way across the creek; later in the season when the water is low, the crossing is an easy boulder hop. On the far side of the stream is another unmarked junction [3], where the left-hand trail heads toward the vicinity of the former Incline Lake.

Veer right and begin a stiff and unrelenting 1.25-mile, sometimes-winding climb, initially under the welcome shade of thick forest. Western white pines, white firs, and mountain hemlocks eventually replace the lodgepole pines of below. Farther up the slope, the trail crosses a seasonal tributary and continues climbing into a more open forest on the way to the signed Mount Rose Wilderness boundary at 1.6 miles. Shortly past this landmark, the grade eases and you break out of the trees to a remarkable ridgetop view of shimmering Lake Tahoe and a portion of the Carson Range crest, including Rose Knob Peak, Slab Cliffs, Relay Peak, Mount Houghton, Mount Rose, and Slide Mountain. In addition, some interesting-looking rock cliffs lie directly ahead. The views are a fitting reward following the stiff ascent, as the trail makes a more enjoyable descent to a junction [4] with the Tahoe Rim Trail, 2 miles from the trailhead. A reliable spring is just below the trail junction.

Turn left and follow a rising path leading southwest across open, view-packed slopes covered by swaths of yellow mule's ears and other attractive wildflowers during the early days of summer. Soon the trail arcs around the basin, above aptly named Mud Lake. With no permanent inlet or outlet, this "lake" alternates in appearance between a pleasant-looking pond when full of water to a veritable mud hole by summer's end. At 2.5 miles you reach a saddle northeast of Rose Knob Peak and meet the east junction [5] of the trail to Gray Lake, marked by a 4 × 4 post.

Turning right (north), you leave the Tahoe Rim Trail and drop away from the saddle to follow a moderate descent back into the forest. Beyond a switchback the trail winds downslope and eventually breaks out of the trees to a fine view of the steep and rocky, avalanche-prone north face of Rose Knob Peak. A short way farther, shin-deep Gray Lake pops into view, surrounded by the grasses of the encroaching meadow. Soon you reach the junction [6] with the short loop trail around the lake, 3.4 miles from the trailhead.

Turn right and follow a counterclockwise circuit around diminutive Gray Lake, immediately encountering the picturesque inlet coursing through wildflower-dotted meadowlands on the way into the lake, the rugged face of Rose Knob Peak providing a marvelously scenic backdrop as pretty as any subalpine setting in the Tahoe Basin. Built-up sections of trail constructed in 2011 help to minimize the potential environmental degradation to the fragile surroundings. Away from the inlet, the trail moves through lodgepole pine forest and arcs around toward the outlet. In former days, the Gray Lake Trail continued downstream above the east bank of the creek, but nowadays the seldom-used path has all but disappeared. Near the outlet are a few campsites, used occasionally by Tahoe Rim Trail through-hikers who don't mind the detour. Shortly beyond the inlet, is the three-way junction [7] with the trail climbing to the west Gray Lake junction with the Tahoe Rim Trail. (If you're interested in the shortest way back to the car, simply veer left, walk the short distance to the end of the loop around the lake, and then retrace your steps to the trailhead.)

INCLINE LAKE Back in the day, the 777 acres of land around the reservoir of Incline Lake was the private playground of some of Nevada's more prominent citizens. Sold to the Forest Service in 2008 for 43.5 million dollars, the property included the lake's dam and several buildings, including an observatory. The original plan was for Washoe County to assume control of the buildings and the Forest Service would oversee the land. Ultimately, the buildings were razed and the lake was drained due to concerns of the dam's safety during a potential earthquake. In 2014, the Forest Service decided not to repair or rebuild the dam, despite a five-million-dollar fund set aside for such purposes as part of the original purchase. Removing the dam and spillway would allow the return of the natural wetlands. The Nevada Division of Wildlife would like to see the lake restored and used as a recreational fishery for the threatened Lahontan cutthroat trout and has asked the Forest Service to reconsider their decision.

To do the full circuit around Rose Knob Peak as recommended, follow the right-hand trail from the junction and make the steady climb back toward the Tahoe Rim Trail, winding through forest for 0.6 mile to the west Gray Lake junction [8] marked by a 4×4 post. Once again, you have supreme views of the Lake Tahoe basin graced by wildflower-covered slopes in early summer. Mildly rising trail leads around the south side of Rose Knob Peak before a down-and-up stretch of trail leads back to the east junction [5] in the saddle above Mud Lake at 6.0 miles. From there, retrace your steps 2.0 miles to the trailhead [1].

MILESTONES

1: Start at Incline Lake Trailhead; 2: Turn right at road and trail junction; 3: Turn right at junction to Incline Lake; 4: Turn left at Tahoe Rim Trail junction; 5: Turn right at east Tahoe Rim Trail and Gray Lake junction; 6: Turn right at east Gray Lake loop junction; 7: Turn right at west Gray Lake loop junction; 8: Turn left at west Tahoe Rim Trail and Gray Lake junction; 5: Turn right at east Tahoe Rim Trail and Gray Lake junction; 4: Turn right at Tahoe Rim Trail junction; 1: Return to Trailhead.

GO GREEN | Until the process is fully completed, comments regarding Incline Lake's status should be made to the Lake Tahoe Basin Management Unit, or the Nevada Department of Wildlife.

OPTIONS | With a few campsites spread around the shore near the outlet, Gray Lake would be a fine destination for an overnight backpacking trip.

Slide Mountain Trail

Slide Mountain (9,702 feet) is aptly named, as landslides seem to occur here with some regularity. Mark Twain wrote about one such slide in *Roughing It* and the last big event in our era occurred on Memorial Day weekend of 1983, when moisture-saturated soils slid into lower Price Lake, propelling a muddy torrent of sludge roaring down Ophir Creek canyon and across US 395 in a matter of seconds. One person was killed, seven homes were destroyed, the highway was closed for days, and lower Price Lake vanished. The scars left behind on the flanks of the peak are easy to see when gazing up at the peak from the valley below. This short trail leaves the ski area parking lot and scales a hill packed with beautiful views of the valley below, the Virginia Range beyond, and Mount Rose and Slide Mountain.

LEVEL	Walk, novice
LENGTH	Three-quarter mile, semi-loop
TIME	1 to 2 hours
ELEVATION	+150′–150′
DIFFICULTY	Easy to moderate
USERS	Hikers
DOGS	On leash
SEASON	Mid-June to mid-October
BEST TIME	Late June to early September
FACILITIES	Interpretive signs, picnic tables
MAP	Humboldt-Toiyabe National Forest: *Mount Rose Wilderness*; United States Geological Survey: *Washoe City*
MANAGEMENT	Washoe County Regional Parks and Open Space at 775-328-3600, www.washoecounty.us/parks
HIGHLIGHTS	Interpretive signs, views
LOWLIGHTS	None

TIP | An early arrival has a couple of benefits. First, for the really early birds, the unobstructed view of the sunrise over the Virginia Range can be quite enjoyable. A little later in the morning, when the air remains still, you may be able to see hang gliders launching from nearby and then riding the thermals above Washoe Valley.

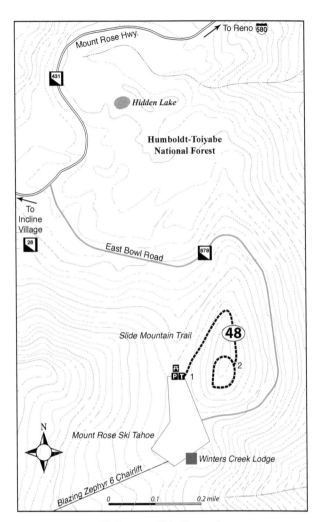

48. Reno to Slide Mountain

KID TIP | Kids will love this trip if the hang gliders are going, otherwise there's not much to stimulate youngsters beyond just the view. However, the distance is short and you might be able to entice them with a picnic lunch after the hike.

TRAILHEAD | 39°19.251′N, 119°52.238′W From Reno, drive southbound on I-580 to the Mount Rose Highway Exit 56 and then head southwest on State Route 431 toward North Lake Tahoe. After 12.5 miles, turn left (south) onto East Bowl Road (SR 878) and proceed to the large parking area for Mount Rose Ski Tahoe. The trail begins at the northeast corner of the parking area.

Mount Rose from the Slide Mountain Trail

TRAIL | From the signed trailhead [1], follow the Slide Mountain Trail on a moderate climb that slices across a hillside sprinkled with a light forest of white firs, western white pines, Jeffrey pines, and mountain mahoganies. Gaining the north ridge of Peak 8448, the trail bends sharply south and continues climbing. On the east side of the peak, over stands of short mountain mahogany trees are fine views of the Truckee Meadows, Washoe Valley, and the Virginia Range. Reach the loop junction [2] just beyond an interpretive sign.

Proceed straight ahead at the junction and wrap around the south and west sides of the peak, passing more interpretive signs and a park bench, placed to take advantage of the fine views of Slide Mountain and the ski runs of Mount Rose Ski Tahoe. Shortly beyond the bench you reach the close of the loop [2]. From there, retrace your steps back to the trailhead [1].

MOUNTAIN BLUEBIRD (*Sialia currucoides*) The state bird of Nevada, the mountain bluebird is found in the higher elevations during summer. The males are beautifully colored, sky-blue birds and rather small at 6 inches long and weighing just an ounce, but they are a stunning sight perched in a whitebark pine tree or in flight. A member of the thrush family, they hunt insects, are monogamous, and nest in cavities.

MILESTONES

1: Start at Slide Mountain trailhead; 2: Go straight at loop junction; 2: Turn left at loop junction; 1: Return to trailhead.

GO GREEN | Although the Slide Mountain Trail is not a park per se, Washoe County Regional Parks and Open Space has an Adopt-A-Park program, where volunteers can donate their time for working in the parks to keep them clean, attractive, and safe. The program is open to individuals and groups. For more information, visit their website at www.washoecounty.us/parks/volunteer_opportunities.php, or contact the Parks Volunteer Coordinator at 775-785-4512, ext. 107.

OPTIONS | The Starbuck's at 18520 Wedge Parkway opens at 5:00 AM if you need a shot of caffeine on the way up the Mount Rose Highway to the trailhead, particularly if you're leaving early to watch the hang gliders. Picnic tables at the trailhead provide a fine spot for a picnic lunch, the ingredients for which could be obtained at Raley's (18144 Wedge Parkway) on the way up the Mount Rose Highway. The full-service grocery store has a deli, bakery, pharmacy, and liquor department.

TRIP
49 | Tahoe Meadows

Tahoe Meadows is one of the larger subalpine meadows in the Sierra. During early to midsummer, the verdant meadows are peppered with an explosion of color from a wide variety of wildflowers. Species you're likely to see include alpine shooting star, buttercup, elephant head, marsh marigold, meadow penstemon, paintbrush, and large-leaved aven. Typically, from late June through July, you could show up weekly to see the progression of wildflowers as the varieties wax and wane through the season. Surrounded by tall peaks and ridges, the mountain scenery around the meadows is superb. The trails in the area are available to just about everyone, as the older Tahoe Meadows Nature Trail is handicap accessible and the newer three loops are pleasantly graded. Interpretive signs along the way offer interesting tidbits about the natural and human history of the area.

49A ▪ Nature Trail

LEVEL	Stroll, novice
LENGTH	1.3 miles, loop
TIME	1 hour
ELEVATION	Minimal
DIFFICULTY	Easy
USERS	Hikers; ADA accessible
DOGS	On leash
SEASON	Mid-June to mid-October
BEST TIME	Late June through July
FACILITIES	Interpretive signs, picnic tables, vault toilets
MAP	Humboldt-Toiyabe National Forest: *Mount Rose Wilderness*; United States Geological Survey: *Mount Rose*
MANAGEMENT	USFS Humboldt-Toiyabe National Forest, Carson Ranger District at 775-882-2766, www.fs.usda.gov/htnf
HIGHLIGHTS	Forest, interpretive signs, meadow, stream, wildflowers
LOWLIGHTS	Sections of trail can be muddy in early season.

TIP | Visiting just after dawn or just before sundown increases your chances of seeing wildlife in or around the meadows.

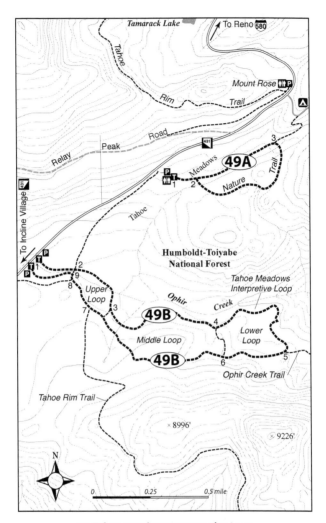

49. Tahoe Meadows Interpretive Loop

KID TIP | This short loop is a great place to bring kids to experience a subalpine meadow, with plenty of trickling rivulets, numerous wildflowers, and a stretch of forest.

TRAILHEAD | 39°18.434′N, 119°54.442′W From Reno, drive southbound on I-580 to the Mount Rose Highway Exit 56 and then head southwest on State Route 431 toward North Lake Tahoe. After 15 miles you pass the large parking lot for the Mount Rose trailhead on the right, near the high point of the highway (8,911 feet), which is the highest road summit open all year in the Sierra Nevada. Continue another 0.7 mile and turn left into the Tahoe Meadows parking area.

TRAIL | From the trailhead [1], head away from the tall trees of the parking area on a wide, well-graded, and stone-lined path into the open meadows, soon reaching a junction [2] with the beginning of a loop circling around the fringe of an upper finger of Tahoe Meadows. Turn right to follow a counter-clockwise circuit, crossing a low wooden bridge above a boggy piece of meadow to the far side, where the path turns east and travels along the fringe through stands of lodgepole pines. Approaching the far end of the meadow, the trail bends to the north and crosses a series of short wooden bridges over damp strips of lush vegetation bisected by tiny seasonal rivulets. At the far side of the loop, you reach a short side path on the left leading to a low overlook on a granite hummock, which, when the trail was originally built, offered a fine view across the rambling meadow. With the advance of time, conifers have matured and blocked most of the view. Just past the side path, is a three-way junction [3] with the Tahoe Rim Trail.

Turn left and follow a section of the old Mount Rose Road southeast toward the parking area, passing to the left of and below the modern Mount Rose Highway, enjoying the fine scenery of the meadows bordered by pine-dotted, granite knolls. Reach the loop junction [2] and continue ahead, retracing your steps to the parking area [1].

MILESTONES

1: Start at Tahoe Meadows trailhead; **2:** Turn right at loop junction; **3:** Turn left at Tahoe Rim Trail junction; **2:** Go straight at loop junction; **1:** Return to trailhead.

GO GREEN | You can assist the Humboldt-Toiyabe National Forest by volunteering for short-term or seasonal projects. Visit the volunteer page at www .fs.usda.gov/main/r4/jobs/volunteer.

OPTIONS | Recent improvements at the nearby Mount Rose Campground have improved the visitor experience. Campsites were $22 per night (2016) and may be reserved through www.recreation.gov. The open season usually runs from late June to mid-September. You can easily connect to the Tahoe Meadows Nature Trail by walking on a section of the Tahoe Rim Trail from the campground access road southwest to the Nature Trail junction.

49B ▪ Loop Trails

LEVEL Walk (Upper Loop and Middle Loops), novice; hike, novice (Lower Loop)

LENGTH 0.5 miles, loop (Upper Loop); 2.3 miles, loop (Middle Loop); 3.3 miles, loop (Lower Loop)

TIME ½ hour (Upper Loop); 1 hour (Middle Loop); 1 to 2 hours (Lower Loop)

ELEVATION	Minimal (Upper Loop); +175′–175′ (Middle Loop); +300′–300′ (Lower Loop)
DIFFICULTY	Easy
USERS	Hikers
DOGS	On leash
SEASON	Mid-June to mid-October
BEST TIME	Late June through July
FACILITIES	Interpretive signs, picnic tables, vault toilets
MAP	Humboldt-Toiyabe National Forest: *Mount Rose Wilderness*; United States Geological Survey: *Mount Rose*
MANAGEMENT	USFS Humboldt-Toiyabe Forest, Carson Ranger District at 775-882-2766, www.fs.usda.gov/htnf
HIGHLIGHTS	Forest, meadow, interpretive signs, stream, wildflowers
LOWLIGHTS	None

TIP | Although subject to the year-to-year fluctuations of Sierra weather, wildflower season usually starts to peak in late June with the arrival of buttercups and progresses with a profusion of other flowers through July.

KID TIP | Between gurgling Ophir Creek and explosion of color in Tahoe Meadows, youngsters should receive plenty of stimulation from the natural world on any one of these three loops, which allows parents to tailor the length of the hike to suit the level and interest of their children.

TRAILHEAD | 39°18.136′N, 119°55.095′W From the turnoff into the upper trailhead, continue on State Route 431 toward Incline Village another 0.6 mile and park on the shoulder as space allows. The trail begins on the east side of the highway (no facilities).

TRAIL | A set of stairs lead [1] away from the highway and down to a dirt path slicing across the lush meadowlands of Tahoe Meadows to a boardwalk alongside meandering Ophir Creek. Soon come to a junction and proceed straight ahead on the boardwalk, quickly reaching a park bench on a wide platform above the stream. The boardwalk matches the serpentine course of the creek on the way to a four-way junction [2] with the Tahoe Rim Trail marked by a sign and map, 0.2 mile from the trailhead.

Continue ahead on the boardwalk following the course of gurgling Ophir Creek. Bending to the right, the boardwalk section ends just beyond where you cross the creek near an interpretive sign. Immediately past the end of the boardwalk, you reach the Upper Loop junction [3], 0.4 mile from the trailhead.

For the shortest loop option, you should turn right and head back toward the highway. Otherwise, veer left at the junction along the shared course of the Middle Loop and Lower Loop trails. Away from the boardwalk protected section, dirt trail moves just above the meadows to travel among

A family enjoys the Tahoe Meadows Interpretive Loop Trail.

scattered lodgepole pines. After a short boardwalk over a sensitive area of vegetation and the crossing of a seasonal rivulet, come to the north Middle Loop junction [4] at 1.0 mile.

For the Middle Loop option, turn right and make the short connection to the Ophir Creek Trail and follow it back toward the highway, as described below. Otherwise, proceed straight ahead and walk above the narrowing finger of Tahoe Meadows approaching the head of V-shaped Ophir Creek canyon. Along the way, you'll notice the increasing rate of descent and the thickening of the forest. As the stream drops even more steeply through the canyon, you come to the low point of the circuit. Here the trail veers south and starts climbing back toward the trailhead. Brief breaks in the forest permit views of Slide Mountain rising above Ophir Creek canyon. Hop over a tributary and reach the Ophir Creek Trail junction [5], 1.7 miles from the trailhead.

Turn right (west) at the junction and follow the wide track of an old road through a mixed forest of Jeffrey pines, mountain hemlocks, western white pines, and white firs. At the 2-mile mark, you come to the south Middle Loop junction [6].

The Ophir Creek Trail continues climbing on a generally westward course. After a bit the ascent ends, giving way to a descent through mostly lodgepole pine forest. Where the grade eases, you encounter the Ophir Creek Trail signboard and reach a Y-junction [7] with the Tahoe Rim Trail angling southeast behind you.

On the shared route of the Tahoe Rim Trail and Ophir Creek trails, continue ahead, soon emerging from the trees to walk along the fringe of Tahoe Meadows. Reach the next junction [8], with a path providing mountain bikers with direct access to the Mount Rose Highway. Follow the right-hand trail and wander around toward the bridge over Ophir Creek and the boardwalk just beyond. Just before the bridge is a junction [9], where you turn left and proceed on single-track trail toward the highway. Just before the road is a short bridge across Ophir Creek. From there, climb the stairs up to the shoulder of the Mount Rose Highway [1].

> **WATER PLANTAIN BUTTERCUP** (*Ranunculus alismifolius*) Perennials, these beautiful yellow flowers with shiny petals usually bloom in Tahoe Meadows around the end of June, the first wildflowers to appear after snowmelt. Emitting a lovely fragrance during the bloom, they last about two weeks before going to seed, succeeded by a buttercup relative, marsh marigold.

MILESTONES (LOWER LOOP):

1: Start at Tahoe Meadows lower trailhead; **2:** Go straight at Tahoe Rim Trail junction; **3:** Turn left at Upper Loop junction; **4:** Go straight at north Middle Loop junction; **5:** Turn right at Ophir Creek Trail junction; **6:** Go straight at south Middle Loop junction; **7:** Go straight at Tahoe Rim Trail junction; **8:** Turn right at mountain bike junction; **9:** Turn left at junction before bridge; **1:** Return to trailhead.

GO GREEN I You can assist the Humboldt-Toiyabe National Forest by volunteering for short-term or seasonal projects. For more information, visit the volunteer page at www.fs.usda.gov/main/r4/jobs/volunteer.

OPTIONS I Recent improvements at the nearby Mount Rose Campground have improved the visitor experience. Campsites were $22 per night (2016) and may be reserved through www.recreation.gov. The open season usually runs from late June to mid-September. You can easily connect to the Tahoe Meadows Nature Trail by walking on a section of the Tahoe Rim Trail from the campground access road southwest to the Nature Trail junction.

Tahoe Rim Trail: Tahoe Meadows to Chickadee Ridge and Incline Creek

A short and relatively easy hike on a section of the Tahoe Rim Trail leads to supremely beautiful views of the Lake Tahoe Basin from Chickadee Ridge. By starting at the Tahoe Meadows trailhead, visitors have the added benefit of passing through verdant Tahoe Meadows, where early and midsummer wildflowers add splashes of color to the lush, green meadows. The view-packed route continues to a pair of Incline Creek tributaries, offering fine lunch spots.

LEVEL	Hike, intermediate
LENGTH	6 miles, out and back
TIME	2 to 3 hours
ELEVATION	+450′–250′
DIFFICULTY	Moderate
USERS	Hikers, trail runners, mountain bikers (even days only), equestrians
DOGS	On leash (first mile)
SEASON	July to early October
BEST TIME	Mid-July
FACILITIES	Interpretive signs, picnic tables, vault toilets
MAP	Humboldt-Toiyabe National Forest: *Mount Rose Wilderness*; United States Geological Survey: *Mount Rose*
MANAGEMENT	USFS Humboldt-Toiyabe National Forest, Carson Ranger District at 775-882-2766, www.fs.usda.gov/htnf; Lake Tahoe Basin Management Unit at 530-543-2600, www.fs.usda.gov/ltbmu
HIGHLIGHTS	Forest, meadow, views, wildflowers
LOWLIGHTS	None

TIP I Hikers may want to avoid encounters with mountain bikes by hiking on odd days only when bikes are banned from the trail.

KID TIP I Some wildlife officials consider feeding birdseed to the chickadees a dubious practice—think carefully about involving children in this activity, especially small ones.

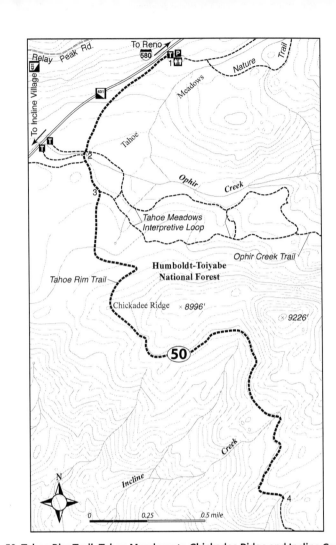

50. Tahoe Rim Trail: Tahoe Meadows to Chickadee Ridge and Incline Creek

TRAILHEAD | 39°18.434′N, 119°54.442′W From Reno, drive southbound on I-580 to the Mount Rose Highway Exit 56 and then head southwest on State Route 431 toward North Lake Tahoe. After 15 miles you pass the large parking lot for the Mount Rose trailhead on the right, near the high point of the highway (8,911 feet), which is the highest road summit open all year in the Sierra Nevada. Continue another 0.7 mile and turn left into the Tahoe Meadows parking area.

TRAIL | This section of the Tahoe Rim Trail begins on the opposite side of the parking area from the Tahoe Meadows Nature Trail. From the west side of the parking lot **[1]**, follow the Tahoe Rim Trail below the Mount Rose High-

A mountain biker on the Tahoe Rim Trail

way along the west edge of expansive Tahoe Meadows, hopping across several sparkling rivulets on the way toward the far end, where the trail bends across the lush, flower-filled meadow and crosses a wooden bridge [2] over Ophir Creek. Shortly beyond the bridge, the trail enters a lodgepole pine forest, passes by an unmarked junction with a use trail over to the highway, and then soon meets a Y-junction [3] with the Ophir Creek Trail, 0.8 mile from the trailhead.

Veer to the right at the junction and begin a gently rising climb through the trees, which eventually becomes steeper on a climb of a forested hillside. Reach the crest to the west of Peak 8996, known locally as Chickadee Ridge for the small birds that will light upon humans with a handful of birdseed. Step across an old dirt road and continue south on a general traverse of the hillside through scattered whitebark pines, which afford stunning views of Lake Tahoe, a fine reward for the little effort involved in getting here. The grand vista extends above the far shore, revealing the line of peaks forming the Sierra crest. Eventually, the trail bends across the south slope of the peak and heads east to a pair of nascent tributaries of Incline Creek [4]. Other than Ophir Creek, these two rivulets provide the only easily obtainable, naturally occurring water sources along this stretch of the Tahoe Rim Trail between Tahoe Meadows and Spooner Summit (a hand pump was recently installed at Marlette Campground). The streams make a good turnaround point for day hikers, although the views and lovely scenery continue for several more miles.

Mountain Chickadee (*Parus gambeli*) These small, black-capped, gray birds of the mountain West are commonly seen and heard in this section of the Carson Range, frequently uttering their *chick-a-dee* call to anyone who listens. They are quite acrobatic, clinging to the underside of branches to pluck insects or seeds from cones with their short bills. A common practice on Chickadee Ridge is to place a small pile of birdseed in your palm and wait for the birds to eat from your hand, which they seem to be more than willing to do, especially in winter when food is scarce. This practice is not recommended by some wildlife officials—if you plan on doing so, make sure you use nothing but birdseed, as offering human food is definitely frowned upon as being detrimental to the long-term health of the birds.

MILESTONES
1: Start at Tahoe Meadows trailhead; 2: Cross Ophir Creek bridge; 3: Turn right at Ophir Creek junction; 4: Incline Creek tributaries; 1: Return to trailhead.

GO GREEN | You can assist the Humboldt-Toiyabe National Forest by volunteering for short-term or seasonal projects. For more information, visit the volunteer page at www.fs.usda.gov/main/r4/jobs/volunteer.

OPTIONS | Extending your trip along the Tahoe Rim Trail is quite easy, as the trail continues south toward Spooner Summit.

Additional Trip in the Mountains

GALENA CREEK VISITOR CENTER INTERPRETIVE TRAIL: 39°21.843′N, 119°51.122′W
As part of a trip to the Galena Creek Visitor Center, the short, paved, and easy trail through a representative sample of the east side of the Carson Range environment is a pleasant and informative way to be introduced to the area.

Index

About the Author

MIKE WHITE grew up in Portland, Oregon, from where he began adventuring in the Cascade Range. He obtained a BA from Seattle Pacific University, where he met and married his wife, Robin. The couple lived in Seattle for two years before relocating to Reno, Nevada, where Robin had been accepted to medical school. For the next fifteen years, Mike worked for a consulting engineering firm, journeying to the Sierra Nevada and other areas of the West as time permitted. During that time, the couple had two sons, David and Stephen, and Robin completed school and residency, and then went into private practice as a pediatrician. Upon leaving the engineering firm, Mike became a full-time writer, eventually authoring or contributing to numerous outdoor guides, as well as articles for magazines and newspapers. A former community college instructor, Mike is also a featured speaker for outdoor and conservation organizations.

About the Photographer

MARK VOLLMER has shared his award-winning outdoor images through books, magazines, scenic calendars, gallery exhibits, multimedia slide shows, photo/music DVDs, and class instruction for thirty years. He believes that nature is often our greatest teacher—a deeper awareness of our natural surroundings and their seasonal rhythms translates to better photography. In turn, photography makes one a better naturalist. A resident artist with the Nevada Arts Council, Mark enjoys sharing his love of science, visual arts, and writing with schoolchildren and community audiences.